RESURRECTION

STUDIES IN COMICS AND CARTOONS
Jared Gardner, Charles Hatfield, and Rebecca Wanzo, Series Editors

RESURRECTION

COMICS IN POST-SOVIET RUSSIA

José Alaniz

THE OHIO STATE UNIVERSITY PRESS
COLUMBUS

Library of Congress Cataloging-in-Publication Data is available online at https://catalog. loc.gov.

Identifiers: ISBN 978-0-8142-1510-4 (cloth); ISBN 978-0-8142-5821-7 (paper); ISBN 978-0-8142-8193-2 (ebook)

Cover design by Christian Storm and Laurence J. Nozik
Text composition by Stuart Rodriguez
Type set in Minion Pro

To the memory of Khikhus (Pavel Sukhikh, 1968–2018)
and Natalya Samutina (1972–2021)
Светлая память

CONTENTS

ILLUSTRATIONS

PREFACE

This book explores the rise—what we might call the kopecks to rubles journey—of Russian comics as an art form and industry after the 1991 fall of the Soviet Union. Though it devotes some attention to the tumultuous 1990s under Boris Yeltsin, when the industry struggled to survive, the book lays emphasis on the Putin era, when after much trouble it found its footing and established itself, particularly after 2008.

To an extent, this study covers ground dealt with in my first book, *Komiks: Comic Art in Russia* (2010), though in much more detail for this period. The bulk of the book takes the story well past the historical limits of that earlier work, as far as the fourth Putin administration, the Covid-19 crisis of 2020, and beyond. In the second decade of the twenty-first century, a bona fide comics culture in the Western sense took firm root in Russia, going well beyond cliques, major urban centers, and the internet, to enter the mainstream.

Russian comics creators (*komiksisty*) have gained much social and cultural capital in the last decade and a half—but as I also try to show, they have given up some things along the way, not least of which being a sense of their own artistic lineage. Indeed, to many young Russian comics-makers today, the origins of their industry and the history of their art form going back no further than the 1980s are a black void. Worse, they often don't know what they don't know. I spend a considerable amount of time in this book investigating how and why that happened.

As a whole, though, the story told in these pages is a happy, even triumphant one: the coming into its own of a national comics industry and culture after many false starts over nearly three decades. Komiksisty produce, publishers print, shops sell, fans devour, conventions and festivals attract thousands. Those facts alone seem miraculous, and something I personally looked forward to for many years, ever since first beginning my study of Russian comic art in the early 1990s, when I was living in Moscow.

One of my manuscript's anonymous reviewers saw *Resurrection: Comics in Post-Soviet Russia* less as a sequel than as the middle book in a projected trilogy. The concluding volume, they surmised, I would write later on, in my emeritus years. Inshallah!

As with my first book, innumerable wonderful people have helped me along the way. Some of them, sadly, are no longer with us. I want to especially thank the late Khikhus and Natalya Samutina (to whom I dedicate this work). Others who proved invaluable were Sasha Kunin, Misha Zaslavsky, Alim Velitov, Dmitry Yakovlev, Vika Lomasko, and Lena Uzhinova. I am happy to call them friends. I also thank the anonymous reviewers of the manuscript and the very patient OSU Press, which helped shape the project in critical ways.

There were too many images to be able to include them all in this book, but readers interested may access more at my blog: https://komiksoved23. blogspot.com/.

The research and writing of this book was made possible in part by grants from the Foundation for Baltic and East European Studies and the Hahn Endowment at the University of Washington.

A Note on Transliteration

In the main body and footnotes I utilized a simplified, more reader-friendly form of transliteration from Russian (e.g., Dostoevsky), while adhering more closely to the Library of Congress style in the bibliography.

The *Maus* That Roared

We can date it almost down to the hour: by sometime just before Victory Day (May 9), 2015, comics in Russia started to matter.

Leading up to what Russians call the *maiskie kanikuly* (May holidays), when Moscow celebrates the Soviet Union's World War II victory over the Germans with period street decorations (banners, posters, slogans), Red Square military parades, and fireworks—that is, a time of peak patriotism—*Maus* disappeared from bookstore shelves.

It's true that Art Spiegelman's seminal 1991 comics memoir about his father's experiences during the Holocaust, released in Russian translation[1] in 2013 by the prestige publisher Corpus Press, had been selling handsomely.[2] But that's not why copies started going missing all at once, in late April. Press reports noted that one suddenly could not find *Maus* at branches of two major Moscow bookstores, Dom Knigi (House of the Book) and Moskva. You couldn't find the book on the latter store's website either. No explanation given. "Why they're removing them, no one has said. We just know they

---

1. The Russian translation of *Maus* followed—in many cases by several years—its appearance in numerous other Eastern European markets: Czech Republic (Torst, 1997–1998), Poland (Post, 2001), Hungary (Ulpius—ház, 2004), and Romania (Art Publishers, 2012), to name a few.

2. Ivan Chernyavsky, co-owner of the comics shop Chuk and Geek, called *Maus* one of the store's perennial best sellers, and the book has gone through several printings (Cherniavskiy interview, 2017).

removed them," one journalist was told when she phoned Dom Knigi. A customer, Margarita Varlamova, wrote on Facebook on April 23 that she had sought *Maus* in Dom Knigi, and when she couldn't find it, she asked staff. According to her account: "The clerk, avoiding eye contact, said, 'Come back after May 9.'" Moreover, the clerk said they had removed the book because of the swastika on the cover. Varlamova managed to convince the staff member to sell her a copy on the sly anyway (Berezina, "Komiks").

So: Mystery solved. The cover of the Russian *Maus,* like other editions throughout the world, sports a swastika with a stylized Hitler cat face.[3] The Russian parliament one year before had passed the Law Against Rehabilitation of Nazism, which punishes "the spreading of information on military and memorial commemorative dates related to Russia's defense that is clearly disrespectful of society, and to publicly desecrate symbols of Russia's military glory" (Kurilla, *PONARS*: 2). Individual store managers and salesclerks had evidently taken it upon themselves to withdraw the "inappropriate" item, at least for the duration of the Victory Day celebrations. The fact that other stores did have the book in stock and in plain view indicates that this was not a top-down, coordinated policy, but the actions of individuals leery of drawing the wrong kind of attention during the most "pro-Russia" time of year (Berezina, "Komiks"). The ad hoc nature of the phenomenon was confirmed when journalist Darya Peshchikova actually did find the book at Dom Knigi on April 26—but when she asked staff about reports it had been removed, "the salesclerk saw the swastika and pulled *Maus* from the shelf herself!" (Rothrock, "Gone").

Speaking to the RBC news service, Corpus director Varvara Gornostaeva declared, "I don't think that anyone explicitly banned anything. [The shop's staff] did it themselves, after the business with the toy soldiers and other lovely things like that. Just in case, they took it upon themselves to put away anything that had a swastika on the cover in whatever form. Even in a form like on *Maus*" (Berezina, "Komiks"). She was referring to an incident from earlier that April, when the state had opened a case against Moscow's Children's World toy store for selling toy soldiers dressed in Nazi uniforms, as a violation of the Criminal Code's statute 282, outlawing "the instigation of hatred or enmity."[4] Gornostaeva added that at the same time—and perhaps

---

3. As Spiegelman told the NPR show *All Things Considered* in response to the Russia developments, a similar situation had previously ensued in Germany upon *Maus*'s publication there (NPR, "Graphic").

4. The case was widely reported, and later dropped. The state clarified that merely displaying such figures was not a cause for an investigation, as long as it was not for propaganda purposes (Berezina, "Komiks"). Other incidents of hyper-patriotic overreaction occurred around this time (see Rothrock, "Gone").

not coincidentally—new volumes on "dear Stalin" and "heroic" Lavrenty Beria (Stalin's sadistic NKVD secret police chief) were just now appearing.[5]

Indeed, the de-*Maus*ification contretemps demonstrates the walking-on-eggshells quality of twenty-first-century life in Putin's Russia. With the country embroiled in a separatist war in Eastern Ukraine after its (illegal) 2014 annexation of Crimea and the crippling Western sanctions incurred as a result, a siege mentality had gripped the nation—a familiar posture throughout Russia's modern history. You could never be too vocal in your love of country. The Moscow city government, in fact, had announced on April 20 that it would conduct spot inspections of shops for products with "banned" symbols such as swastikas (Rothrock, "Gone"), which had obviously led to some preemptive curating of the bookstores' stock, in any case until the May 9 patriotic fervor died down.

Speaking to another journalist, Gornostaeva said, "One person doing it is always enough for everyone else to do the same thing in a panic." The publisher seemed especially irate about the twisting of Spiegelman's message—that anyone could mistake the cover's swastika for a pro-Nazi statement: "It's completely caricatured. All you have to do is look at it to understand that this is not fascist propaganda, but a powerful antifascist expression." She concluded: "[*Maus*] is a work about the triumph of the human spirit and reason, but now what's triumphing is cowardice and stupidity" (Polygaeva, "Dokopalis'").

It seems, though, that it was *Maus* and Corpus that triumphed after all: Sales of the book skyrocketed as a result of the press coverage. Ivan Chernyavsky, co-owner of Moscow's first comics shop, Chuk and Geek, told me in 2017 that "within a week of the scandal, the publisher sold out of its fifth or sixth printing. It sold out immediately [at our shop]." (They had refused to clear the book from their shelves.) In fact, Chernyavsky identified *Maus* as still the best-selling and best-known auteur comics work in Russia. "I think everyone was overjoyed at the scandal, since it brought attention to the book," Alexander Kunin, director of Moscow's Center for Comics and Visual Culture (TsKVK), told me in 2017 as well.

Besides, the 2015 *Maus*gate contrasts sharply with previous attempts to censor comics in postcommunist Russia, which had largely amounted to scattershot moral panics about "protecting" children. For example, during the second KomMissia Comics Festival (2003) in Moscow, the directorship of the Andrei Sakharov Museum and Public Center, which hosted the event, expressed alarm about what it considered the sexually risqué comics of animator Ivan Maksimov. (The center was still reeling from the "Caution, Religion!"

---

5. Gornostaeva had in mind the actress and singer Lyubov Orlova's memoir *On Stalin with Love* and Beria's diaries, which indeed were freely available.

scandal it had hosted earlier that year, which resulted in vandalism—one of the great controversies of post-Soviet art.) So the festival organizers cheekily covered up the "dirty parts" of Maksimov's work with yellow slips of paper and put up a disclaimer: "You must be at least 18 years old to raise these slips of paper" (Ignatenko, "Khikhus"). Other cases did not end so cheerily: The Nabokov Museum in St. Petersburg, which participated in the 2015 Boom-fest Comics Festival, took down an exhibition by German artist Kai Pfeifer and Belgian artist Dominique Goblet due to nudity concerns (Naylor, "St. Petersburg"), and in 2013 a parents' association in Ekaterinburg implicated the Tsugumi Ohba and Takeshi Obata manga series *Death Note* in the tragic suicide of fifteen-year-old Yulia Makarova (the case against the publisher was eventually dropped; see Gorbunov, "Pavel").[6]

Only the rare politically charged instances of censorship, such as that of Denis Lopatin's explicitly anti-government comics at the 2008 KomMissia (see Alaniz, *Komiks*: 218–219), could compare to what happened with *Maus*. But whereas those other cases never went beyond the confines of the local (a provincial city) or the elitist (the Moscow and St. Petersburg art scenes), *Maus*-gate penetrated everywhere, involving well-known mainstream bookstore chains, eliciting media coverage throughout Russia (and worldwide).

As Russian pop culture scholar Eliot Borenstein puts it: "You can tell a lot about a community based on what it decides to censor" (*Plots*: 1).

And so I repeat, comics in Russia now mattered. They mattered because—in a time-honored tradition—Russians of the twenty-first century, on a wide scale, once more considered them dangerous objects that had earned the right to be banned. (Even if informally, and on hysterical grounds.)

To get to this point, where comics were newly deemed worthy of repression (as opposed to mere disdain), they had had to negotiate many twists, turns, and disasters since the collapse of the Soviet Union.

Clearly Russia had changed since the early 1990s.

What a long, strange trip it had been.

---

6. Most other notable instances of Russian comics censorship also involved foreign works, including a 2014 issue of *The Avengers* (for its representation of the Russian heroes Winter Guard; see Parker, "Censoring") and a 2016 episode of the digital comic *Overwatch*, disallowed due to the representation of a same-sex kiss in violation of Russia's "anti-gay propaganda" law (Grayson, "Overwatch").

CHAPTER 1

A Time of Troubles

The First Post-Soviet Decade (1990–1999)

What a long, strange trip it had been.

Under the Soviets, comics suffered the twin curses of political repression and societal contempt. Such at least is the governing myth about that era, even up to today. As I tried to show in my book *Komiks: Comic Art in Russia* (2010), the reality was more nuanced. But certainly no comics culture of the sort familiar to Americans, Western Europeans, or the Japanese had purchase throughout the history of the USSR, where the first studio exclusively dedicated to comics production, KOM, did not form until 1988.

As it turned out, that was very late in the country's history.

General Secretary Mikhail Gorbachev, the last leader of the Soviet Union (1985–1991), had just ushered in the reformist policies known as Perestroika; the sociopolitical revolutions they uncorked throughout the empire were already fast spinning out of his control. By 1989, the Soviet Bloc itself would collapse—before KOM had even released its first actual book. With the collapse of the Soviet Union itself in 1991, the prospects for Russian comics as art form and business—which many thought a free market would greatly expand—in fact diminished greatly.

In the new economy, the ruble—and even more so the dollar—ruled.

Could Russian comics survive?

The answer to that question turned out: not very well.

Two works, about eleven years apart, by the ultra-conservative painter Ilya Glazunov crystallized the difficult journey Russians had undertaken since Perestroika. In his *Eternal Russia* (1988), Glazunov hails 1,000 years of Christianity in the country, with a massive parade of czars, saints, patriarchs, and other religious figures from history. The end of communism would spiritually purify Russia, the image declares, allowing it to resume its age-old role as messiah of nations. A follow-up painting, *The Market of Our Democracy* (1999), shows what actually happened in the interim—from a very right-wing point of view. This also shows a parade, but one of perfidy: Russia's enemies, including Jews, pornographers, pedophiles, child-sellers, drug addicts, fascists, a tipsy Yeltsin, even Marilyn Manson, crowd each other against a backdrop of US-style skyscrapers, military jets, the Statue of Liberty, and US corporate brands, while an old lady and her child beg on the streets.

We may assume Glazunov would not want to shake the hand of Yeltsin's acting prime minister Yegor Gaidar, who spearheaded the country's "shock therapy" economic reforms and was thus one of the primary architects of the world envisioned in *The Market of Our Democracy*. Looking back, he tried to put the best face on the immense human toll his policies unleashed in the '90s:

> In the course of those years a young and imperfect democracy was created. It had elements of populism, political irresponsibility, and corruption. Nevertheless, the country had a system of checks and balances. This let us hope that once the most difficult consequences of the socialist experiment were overcome, the country would have in place the preconditions for sustainable development on market and democratic bases. Naturally, interethnic conflicts, especially in the Caucasus, remained a serious challenge to the country's security and political stability. Still, the system of federative regulations gave reason to hope that the system was flexible enough to ensure stability in the organization of life and political processes in the huge and ethnically heterogeneous country. (*Collapse,* 251)

Things of course could look very different on the ground. Let me describe to you a bit of what I saw. My work as a journalist in 1990s Moscow showed me on a daily basis the jarring differences in life experience of those with and without money. I recall covering stories like that of a young girl with cancer, in a hospital that more resembled a sparsely furnished dormitory for the dying. Due to budget cuts, the staff told me, most of the medicines administered were those brought in by the parents themselves. Many couldn't afford them.[1]

---

1. Things, sadly, have changed too little since the early '90s, with Russian health care still drastically underfunded. See Mikheev, "Onkolog."

On the same day, I might also cover a Chiquita banana press conference, with smiling women dressed as the corporate namesake and lavish buffets laid out for reporters (many of whom slipped food into their pockets to take home). I could finish off the evening at the ultra-chic Metropol Hotel, with balcony views of the Kremlin, at a very expensive reception attended by brother film-makers Nikita Mikhalkov and Andron Konchalovsky, champagne flowing. The price of the haute couture on display alone would cover a lot of cancer medicine for a child, I might muse. Leaving the reception, on my way to the Revolution Square metro nearby, I see, not ten paces from me, a filthy home-less man lying on the sidewalk. He's masturbating, in plain sight, right across from the Bolshoi Theater.

This was Moscow to me then.

Literary culture in Russia changed a lot in the 1990s; many who still par-ticipated in it would say for the worse.[2] It steadily ceded ground to other entertainment venues, such as popular music. Yet no work I know more capa-bly bottled the profound psychological turmoil, chaos, humor, mixed feel-ings, and lingering shadow of Sovietism of the first post-Soviet decade than Viktor Pelevin's[3] 1999 novel *Generation "P"* (translated into English as *Homo Zapiens*).

The *P* of the title stands for a number of things, such as Pelevin, or Pepsi—the novel begins with a paean to the first Western soft drink allowed in the Soviet Union—but by the end we come to understand the most salient word for the letter is *Pizdets*. This refers to a mythical dog, a part of the goddess Ishtar's body, which must "sleep forever in this distant country in the north" (238) lest the world end. Pizdets is also a vulgar Russian term meaning, basi-cally, "fucked." So for Pelevin, the *P* in *Generation "P"* stands for "pizdets," that is, the first post-Soviet generation, Generation Fucked. From where he was writing, near the turn of the century, it sure looked that way. It may well have felt that way to the homeless man in front of the Bolshoi.

The 1990s, which most Russians today look back on as a time of socioeco-nomic chaos, impoverishment, and national humiliation, proved disastrous

---

2. Russian popular fiction in the 1990s tended toward the sensational, graphic, and crude in such genres as the *boevik* (action story) and *detektiv* (murder mystery); see Lovell and Men-zel, *Reading*. Sergei Pugachev's torture novel *You're Just a Slut, My Dear!* (1999) represents a sort of nadir for such material, evoking *bespredel*, a "without limits" outlook on life (it comes from underworld and prison slang meaning "an unjustified act of violence"). See Borenstein, *Overkill*: chapter 7.

3. Viktor Pelevin (b. 1962), the first major star of post-Soviet Russian literature, combined drugs, Eastern mysticism, Soviet science fiction, Buddhism, cosmopolitanism, and satire in his prolific output.

for those trying to build a Russian comics industry too.[4] Foreign corporate brands, such as Mickey Mouse, took their place at the newsstand and kiosk racks, with precious little domestic product to compete with them. But impediments to the industry rose not only from the fraught market conditions; they were cultural as well. As noted by Viktor Erofeyev and others, Russians refused to consider graphic narrative a legitimate art form for grown-ups for longer than any other developed nation. Writing as late as 2010, Lyudmilla Gorlova could still claim:

> Mexican soap operas, action films, fantasy and love stories, for example, were readily accepted by the [post-Soviet Russian] viewer, who started consuming them with relish. The new availability of comics, however, met with a host of obstacles. In a verbal, literarily-oriented local context, comics found itself less in demand than all other genres; over the last 20 years of their presence in the Russian market they have yet to become a factor [*fakt*] in the culture industry. Today we can say that the Russian spectator does, to a degree, have available to them this item of mass culture, though predominantly in the form of imported product and in the almost total absence of a domestic comics industry. ("Komiks": 65)

Readers of *Komiks: Comic Art in Russia* may recognize this as more or less where the story left off at the end. Despite many great artists producing great work, and fitful attempts since the late 1980s to create a viable industry, the comics scene remained a subcultural phenomenon in Russia, marked by a few festivals in Moscow and St. Petersburg, informal clubs, internet communities, and a smattering of publishers. All of which seemed a bit puzzling for a nominally democratic European country of 140 million.[5]

But we're getting ahead of ourselves. From the perspective of 1998, one could still ask whether Russian comics existed at all—and if so, in what guise. Such was the motivation behind one of the first major exhibits devoted to the question, "100 Years: Comics in Russia," which opened at the Borey Arts Center in St. Petersburg on March 17 of that year. Art historian Ivan Chechot, writing in the exhibit program, seized on the matter at hand, that is, the "Russianness" of the art form in dispute:

---

4. See Alaniz, *Komiks*: chapters 3 and 4 for more details.

5. This contrasts sharply with the comics industry of another former Soviet bloc country, the Czech Republic (see Alaniz, "Czech") and resembles more closely the experience of other former Soviet republics, like Ukraine (see Kuhlman and Alaniz, "General").

I'm afraid that Russian comics exist only as a replica [*model'*] of the world and as virtual reality, but not as a Russian version of solitaire. Instead, comics exist in the form of a separate branch, like something untranslatable and universal, similar to cognac, rum and whiskey. All the same it's interesting to consider to what extent Russian comics exist: is it like Russian ballet (100%), or only like Russian opera (50%), or on an even smaller scale, like Russian rock (?%). (quoted in Y. Aleksandrov, "Desiat'": 7)

The exhibit inspired a collection of essays coedited by the conceptualist artist Yury Alexandrov,[6] *Russian Comics,* which appeared in 2010.[7] The first Russian-language book-length study of the subject, its contributors explored the history and aesthetics of the form as it had manifested in a "comics-denying" culture: religious icons; *lubok* (woodblock prints); revolutionary-era ROSTA windows (a form of propaganda poster); Soviet children's books and journals such as *Chizh*; instructional diagrams for putting on leggings; *diafilmy* (film strips); tattoo art; and other such examples. When examining the modern era, the collection's authors (mostly art historians) emphasized Russian comics work made by artists in the vein of Keith Haring and Takashi Murakami, such as the Mukhomory (Toadstools), the Mitki group, and the Novye Khudozhniki (New Artists). These include Konstantin Zvezdochetov, Oleg Kotelnikov, and Oleg Zaika. Such representatives of fine art contrast with more obscure choices, such as Yevgeny Kozlov's *Leningrad Album,* a startling work of early 1990s erotica; Mikhail Efremenko, a self-taught artist who had produced comics since the late 1970s; and Danzig Baldaev, a prison guard and tattoo artist who during the late Soviet era depicted the sadistic tortures of the Gulag system in unpublished vignettes.

While a breakthrough work of Russian comics studies, *Russian Comics* betrays its fine arts biases by almost completely ignoring what comics-related phenomena were taking place in post-Soviet mass culture. As mentioned, Russian comics publishers struggled mightily in this era, with journals and other ventures often closing soon after launch, but that doesn't mean *nothing* was going on. They also passed over manga and anime, which by the turn of

---

6. Alexandrov had since the 1970s been producing conceptualist works that quoted and repurposed Soviet children's books.

7. The book's cover uses imagery evocative of the early Soviet-era artist Lev Yudin, who produced illustrations for children's journals and books, such as for the poet Alexander Vvedensky's *Who?* (1930). An article in the collection, "Lev Yudin: Multicolored Stories" by Irina Karasik, argues for Yudin as part of Russia's comics patrimony.

the century were starting to exert a strong influence on the development of Russian comics, especially among younger artists.[8]

As Daria Dmitrieva explains, the first post-Soviet comics "which had as their goal to provide entertaining adventures to young and grown-up readers, were created 'out of nothing'—often through a direct re-planting of Western traditions onto Soviet soil" (*Vek*: 300). Not for nothing do Russian comics scholars call this era the Wild Age (*Diky vek*).[9] Journals such as *PiF* (*Prikliucheniya i Fantastika* [*Adventures and Fantasy*], Ekaterinburg, 1990–1991), *Mukha* (Ufa, 1991–1995), *Vova* (Moscow, Ufleku, 1991), *Blaster* (Moscow, 1995), *Veles* (Ekaterinburg, 1992–1995, in which appeared the remarkable war series *Red Blood*), and *Komikser* (Moscow, 1999) all had to contend with a public largely hostile to the notion of comics as suitable reading material for anyone not a child, even as they adapted Western genres such as war, sci-fi, adventure, superheroes, *Mad*-style parody, and European autography to local tastes. The collection *Reanimator* (1992, among the last KOM publications) typified this approach (see figure 1.1). Some, like *Veles*, sought inspiration closer to home, in Russian folktales and myth, or Soviet sci-fi. Pyotr Severtsov's *Andrei Bryus: Agent of the Cosmofleet* (1993), based on a story by iconic Soviet sci-fi author Kir Bulychev, followed this model. Viktor Agafonov's *The Russia of the Epics: On the Famed and Mighty Russian Knight Ilya Muromets* (Bylinnaya Rus', 1992), released by Panorama Press and since become a collectors' rarity, used Russian folklore and myth to appeal to readers (see Majsova, "Hazy").

The journey to print of Alexander Eremin's sci-fi epic *Maksim: Star Patrol—The Contagion* tells us something of the conditions that comics artists had to negotiate during the period of "transition." Eremin began drawing the Maxim stories as the Soviet Union collapsed, from 1989 to 1992, but he could not find a willing publisher until 1998, when they appeared piecemeal in the journal *Game World Navigator*. But he did not manage to conclude the series then. Only in 2013, after properly securing the rights to his own work, did he manage to self-publish it in its entirety. According to Olesya Shamarina: "If *Reanimator* and *Andrei Bryus* were published much more 'democratically' and—through the power of what was left of the Soviet publishing system—in print runs of thousands, then in the land conquered by capitalism, on his own dime, the author could afford to bring joy to the readers of only a few hundred copies" ("Realii": 89).

---

8. See the articles by Russian manga scholar Iulia Maguro in the bibliography.
9. See, for example, Pavlovskiy, "Proshloe": 33 and Zaslavsky, "Ul'ianovskiye": 22.

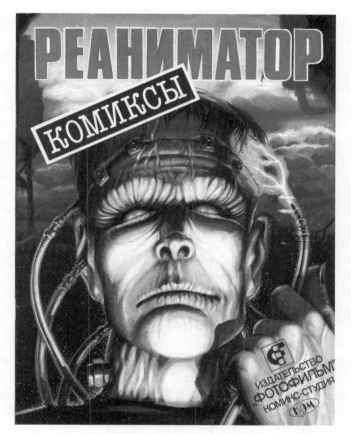

FIGURE 1.1. The cover to *Reanimator,* a late KOM studio
publication of horror comics from 1992. Used with permission.

The remarkable success of the children's journal *Seryozhka* (1994–January
1997, afterward named *Watermelon*) tells us something else. Published in Ulyanovsk (birthplace of Vladimir Ilyich Ulyanov, aka Lenin), it holds the record
for longest-lived Russian comics journal of the Wild Age; it stayed in print
for fifty-two monthly issues, up until 1999, in runs of 20,000 (Zaslavskiy,
"Ul'ianovskie": 22). (This seems a good opportunity to issue a correction: On
page 96 of *Komiks: Comic Art in Russia* I embarrassingly reported that *Watermelon* lasted only one issue.)[10]

10. For those who want a fair and balanced recounting of my book's shortcomings,
see Aleksandr Sobchan's review "Alaniz, José. *Komiks: Comic Art in Russia*" in *Novoe Literaturnoe Obozrenie,* no. 115/3 (2012). https://www.nlobooks.ru/magazines/novoe_literaturnoe_
obozrenie/115_nlo_3_2012/article/18808/.

The journal, published through the auspices of the newspaper *Simbirsk Governorate Bulletin,* benefited greatly from the support and material investment of the paper's editor, publishing magnate Aram Gabrelyanov (he would go on to invest in his son Artyom's venture, Bubble Comics, decades later; see below).[11] Unfortunately, most comics journals did not have a patron like Gabrelyanov; according to KOM founding member, publisher, and comics scholar Mikhail "Misha" Zaslavsky, practically no such journals remained in Russia after the economic crisis of 1998, when the ruble collapsed and the country defaulted on its international loans (Evdokimova, "History").

What would lead someone in this most inhospitable of times to pursue comic art? A closer look at the career of Ekaterinburg's Oleg Kozhevnikov provides one answer. Born in 1967, early on Kozhevnikov had little exposure to Western comics, though at twelve he did read an article in the journal *Smena* that critiqued them as bourgeois trash. Like many of his generation, he grew up reading Soviet children's journals that featured some comics, such as *Murzilka*. Friends also showed him comics magazines from Yugoslavia. Gradually he saw more foreign work, including *Pif* (a French Communist Party publication for children) and *L'Umanita* (from Italy, in which he first saw Superman) (Kozhevnikov interview, 2013).

Kozhevnikov put together his first collection of comics at fifteen, on risograph, with two friends. The stories, influenced by French comics, featured, among other things, Masad (the Israeli intelligence service). He finished school, served in the army. His friends gave up on comics, but not him. He kept drawing and sent his work to Soviet magazines. "I had a calling," he told me. But no luck. They didn't want superheroes. "There was no hope of getting published," he said, "so I just drew for myself." By that point he had gotten married and had a family. Then: "My father came in one day and saw me drawing comics. He told me I needed to go out and do something serious to support my family. My father was an electrician, he had a trade, he was from the working class." He advised his son to give up childish things. He turned to illustration work and eventually went to art school (Kozhevnikov interview, 2013).

With Perestroika came new possibilities. Sometime around early 1988 a friend told him he was organizing a business venture to publish reprints of US and European comics, because that was cheaper than producing new material.

---

11. Gabrelyanov is the director of News Media Holding, which owns the newspapers *Izvestia* and other media properties. Fifty percent of News Media is itself owned by the National Media Group of Yury Kovalchuk and Gennady Timchenko, billionaire supporters of Russian president Vladimir Putin. They wound up on the Western Sanctions list after the 2014 annexation of Crimea (Miller, "Tabloid").

Comics from other parts of Russia started trickling in, like *Mukha* from Ufa. They heard about KOM. But Ekaterinburg's remote location (near the Ural Mountains, over 1,700 kilometers from Moscow) and poor distribution infrastructure meant comics artists and publishers there remained largely cut off from what was going on elsewhere. "Only Moscow publishers could make and distribute product on a national level," Kozhevnikov said. "Provincial presses like ours had no such possibility to finance that, so we received only Moscow stuff, not other stuff. We didn't meet up with comics artists from any other city then—we didn't have such opportunities" (Kozhevnikov interview, 2013).

In 1991 Kozhevnikov, along with two others, founded Veles-VA, a comics press that launched the aforementioned anthology journal *Veles* in 1992.[12] Responding to the influx of Western imports, the stories relied on "traditional" Russian/Slavic folk and myth imagery in a Bilibin-like vein, such as "Veles. The Jimson Blossom" and "Ivan the Peasant Son and the Dragon."

Comics scholar Alexei Pavlovsky sees the Veles publications as engaged in a reparative mission, to smooth over the transition from communism to the free market with "patriotic" comics works that featured everything from "the covert traditionalism of pseudoslavic fantasy[13] to the processing of trauma in comics about the Afghanistan war" ("Proshloe": 44). Some of the material got rather grim, reifying many of the national anxieties that Russians experienced in the early 1990s, and which only got worse when hopes soured as the decade progressed.

The post-apocalyptic tale "Through Blood and Suffering" (1992),[14] written by Mikhail Pudovkin with art by Kozhevnikov, stands among Veles's most disturbing visions. Its opening splash shows a lone, armed figure striding through a blasted urban landscape, fires still smoking. A textbox reads: "Russia, 199—. There is no government. There is no army. Youth gangs in fatigues kill and rob citizens, who shelter in their tiny rooms" (Kozhevnikov, *Cherez*: 5). Heavily armed, in military dress, the cynical tough-guy hero Andrei survives in this dark world through quick thinking and an even quicker trigger finger. As Pavlovsky describes it, the story "promised readers bleak realities, in which . . . 'monarchists' and 'democrats' wage a civil war on each other,

---

12. The three had previously collaborated on *PiF*, a short-lived Ekaterinburg-based journal that published primarily translations of foreign sci-fi works (Pavlovskiy, "Proshloe": 45).

13. Menzel, "Russian" and Bassin and Kotkina, "*Etnogenez*" link post-Soviet sci-fi/fantasy to extreme Russian nationalism.

14. "Through Blood and Suffering" first appeared in Veles-VA's *Comics Collection* (Sbornik komiksov) #s 1 and 2, 1992. It was reprinted in the 2015 Tien Press anthology *Through Blood and Suffering*, to which I refer.

while vampire-cyborgs and cannibal savages seek out their ecological niche" ("Proshloe": 50–51).

In "Through Blood and Suffering," ordinary people barricade themselves in enclaves against myriad human and supernatural threats. For all that, on the level of the social, things go on much as before. As Andrei opines, "When life slammed into an obstacle, it didn't just get smashed to pieces. It found a way to carve out a new channel. It flowed alongside the new barrier and just kept on going with its existence, adapting its old habits to the altered circumstances. Like always" (7). Such a description all too readily maps onto the post-Soviet chaos of the 1990s, with government broken, institutions collapsed, but people still living day by day on the ruins of historic disaster. Like always.

The story's plot involves Seryozhka, an orphan who, Andrei discovers, has begun the transformation into a vampire-cyborg, his face covered with "iron-like growths" (13). The boy, scared and confused, turns to our hero—who for once cannot bring himself to do the smart thing: "To kill, to shoot this trusting child clinging to me—even if it rid me of a mortal threat—I couldn't do it" (14).

The mounting tension—will Andrei kill an innocent child who calls him Uncle, even as that child is slowly becoming a bloodthirsty monster—starkly allegorizes the Oedipal dynamics of the post-Soviet generation gap: Is Andrei (read: older people raised in communism) doomed to die in a terrifying new environment, at the hands of Seryozhka (the younger generation), who is better suited to it? The authors crystallize the dilemma in a blood-chilling moment, after Seryozhka has used his extraordinary new body to massacre a horde of cannibal savages. A sweating Andrei sits with his back to the boy, as a textbox recounts: "Tiny iron fingers latched onto my shoulder—and I was seized by a deathly horror." Behind him, a half-robot Seryozhka inoffensively asks, "Andrei, what's the matter?" (21) (see figure 1.2). Later, at the story's climax, the inevitable happens—bringing the theme to an explicit conclusion. "Who am I, Andrei?" Seryozhka pleads. "You're my death," Andrei answers. As the vampire-cyborg contagion takes over completely, Serezhka sinks his iron fangs deep into Uncle's throat (31).

If "Through Blood and Suffering" functions as a twisted version of Turgenev's *Fathers and Children* (1862) by way of cyberpunk horror, then Kozhevnikov's *Batman in Russia* (1992)[15] offers a tantalizing "alternate universe" view of how superhero comics might have operated in a Soviet Union

---

15. The story originally appeared in *Humor Comics* #1 (Veles-VA, 1992). Veles also used Western characters in *The Ninja Turtles and Russian Mishka* (1994), with art by Kozhevnikov. Batman guest-starred in a series of unlicensed 1990s illustrated novels devoted to the Teenage Mutant Ninja Turtles put out by Minsk Press.

FIGURE 1.2. "Through Blood and Suffering" by Mikhail Pudovkin and Igor
Kozhevnikov, a Veles publication from 1992. Used with permission.

with a Western-style comics culture.[16] One of the true oddities of the early Wild Age, Kozhevnikov's one-shot takes Bruce Wayne away from 1921 Gotham—"Looks like I've cleaned out all the filth from the city" (Kozhevnikov, *Betmen*: 3)—to the USSR, at that time in the middle of a ruinous famine.[17] "Lenin and Trotsky can't feed the starving," he says. "Therefore, it is the duty of civilized people to help suffering Russia" (4). Wayne uses his fortune to open a shelter for homeless children in Samara and feed the hungry in the Volga region.

This despite suspicious (and odious-looking) Cheka[18] operatives who point a gun and threaten "merciless" punishment for any counterrevolutionary activities on the part of the "capitalist-humanitarians" (4). To a man, the Soviet authorities are portrayed unsympathetically; even Lenin's portrait seems to sneer from its frame (6).

Wayne and his right-hand man Harvey (who more resembles Commissioner Gordon) soon find themselves battling a mysterious abductor of children, an axe-wielding maniac who houses his victims in a church confiscated by the Bolsheviks. The villain, bearded, barrel-chested, in traditional peasant dress, seems to emblematize "Russianness" (as well as evil), while the exotic Batman stands for modernity, foreignness, and "cool" (along with good). The twenty-page story, while slight, cleverly plays with superhero conventions and their inapplicability to Russian circumstances. If Bruce Wayne dons a bat costume to "strike fear into [criminals'] hearts" (Finger and Kane, "Legend": 139), in the Volga region he has to explain to the terrified children that, even though "he looks like a devil" (9), he has come to save them (15).

Batman in Russia is a derivative work, in more ways than one. Most directly, it lifts plot points, poses, and mise-en-scène from *Gotham by Gaslight* (1989)[19] by Brian Augustyn and Mike Mignola. The examples of obvious swiping include our first glimpse of Batman atop a gargoyle overlooking a Gotham skyline at night (3) and Batman run over by a horse (12). But as for its roots, Kozhevnikov's admittedly fun tale participates in an age-old tradition: the Russian literary knock-off of Western popular culture. In particular it recalls P. Nikitin's novella *The Strangler* (1908), which likewise transplants

---

16. For a detailed, relevant discussion of "transnational" superheroes, see Daniel Stein's analysis of Jiro Kuwata's *Bat-Manga* (Stein, "Popular").

17. The 1921–22 famine in Russia's Volga and Ural river regions killed up to 5 million. Cannibalism, referenced in Kozhevnikov's story, was documented. On the famine and the US humanitarian assistance mission, see Husband, "New": 275 and Weissman, *Herbert*.

18. The All-Russian Extraordinary Commission (VChK), popularly known as the Cheka: the much-feared early Bolshevik security agency.

19. Though its first edition was not labeled as such, the book has the reputation of being the first Elseworlds work, featuring DC heroes in alternate universes outside standard continuity.

Sherlock Holmes to the Motherland, subtly mocking his "fish out of water" English mores.[20]

The tale's boldest (and bravest?) choice has to do with its representation of the Revolutionary-era Soviets. Not only, as already noted, does the artist draw them to look as ugly as possible, but their behavior vis-à-vis the masses comes off as callous, too. In one scene, they greedily gorge on "good meat" and moonshine, in the middle of widespread hunger (6). Even worse, the conclusion exposes their cook, Demyan, as the culprit who has been stealing children, killing them, and serving them up in cannibal feasts. As Harvey tells the stunned Chekists, "Now do you understand what meat it was you were eating?!!" (20).[21] It goes without saying that, had Kozhevnikov tried to publish something like this only ten years before—it might not have gone well for him.

Veles plied the stormy seas of 1990s Russian comics publishing as best it could, but by mid-decade it was no longer releasing material, while a fire in 1997 destroyed much of what it had intended to release. Hyperinflation and the 1998 financial crisis finished it off (Pavlovskiy, "Proshloe": 46). Kozhevnikov, who had converted to Russian Orthodoxy, once more left comics to pursue other work.[22] They just couldn't compete with video games and computers, he told me. Those who tried to build a national comics industry in the first post-Soviet decade picked the absolute worst time. "Just as it became culturally possible," he said, "it became financially impossible" (Kozhevnikov interview, 2013).[23] (Sadly, I don't know if we can even say it was culturally possible then.)

Speaking with me in 2013, Alexander Kunin of the Center for Comics and Visual Culture (TsKVK) saw the period from the 1990s to the 2000s as an era of flailing attempts to create things absent an infrastructure:

> It was a time of non-cultured developments, cultural experiments. Veles was a cultural experiment. But an economic crisis comes, and it closed. The KOM studio, it was also a kind of experiment. But then people lost interest and other interests came up. Studios closed, people scattered in different directions. A work of art had never been taken as entertainment in Russia before then. "It should always be the idea, something new." And there was

---

20. As is the case with Nikitin's Holmes, in *Batman in Russia* we get no explanation as to how Bruce Wayne learned to speak the local language fluently.

21. As Kozhevnikov gleefully admitted to me, "I like to shed lots of blood in my comics" (Kozhevnikov interview, 2013).

22. Kozhevnikov today teaches at St. Peterburg's Repin State Academic Institute of Fine Arts, Sculpture and Architecture.

23. Despite its short life, *Veles* is fondly regarded by an influential cohort of contemporary Russian comics industry figures, including writers Alexei Volkov and Filipp Sosedov, and TsKVK director Alexander Kunin (Pavlovskiy, "Proshloe": 45).

a defined way of positioning it. In the 1990s some of the shibboleths of our culture were destroyed, including what an author is and what he should do. (Kunin interview, 2013)[24]

A time, then, of much ferment and great disillusion. Of great masterpieces, as well: graphic novels such as Alexei Lukyanchikov's *The Crew* (1992) and KOM artist Igor Kolgarev's uproarious and ambitious *War with the Snowmen* (1992); the Belarussian Andrei Arinushkin's historical epic *Waterloo* (Makhaon, 1993); fine artist Georgy "Zhora" Litichevsky's conceptualist strips in *Art Magazine* and other venues; and perhaps the most original of all, Alexei Nikitin's cycle of stories *Kharmsiada. Anegdote: Comics from the Lives of the Greats* (LIK, 1998), based on the writings of Soviet absurdist poet Daniil Kharms.[25]

One of the most remarkable unpublished works—which might have actually sold well in the 1990s (it's a bit more "uptown" than *Batman in Russia*) was *The Master and Margarita,* a comics adaptation of Mikhail Bulgakov's 1940 novel (considered by many the greatest Russian novel of the twentieth century), by KOM veterans Zaslavsky and Askold Akishin. It appeared in print only in 2005—in France (from Actes Sud). In its brisk 120 pages, the book distills the essence and more importantly the atmosphere of Bulgakov's opus; not an easy feat. As an unsigned synopsis of that edition explains:

> The authors of *The Master and Margarita*'s adaptation, Misha Zaslavsky and Askold Akishin, could not convey the whole of Bulgakov's novel, which, revisiting the Faust legend and the drama of Pontius Pilate, comprises more than 506 characters. They have chosen to present the great unavoidable scenes: the decapitation of Berlioz, the psychiatric clinic, the hypnosis session at the Variety Theater, Pontius Pilate, Jesus, the Grand Ball. (n.p.)

Moreover, the graphic novel duplicates Bulgakov's temporal and mood shifts between the primary locations of first-century Palestine and 1930s Moscow through a visual equivalent: Akishin renders the ancient world in a "borderless" scratch technique, while the modern era appears in crisp, solid blacks and whites in conventional panels, as in the phantasmagoric "Satan's Ball" scene (97).[26]

---

24. Kunin's remarks here resonate with the aforementioned writer and literary critic Viktor Erofeyev's 1990 essay "Soviet Literature: In Memoriam."

25. *Anegdoty,* a willful misspelling of *anekdoty* ("jokes"), references Kharms's own *Anegdotes about Pushkin* (1939). Boomkniga released a subsequent edition of Nikitin's work, *Kharmsiniada. Comics from the Lives of Writers,* in 2017.

26. Artist Rodion Tanaev later released his own adaptation of Bulgakov's novel (Terra, 1997).

Among other accomplishments of the comics medium in the '90s I would count Andrei and Natalya Snegirov's *Keshka* (see Alaniz, "Nice"), a home-grown Russian brand aimed at children, to compete with foreign interlopers like Mickey and Donald; the first published autobiographical pieces by Lena Uzhinova in *Komikser* (1998); and late in the decade, the launch of the Komiksolyot online portal and gallery.[27]

Even Spiegelman's *Maus* made an appearance in the Wild Age, decades before its swift removal from bookstore shelves in 2015: Its first Russian-language excerpt appeared in Ilya Kitup's zine *Pinoller* #0 (1994) (Kunin, "Istoriia": 5). So, with all that, I am hardly prepared to write off the years 1991 to 1999, as some contemporary Russian comics artists and fans are wont to do (see below).

Under Boris Yeltsin, Russian comics—like Russia itself—went through a traumatizing age of constant failure, anticipation, rebuilding, and failure anew. Not much outlasted the Wild Age.

But it broke vital new ground for the future.

---

27. Komiksolyot, according to KOM veteran Alexei Iorsh, was "after KOM the second great milestone in the history of Russian comics" (Kunin, "O zhizni": 48).

CHAPTER 2

Russian Comics under Putin
(2000–?)

For better or worse, Russians of that future—and maybe not just them—will remember our era as the Age of Putin.

Vladimir Vladimirovich Putin (b. 1952), president (2000–2008), prime minister (2008–2012), and again president (2012–?) of the Russian Federation, was plucked from obscurity by the ailing Boris Yeltsin very late in his term, and installed as leader of the nation in a surprise announcement on December 31, 1999. Very much unlike the despised drunkard Yeltsin,[1] Putin was a teetotaler, young and dynamic, with a KGB background and no-funny-business mien.

Helped by high oil and natural gas prices (Russia is a major supplier to Europe and the world), Putin presided over a stabilizing economy and rising standard of living, thus restoring a sense of national prestige to Russia after the humiliating disaster of the 1990s. On the international stage, he worked closely with the West on security issues, such as the safeguarding of Russia's vast arsenal of nuclear weapons and anti-terrorism initiatives, especially after September 11, 2001. Foreigners no longer regarded the country with pity and condescension, many felt. In short, Putin came to epitomize a resurgent twenty-first-century Russia.[2]

---

1. In surveys Yeltsin's approval rating in 1999 hovered at about 6 percent; see UPI, "Yeltsin's."

2. On Putin as a restorative figure, see Cassidy and Johnson, "Personality"; Remnick, "Tsar's"; Gessen, *Future*: 201–202; Belton, *Putin's*: chapters 8 and 9.

But over time he reconcentrated more and more power in the Kremlin—this after years of decentralization policies under Yeltsin. For example, from 2005 the Russian regions could no longer elect their own governors; they would henceforth be appointed by a rubber-stamp parliament on the "recommendation" of the president.[3] Putin strengthened the state's ties to the Russian Orthodox Church, reinvigorated after decades under the Soviet yoke—even though some felt uneasy at such a close relationship between the government and the church in a country that, according to its constitution, has no official religion. Smaller Christian groups, such as Baptists, Catholics, and Mormons—often perceived as "foreign," despite long histories in Russia—reported an upsurge in state harassment.[4]

Coupled with a rollback of free expression, especially of speech directed against the president or his supporters, and renewed Kremlin control of mass media, the atmosphere began to resemble something more akin to authoritarianism, if not to the Soviet era. A seemingly trivial example, but one that proved prophetic: the shutting down of *Puppets* (*Kukly*), a highly popular satirical TV show that viciously spoofed Russian politicians. A mainstay during the 1990s (Yeltsin didn't seem to mind getting mocked), it was abruptly cancelled in 2002, after an episode spoofing Putin (who very much did seem to mind). At the time, *Puppets* was the highest-rated show on the air. Lead writer Viktor Shenderovich's TV career was blackballed for years (Bennetts, *I'm*: 22–23).

As this incident shows, the new president jealously guarded his image. It soon gelled into that of a virile, "in-charge" father figure. Fawning press coverage showed him reveling—often shirtless—in such traditional Russian masculine activities as fishing, horseback-riding, and hunting. His handlers even made much of the fact that their boss had a black belt in judo; on TV Russians could watch their leader toss sparring partners onto the mat like a "real" man. Could the French say the same of François Mitterand?[5]

---

3. As journalist Masha Gessen wrote in 2017: "In Putin's Russia, most elections had been eliminated altogether: governors and senators were now appointed and the lower house of parliament was formed by parties, through a depersonalized form of voting. The candidate for president also in effect ran unopposed in every election beginning with the year 2000. Still, there were banners, billboards, concerts and other accoutrements of a campaign, and there were ballots. It looked more like a Western democracy, but felt like the Soviet Union. After a while, the term 'hybrid regime' supplanted 'liberal democracy'" (*Future*: 385). From 2012, a new law restored the right of the regions' voters to directly elect their own governors.

4. See the Bureau of Democracy, Human Rights, and Labor's "2018 Report on International Religious Freedom: Russia."

5. Writing in 2008, Borenstein could claim that "Recent popular culture is attempting to move beyond male insecurity (Yeltsin) to a manly grip on power (Putin). . . . [P]utin's specific policies and actions arguably matter far less than his reassuring symbolic function as a 'real man' who can husband the nation's resources and promise a return to greatness" (*Overkill*: 227).

Another vestige of the Soviet period reemerged: the personality cult, which the president did nothing to discourage, especially among the young. Throughout the 2000s, pro-Putin youth groups like Nashi ("Ours") held mass rallies, protests against the Kremlin's political opponents, and summer gatherings that some likened to indoctrination camps. "Generation 'P'" now meant "Generation Putin!"[6] In 2000, a "very young" reporter at the opposition *Obshchaya Gazeta* presented his resignation to editor-in-chief Yegor Yakovlev, a member of the liberal Khrushchev-era "Thaw" generation. When asked why he wanted to quit, the young man replied, "Because life is moving forward and you are stuck in the past. . . . I see in Putin a young and strong politician who wants to change the country for the better, and I want to be a part of this. All you do is criticize" (Rykovtseva, "Youth's": 35).

Popular culture responded to such sentiments with the 2002 release of a joke song, "One Like Putin" ("Takogo kak Putin"), by the girl group Singing Together (Poyushchie vmeste)[7]—a pun on another pro-Kremlin group, Walking Together (Idushchie vmeste).[8] Over a throbbing techno beat, the song and video likened the president to the dream partner Russian women had craved for far too long:

My boyfriend is in trouble again,
He got into a fight and got stoned on something,
I'm sick of him and so I told him, "Get out of here,"
And now I want a man like Putin.

One like Putin, full of strength,
One like Putin, who doesn't drink,
One like Putin, who wouldn't hurt me,
One like Putin, who wouldn't leave me.

Though comparable to the parody song and internet video *Crush on Obama* from the 2008 US presidential campaign,[9] "One Like Putin" had the distinction of truly blurring the line between reality and satire; the fact was that many Russians really did see Putin as a transcendent, virile, flawless sav-

---

6. "Forward, Generation Putin!," as a mid-2000s billboard with his portrait announced.

7. The duet was made up of Yana Dayneko and Irina Kozlova. The song topped the charts in 2002.

8. Like Nashi, formed later, Walking Together had close ties to the Kremlin, especially to first deputy chief of the presidential administration and ideologist Vladislav Surkov.

9. The June 2007 video was released on YouTube by BarelyPolitical.com, written by Leah Kauffman and Ben Relles, with vocals by Kauffman and lip-syncing by model Amber Lee Ettinger (aka "Obama Girl").

ior, who was finally putting the nation on the right path. Throughout 2008, at the end of his second term in office, Putin's national approval rating, according to the highly regarded Levada Center polling agency, never dipped below 83 percent.[10] Fans nodded along to "One Like Putin," even as they laughed.

But not everything about those first two terms was fun and games.

After two terms, Putin, despite his great popularity, could not legally run for a third, and so Dmitry Medvedev (b. 1965) became the third freely elected president in the history of the Russian Federation. He assumed office on May 7, 2008. Medvedev, younger and more moderate, championed some policies and had affectations that gave the rapidly diminishing Westernizers hope (for instance, he invited his favorite rock band, the British group Deep Purple, to the Kremlin).

But no one was fooled. When Medvedev took over the presidency, Putin moved to the post of prime minister—and while on paper the former is the far more powerful office, Putin was still solidly in charge. The so-called Tandem era had begun. Even if one knew nothing about the context or did not understand Russian, the two's body language in press photos and television broadcasts made it obvious who was giving orders and who was following them. Furthermore, no alternatives to the tandem existed.

Bald, Hirsute, a 2008 cartoon by Denis Lopatin (see figure 2.1), captured the situation brilliantly. Playing off an old joke about the alternating hairstyles of successive Russian leaders, a sixteen-panel grid shows the bald Lenin, then the hirsute Stalin, then the bald Khrushchev, then the hirsute Brezhnev, and so on, until we get to the bald Putin and the hirsute Medvedev—at which point they simply alternate between each other, growing progressively older and more decrepit over the final six panels. We're struck with these guys forever, Lopatin says.[11]

Putin's announcement in 2011 that he would seek a return to the presidency sparked the largest mass protests since the Soviet era. This served as backdrop to the most famous crime of the post-Soviet era: On February 21, 2012, members of the feminist punk collective Pussy Riot staged an unauthorized protest/performance in Moscow's Cathedral of Christ the Savior, a sacred site for Russian Orthodox believers. They sang a song with the lyric, "Mother of God, Everlasting Virgin, drive away Putin!"

---

10. See the Levada Center's presidential approval tracking at https://www.levada.ru/en/ratings/.

11. Lopatin, formerly based in Petropavlovsk-Kamchatsky, in the Russian Far East, emigrated to France in 2018. For years he had faced bans, court calls, and persecution under Article 282 for his politically charged work (see Eurocature, "Denis" and Alaniz, *Komiks*: 218–219).

FIGURE 2.1. Denis Lopatin's *Bald, Hirsute* (2008)

The popular uproar and contempt for Pussy Riot (notwithstanding their positive reception abroad) demonstrated the nation's predominantly conservative posture under Putin. It says much, too, about the present moment that, despite his crimes, many in modern-day Russia profess admiration for Joseph Stalin—and not only among the older population. Public buses in Volgograd (site of a crucial WWII battle) prominently displayed his portrait to commemorate the seventieth anniversary of victory in 2015, while four years later in Balakhan (Nizhny Novgorod region), there appeared a huge banner with Stalin in dark glasses and a motorcycle jacket, holding a rifle against the Kremlin's Spasskaya tower, with the English inscription: "I'll be back." The Terminator-Stalin had appeared in commemoration of the dictator's 140th birthday (*Novaia Gazeta,* "V Nizhegorodskoi"). Other such monuments have been unveiled throughout the country in recent years.

In 2011, a cartoonist from Novorossisk, Anton Chadsky, distilled what he considered the nation's simmering brutality and chauvinism into Vatnik,[12] an adult parody of SpongeBob Square Pants with a blackened eye and unkempt look—and hit "upload." A post-Soviet Runet (Russian internet) star was born. In one widely shared image, "The Ideal Patriot," our gap-toothed lout sneers at the viewer, holding a bottle of booze, his stunted physique colored to resemble the Russian flag. Each color corresponds to a character trait: white—"33% envy"; blue—"33% stupidity"; red—"33% hatred." The 1 percent left over is attributed to "vodka."

AT THE DAWN of the twenty-first century, a nascent Russian comics scene existed in three forms: internet communities (with the 1999 launch of *Komiksolyot* a major development); freelance artists occasionally publishing in magazines and newspapers; and scattered informal clubs of devoted readers (especially of scanlated manga). The lion's share of the market belonged to imported product. Comics were a subculture, an exotic niche for the in-crowd.[13] Those few who knew, for example, that celebrities Konstantin Ernst (TV mogul and later producer of the 2014 Winter Olympics opening ceremony) and Andrei Venediktov (head of the liberal radio station Echo of Moscow) were avid comics collectors, tended to dismiss the fact as two rich men's eccentricities.[14] I recall the cartoonist and impresario Khikhus (Pavel Sukhikh) telling me in 2004, "You know, Ernst collects comics." He said it as a way to show how "cool" and "insider" comics were—and I admit it did impress me to learn someone that famous and connected had the itch.

We can also draw a correlation between Putin's escalating crackdown on citizens' freedoms and the increasing politicization of comics, especially after his 2012 reelection. As the selfsame Khikhus told an interviewer in 2012, during the peak of anti-Putin mass movements:

---

12. Vatnik originally referred to a type of padded jacket worn by Soviet soldiers and Gulag prisoners. On Vatnik, see Borenstein, "Coat" and Karpova, "Sozdatel.'" Chadsky openly refers to his Vatnik imagery as "Russophobic comics" (Karpova, "Sozdatel'").

13. Comics would pop in Russia in unexpected places, though. It bemused me to read in *National Geographic* in 2008, in an article about exploring Moscow at night, that "it was reassuring to find two uniformed security men sitting in the walkway, even if one was reading a comic book and the other was asleep" (Smith, M. C., "Moscow": 132).

14. See Anikina, "Aleksey."

One way or the other, the government—with its dirty tricks [*vykhodkami*] and sending people to prison—will turn us all into social activists. When you've got seven years in prison just for singing in the wrong place,[15] you'll scream, "Hey, what's up with you?" I have a feeling that in Russia we're following the script of Germany in the 1930s. They start by jailing conscripts, drug addicts and gay people. These are the social groups that no one stands up for. (Ignatenko, "Khikhus")

Whereas Putin's first two terms saw the emergence of major festivals (KomMissia in Moscow, founded in 2002, and Boomfest in St. Petersburg, in 2007); a handful of publishers; and even a breakthrough Western publication (by Nikolai Maslov, whose autobiographical comics appeared in two volumes in France in 2004), after 2010 Russia at last saw the establishment of a viable comics industry through such mainstream presses as the superhero-based Bubble (launched 2011), as well as greater attention to alternative work. The St. Petersburg publisher Boomkniga played an outsize role in the latter, through translations of such seminal Western graphic narrative as David B.'s *Epileptic* (2000, Russian translation 2011) as well as home-grown releases. Also important: the organization of comics centers and comics clubs attached to libraries, which proliferated starting in 2010. Russia saw its first comics shop, Chuk and Geek (Chuk i Gik), open in Moscow in 2010. Many more followed over the course of the decade. Comic Con Russia, first held in 2014, has become a major annual event, drawing over 150,000.[16]

What Alexander Kunin of the TsKVK said the 1990s needed but never had—comics as a viable cultural institution—now at last coalesced into a full-blown Western-style comics scene.

In what follows I delve into this and other matters in detail.

The Role of Festivals

A 2006 cover of the journal *ArtKhronika* reproduced Roy Lichtenstein's *Grrrrrrrrrr!!* (1965), showing a head-on portrait of an angry dog, partly lifted from *Our Fighting Forces* #66 (February 1962).[17] The cover read, "Why There

---

15. Khikhus here is referring to the stiff fines and jail time handed out by the authorities for "unauthorized protest." Comics journalist Viktoria Lomasko also told me about repeated harassment by police and right-wing organizations who disapproved of her work (Lomasko email interview, 2012).

16. Sergei Karandayev, curator of the Library of Comics in St. Petersburg, dates the start of the boom to 2014–2015 (Kolokoltsev, "Vidish'").

17. Lichtenstein took as inspiration a frame from the story "Trail of the Ghost Bomber," written by Robert Kanigher and drawn by Jerry Grandenetti.

Are No Comics in Russia." Within its pages, the journal devoted several articles and interviews elaborating on that statement, in the process presenting
a primer on the scene of that period, half a decade on from the economic
turmoil of the 1990s. It made for at times grim reading. Georgy "Zhora"
Litichevsky, one of the few fine artists who had been making comics in Russia
since the 1970s, said to an interviewer:

> [The question of why comics are not popular in Russia] I have not been able
> to resolve to this day. One could make reference to the elitism of Russian cul-
> ture. Even Belinsky[18] in his era complained that in Russia there existed only
> great literature, not popular fiction. We're not living in the time of Belinsky,
> but even post-Soviet kitsch has traditionally oriented itself to high culture,
> while comics are too democratic. But such an answer would be too sche-
> matic. After all, in Russia there existed the developed folk culture of the
> *lubok*. (Miskarian, "TV": 88)

It would become standard to identify the native lubok (woodblock prints
dating back to the eighteenth century) as part of the lineage of comics in
Russia, along with ROSTA windows (early Soviet propaganda posters) and
some conceptualist art works. Litichevsky does so, as do the curator Andrei
Erofeyev (he called comics a "full-fledged genre of contemporary visual art")[19]
and Yury Alexandrov and his collaborators in the aforementioned 2010 *Russkii
Komiks* essay collection. As indeed do I. Without re-presenting the arguments
in my first book, let me just say that such a genealogy was available (and had
been for a long time) for anyone in Russia who wanted to defend comic art
against attacks that it was somehow irreducibly "foreign."

Yet precisely this disparaging association, among others, bedeviled Russian comics even up to very recently. By 2006, though, the leading edge of
a revolution had already been pushing back against such prejudices for four
years. The fact that this revolution would not fully ignite until the latter half of
Medvedev's term only makes the achievements in this era all the more notable.

KomMissia, the first annual comics festival in post-Soviet Russia, was
founded by Khikhus[20] and Natalia Monastyrova in 2002. It first took place
on February 1 to 3 of that year at the Zverev Center for Contemporary Art in

---

18. Vissarion Belinsky (1811–1848), a prominent nineteenth-century Western-oriented
critic.

19. Kravtsova, "Marginal'niy": 91.

20. Prior to KomMissia, Khikhus had worked in Russian media, including as editor of the
comics-friendly journal *Fantom*. He later founded the artists' association People of the Dead
Fish (2003–2009).

Moscow. Later iterations under Khikhus[21] convened at the Sakharov Museum and Community Center, M'ars Gallery, and the Contemporary Art Center Winzavod. It offered exhibitions of Western and Russian comics (in reproductions), workshops, guest talks, awards, and small book fairs. Among its most notable guests: France's Moebius (Jean Giraud), Russian playwright and author Lyudmilla Petrushevskaya, and the US's Richard McGuire.

The festival, while at times disorganized and chaotic, created vital space for fandom and artists in Russia to meet and do what comics communities do the world over. As one fan put it, at KomMissia one could "discover for themselves all the rich diversity of the world of drawn stories!" (Kunin, "KomMissiia": 11). And while often KomMissia looked more to Western or Japanese models for inspiration—and saw itself as a bridge to those faraway worlds—it also on occasion paid homage to the past achievements of domestic comic art. Such was the case with the festival's grand prix award handed to Vadim Rubtsov in 2006 for the continuation of his *School of Mages*, a series begun in the pioneering Ufa journal *Mukha* (*The Fly*) in the early 1990s.

All the very real enthusiasm notwithstanding, however, KomMissia suffered the tragic fate of arriving too early, in essence celebrating comic art in a culture that had no viable comics industry. Such circumstances led to charges that the festival in its early years, though it attracted hundreds of visitors, amounted to nothing more than a *tusovka* (clique), a hang-out for a small group of young people with money to burn. Publisher Yevgeny Nitusov shared this opinion, adding, "I think the festival should open itself up to children who read Spider-Man comics" (Kunin, "Pro KomMissiiu": 9).[22] This the bohemian Khikhus resolutely refused to do, opting instead to foster a less "commercial" image of comics for public consumption (as he told me more than once). But Nitusov and others argued that KomMissia's stance only retarded the development of the industry by alienating prospective customers (like parents) who might have responded better to more mainstream fare.

Other problems beset the festival, as they did the vast majority of those working to build a Western-style comics scene in the inhospitable environment of the early 2000s. The biggest concern: not enough jobs to go around, and no opportunities to publish beyond small pieces in festival catalogs, magazines, or online. Feuds, divisions, and professional envy corroded the scene in its infancy (see Alaniz, "Notes"), as shown by the absurdly cruel case of Nikolai Maslov—who despite being the most famous and most translated Rus-

---

21. Monastyrova died of cancer in 2006.

22. In the early 2000s, Nitusov Press released several French graphic albums in Russian translation, as well as Anna Anosova and Konstantin Komardin's graphic novel *Site-O-Polis: Subterranean Networks* (2004). See Alaniz, *Komiks*: 127–128.

sian comics artist in the world, as well as the progenitor of a new genre (the Russian graphic autobiography), could not get invited as a guest to KomMissia (see Alaniz, *Komiks*: chapter 7). Khikhus himself openly traded insults and nearly came to blows with, among others, Mikhail "Misha" Zaslavsky, the KOM veteran and publisher. Despite its many breakthroughs, then, the Russian comics scene during Putin's first two terms was a community riven by conflict.

By 2010 Khikhus was desperate to drop KomMissia. He had in fact complained to me and others over the years that he wanted to quit, that the festival—especially after Monastyrova's death—had turned into a monster out of his control. (Though some of his troubles, as noted, were self-inflicted.) Sponsors and the media only wanted to deal with him, the "face" of Russian comics, familiar from television. But Khikhus didn't care the way he used to; among other things he was sick of the political and economic situation in Russia, and wanted to spend more time abroad to work on his animation projects.[23] (His health problems may also date to this time.)

So in 2009, when an acquaintance, Alexander Kunin (a stylish man in his early twenties, recalling a young Truman Capote), approached Khikhus at the festival to give him his critiques—bad organization, poor mounting of the exhibits, labels hard to read—he didn't just brush him off, as was his wont in such situations. "He got upset," Kunin told me. "He said, 'Since you're so smart, why don't you do something yourself?' That was all I needed to hear" (Kunin interview, 2013).

Kunin had a background in journalism, graphic design, and book editing, and had taken an interest in comics only in the last few years. For the 2010 KomMissia, he along with editor and translator Olesya Shamarina organized a "Day of Manga," which included a groundbreaking roundtable that brought together librarians, publishers, booksellers, and manga specialists (Kunin, "KomMissiia": 20). In time that event led to some critical developments for the scene, such as the founding of the first Center for Comics and Visual Culture at the Russian State Library for Youth (RGBM); sitting in the audience, I mostly wished the acoustics in the cavernous halls at Winzavod weren't so terrible.

During the 2012 KomMissia, a disagreement between Khikhus and the new Winzavod directorship erupted into a public scandal when, outraged that the center had relegated the festival to an inadequate space, Khikhus moved all the exhibits out, literally in the middle of the night. He accused Winzavod

---

23. Khikhus had also been devoting more time to grant-funded projects, such as the social activist comics initiative Respect, formally launched at the 2011 KomMissia (see Alaniz, "Flashy").

of "violating the norms of exhibition and mass culture work" (Kunin, "Kom-Missiia": 22).[24] Winzavod did appear the party at fault here—though in any case Khikhus always seemed to thrive on drama. Whether any of this was actually helping Russian comics was another matter.

That KomMissia would prove the last under the full control of its cofounder. The next year, Kunin took over many of the organizational duties—though again, things happened in less smooth a fashion than one might have wished. In spring, not long before KomMissia traditionally took place (during the May 9 Victory Day holiday season), Khikhus announced he was dropping the festival, in part for health reasons. Kunin frantically reached out to him (Khikhus had already left for Cambodia). As he related it to me: "'How can you do that?' I told him. 'Thanks to KomMissia the comics center came about, comics shops like Chuk and Geek, everything, publishers, Zangavar!'" He answered: 'If you need it so much, then you do it.'" By then Kunin was directing the Moscow comics center he had helped create; he explained the situation to his superiors, arguing, "If we don't take this on ourselves, it will be a big blow for the Russian comics movement" (Kunin interview, 2017). In record time, Kunin, his staff, and volunteers put on a downsized version of the festival that May at RGBM.[25]

By then, the environment for comics in Russia was changing fast, to the point of making KomMissia, the first event of its kind, increasingly irrelevant. In his last major interview, from 2018, Khikhus took stock of the festival's accomplishments and shortcomings under his leadership. KomMissia, he said, had gone from a modest apartment exhibit in the early 2000s to fostering something new and exciting in the culture:

> These were years of blossoming for Russian comics. It's a fact that I and KomMissia positioned comics as an expressly modern art form, which was important to me. Although because of that the whole time we were disappointing the hopes of many artists, who asked, "Where's the industry?" To which I always answered and will continue to answer: an industry kills everything, everything interesting. For a while, at least.

---

24. See also Po, "Festival."

25. The other, mass-culture "half" of KomMissia 2013 took place in the fall at the Flacon Design Factory as part of a new festival, Day of Open Worlds (DOM), which featured video games, cosplay, and comics—in short, the sort of "commercial" event Khikhus had once refused to put on. It was funded by a grant from Synergy University (a private institution where Khikhus had launched a professional comics program in 2011). See Khikhus's announcement on his Live Journal page from October 31, 2013: https://xixyc.livejournal.com/206212.html.

He added:

> One more tragedy for Russian comics is that money and talent never crossed paths. All the time we had all sorts of people popping up, waving around wads of cash, with their heads full of unbelievably crappy ideas. Meanwhile really awesome projects that could have had commercial success were ignored. Another problem was that Russian *komiksisty* back then, who had learned the ropes from the French, at a certain point they fell really easily into a euphoria, thinking that they should absolutely get paid 400 euros per page. But here you have to keep things straight: for an ad job, sure; but for creative work—that you could do even for free. (Kunin, "Khoroshikh")

KomMissia came about at a moment when what it meant to be a Russian comics fan and a Russian comics artist—a komiksist—had yet to fully crystallize in professional and creative terms. The festival, though often dancing on the precipice of disaster, helped to create that very identity. Russian culture of that era needed something like KomMissia, even if it didn't know it. One portion of that interview in particular touched me: when Khikhus described racing to the venue for the opening of the very first festival in 2002—late as usual. Loaded down with catalogs, he and his staff slipped on the February sidewalks: "We were thinking, 'No one's gonna come with ice like this.' And we rush in like that—and there were pe-e-ople there! It was packed. Sixteen TV cameras, everybody yelling—it was a fun time!" (Kunin, "Khoroshikh").

A few months after giving that interview, Khikhus (who by then had been living abroad for years) died in Israel, of cancer, on June 30, 2018. He was fifty years old.

KOMMISSIA WITHOUT A DOUBT broke open the modern Russian comics scene, forming a vital stage in the creation of the nation's comics culture at a time when many doubted it would ever arrive. Today, though, it has a mixed legacy in the eyes of those who live, breathe, and benefit from that selfsame culture.

Ivan Chernyavsky, co-owner of Chuk and Geek, Russia's first comics shop, told me in 2017 that KomMissia was no longer a factor in the scene, which had moved on to bigger and better things:

> [KomMissia] appeared before the existence of an industry. They brought the great Moebius over before it was possible to buy Moebius' books here. They brought over the author of *Blacksad* [Juan Díaz Canales] back when

you couldn't buy *Blacksad* in Russia. I really didn't see the point in doing that. . . . [Y]ou need to be able to read the material to have a festival, otherwise you just have an exhibit of drawings from a work that you have never read. Unfortunately, KomMissia took that path of an inward-focused, closed community, and didn't respond to the emergence of a comics industry. That's why the last couple of years we haven't taken part. There's very few people there. . . . [Today] they have other problems. They bring guests over based on what grant they can get, not based on what real interest there is. (Cherniavskiy interview, 2017)

Artyom Gabrelyanov, founder of Bubble, the first successful US-style superhero comics publisher in Russia, put it even more bluntly when he told me in 2013:

[KomMissia] had a big plus in what it did for the country, and a big minus. . . . It was good to show that comics in Russia is not just kids' reading. But they went into total overdrive and created this version of comics that was totally art-house, alternative, for smart people, for brainy people in glasses, for hipsters. . . . It was all for an in-crowd, drawings for yourself and your circle. It's the same mistake that KOM made. It was a total *tusovka.* We don't need *tusovki,* we need work, we need business. After that you can get together with your friends, sure, but work first. (Gabrelianov interview, 2013)[26]

Modern-day businessmen like Chernyavsky and Gabrelyanov, who operate in a much more hospitable environment for Russian comics than did their 1990s predecessors, look upon KomMissia and other early festivals with what seems like barely concealed (perhaps even Oedipal) disdain. Yet these very institutions sustained Russian comics culture in the lean years of rebuilding during Putin's first two terms. Rather than berate KomMissia for bringing Moebius before his works had appeared on the market, why not thank KomMissia for bringing a world-class artist to Moscow, to meet with those who knew his work and inspire those discovering it for the first time? Indeed, several komiksisty told me it was Moebius who had revealed to them the potential of comics in the first place, and thus in a real sense helped launch their careers. They treasured the memory of his Moscow visit. Chernyavsky's argument had an odd circularity to it, too: Don't bring artists until every-

---

26. Even Kunin conceded that KomMissia, especially in its early years, was vulnerable to accusations that it was largely a grouping of friends: "It could not form into a cultural institution. There was no culturological line in it" (Kunin interview, 2013).

one already knows them, even though no one will know them without major events like festival exhibits, visits, and the press coverage that follows—making it more, not less, likely that those artists will get published.

In addition to the many talks and workshops of KomMissia, smaller events—most of them organized on a volunteer basis, out of sheer enthusiasm—defined much of Russian comics culture in the first decade of the new century: exhibitions like Comics Underground, organized by Tanya O (Tatyana Orlova) and Elizabeta Abdulina in the Moscow arts studio U Divleniya in December (2005); in St. Petersburg in conjunction with Boomfest (2007); and at Moscow's Zverev Center of Contemporary Art in 2009, with the themed exhibit "Lost in Time." The modern, more monied events, like the documentary comics presentations by Swiss artists Kati Rickenbach, Christoph Schuler, and Andrea Caprez at the 2015 Krasnoyarsk Book Culture Fair (Antonshchenko, "Ia—nastoiashchiy") or the many comics presses who participated in Moscow's seminal 2019 Non/Fiction Book Fair, to the largest event, Comic Con/Igromir (launched in 2014),[27] were built on the previous decades' fan activism.

No comics industry figure has better threaded the needle between art and commerce than Dmitry Yakovlev, founder of the Boomfest Comics Festival in St. Petersburg. Originally from the midsize city of Kirishi, the soft-spoken Yakovlev (in terms of personality the opposite of Khikhus) first started taking comics seriously in 2001, when new friends from Canada introduced him to the Western alternative scene (he called the Canadian cartoonist Julie Doucet a "discovery"). He learned of KomMissia in 2003. He attended that and the Angoulême festival in France. This confirmed him in his mission to create something similar to KomMissia in St. Petersburg, but more in keeping with that city's reputation as a Western-leaning arts mecca. Leveraging his experience at the major children's books publisher Samokat, he co-organized small exhibitions and anthology publications under the banner SPb. Nouvelles Graphiques in the mid-2000s; made further contacts through the Slovenian comics journal *Stripburger* (one of the first to publish Russian artists such as Litichevsky in the '90s); approached sponsors; and in September 2007, launched Boomfest at various galleries, museums, and other venues in the city (Nenilin, "Dmitriy"; Fomenko, "Risovannye").

The BD specialist and translator Mikhail Khachaturov calls Boomfest "a festival of European standard, to which one need not feel embarrassed to invite foreign stars of the first order " (Khachaturov, "Boomfest": 24). Indeed,

---

27. For the inaugural Comic Con/Igromir in 2014, KomMissia organized the comics trade fair. Guests included British artist David Lloyd (Kunin, "5 let," 9–10).

Yakovlev's festival has a much more "European" feel than KomMissia, and has consistently attracted well-known Western artists, including Gary Baseman, Joe Sacco, Jessica Abel, David Lasky, T. Edward Bak, Gabrielle Bell, and Ben Katchor (US); Tom Gauld (UK); Simon Hanselmann (Australia); Dominique Goblet (Belgium; as noted, she was censored); Lorenzo Mattotti (Italy); Hanneriina Moisseinen (Finland); Miguel Gallardo (Spain); and Mawil (Markus Witzel, Germany), to name a few. As the Russian scene developed, the festival devoted more attention to domestic artists, with exhibitions and presentations by Khikhus, Askold Akishin, Nikolai Maslov, Lena Uzhinova, Oleg Kozhevnikov, Olga Lavrenteva, Viktoria Lomasko, and others, as well as historical exhibits such as the first Russian show devoted to Hugo Pratt and another devoted to Soviet-era cartoonist Nikolai Radlov (both in 2011). Boomfest has largely avoided the mainstream in favor of what Russians call auteur (*avtorsky*) or art-house comics: alternative works that for their creators represent a means of "creative self-realization" (Khachaturov, "Boomfest": 24). In 2008 Yakovlev founded Boomkniga, the most important Russian press for alternative comics, both domestic and in translation (discussed below).

Since its inception, KomMissia, which once had the field to itself, has ceded ground to an array of comics, comics-related, and pop-culture festivals that today pepper the Russian cultural calendar. These include the All-Russian Festival of Japanese Animation (VRNFEST) (Voronezh, launched 2000); Geek Picnic (St. Petersburg/Moscow, 2011);[28] Starcon (St. Peterburg, 2012); ComXfest (Moscow, 2012); Comic Con Russia/Igromir (Moscow, 2014); Epic Con Russia (Moscow, 2014); Bigfest Festival of Comics, Cosplay and Nostalgia (St. Petersburg, 2016); Epic Con St. Petersburg (formerly Comic Con St. Petersburg, launched 2015, renamed 2017); Astro Con (Ekaterinburg, 2016); Immersion: Days of World Comics Culture (Ekaterinburg, 2017, supported by the US Consulate); Comic Arts Tyumen (2017); Comic Con St. Petersburg (2019); and §Graphica Festival of Book Illustration and Independent Publishing (Arkhangelsk, 2020).[29]

A single iteration of Moscow's mammoth Comic Con Russia/Igromir alone welcomes more attendees than KomMissia had over its entire first decade; the 2019 event, held at the Crocus Expo International Exhibition Center, topped

---

28. Geek Picnic, a festival devoted to science, technology, and art, got caught up in a number of scandals over the years, including the uproar sparked when it invited representatives of an ultranationalist movement to speak (Dobrynin, "Evoliutsionisty").

29. Smaller events also took place throughout the country, including the Sam Izdam (I Will Publish It Myself) Samizdat Festival, held from 2013 to 2015 in Tomsk, Novosibirsk, and other cities. Not everywhere were they greeted with open arms. The AniDag Festival in Makhachkala, Daghestan (held in November 2018), was marred by mobs of men screaming at the cosplayers, accusing them of "stripteasing" and calling them prostitutes (Vagabova, "Not").

180,000 visitors over four days. As has become the norm in Western conventions, many of those fans did not come for the comics, at least not primarily: The show featured a cosplay contest; presentations by major Russian TV and film directors, producers, and actors; preview screenings, including of *Zombieland: Double Tap*; a merchandise area; and an artist alley.[30] International guests included *Star Wars: Rogue One* star Mads Mikkelsen (Comic Con Russia). And as cartoonist and Comic Arts Tyumen founder Georgy Elaev points out, Comic Con Russia takes place simultaneously (and overlaps with) Igromir, a popular video games festival organized by the same firm, the Russian Game Developers Conference (KRI), since 2006.[31]

In short, Russians (like comics convention fans in much of the world) are drawn to these events by the transmedial versions of characters and worlds they've seen in films, TV shows, games, and the like; only a small minority actually read the comics. Many of those cosplayers may not know the comics histories of the figures they are portraying—not that there's anything wrong with that. It simply demonstrates how, as geek culture went more mainstream in Russia, the kind of person who attends comics-related events changed dramatically in the 2010s. All to the good, especially if it brings spillover business to the industry; as Gabrelyanov said, "Marvel films helped us a lot, they attracted a new audience to comics" (Gabrelyanov interview, 2013).

Few were better poised to appreciate the transformation throughout the scene than KomMissia and TsKVK director Alexander Kunin, who wrote:

> It's hard to overestimate Comic Con's role. We ourselves already understood this perfectly during KomMissia 2015. Whereas before we would see students from art institutes; comics artists (professionals or those just starting out); and people more or less involved in the process of creating comics, now our attendees were 60% regular geeks and fans of the comics universes and series. (Kunin, "5 let": 10)

When asked in 2017 about the importance of festivals to his business, Chernyavsky said:

> They played an important role in the first years for our shop, when they were a space for promotion and advertising, so people could know about

---

30. KomMissia, under Kunin, organized the artist alleys for the first two Comic Con Russia festivals, in 2014 and 2015.

31. Elaev expressed this attitude to me in conversation in 2019. Others have told me the same. The logical extension of such thinking is that Comic Con Russia/Igromir should not "count" as a comics festival at all—certainly not a "pure" one.

us, and it was good for sales during the event. We had a stand at KomMissia. Over the seven years that we have existed, things started changing a lot. Now the last two-three years, we hardly participate in festivals because it isn't worth the outlay. The only festival that we find profitable for us is Comic Con Russia, because a huge amount of people will come through our stand. (Chernyavsky interview, 2017)

Alternative Russian comics artists, on the other hand, sometimes found more receptive audiences abroad. Such was the case especially for the autobiographer Maslov and the social activist artist and muralist Viktoria Lomasko, who regularly exhibited in Western Europe, and whose book *Other Russias* (2017) appeared in English, French and Spanish, but not Russian. In 2010, a delegation of Russian comics artists headed by Yakovlev attended the Angoulême International Comics Festival, to much interest (Kunin, "Dmitriy").[32] Another group of Russian comics industry figures toured the US under the State Department's International Visitor's Leadership program in 2016.[33] That same year Russian comic art was exhibited as part of the Far From Moscow Festival in Los Angeles.[34]

By the new millennium's second decade, Russian comics had made it onto the world map like never before.

32. The group included Lena Uzhinova, Varvara Pomidor, Alexei Nikitin, Viktoria Lomasko, and Anton Nikolaev. They went as part of the "Year of Russia in France and Year of France in Russia" cultural initiative of that year, which led to publications and translations, including of David B.'s *Epileptic* (2000), into Russian.

33. Participants included Anna Voronkova, KomMissia's director of International Projects; Konstantin Dubkov, artist, of the Yekaterinburg Cultural Center; Alim Velitov, artist, KOM veteran, and director of the Moscow Comics Club and, starting in 2020, of the KomMissia festival; and Ekaterina Yakovleva of Boomfest.

34. I consulted and translated works for the FFM exhibit. Also, as chair of the International Comic Arts Forum, I helped bring Yakovlev to the 2013 conference in Portland, Oregon.

CHAPTER 3

The Publishers

Why Now? And What Comes Next?

As much of Russian cultural history has shown, one can still have comic art without an actual comics industry. But how much easier, more lucrative, and accessible that comic art will be with publishers whose products readers actually want to buy! And so, unlike the debacle of the 1990s, domestic comics publishers have flowered under Putin. Misha Zaslavsky, himself an active figure in the field, estimated that periodical comics hit an all-time high in 2008, with some twenty journals and a combined print run of 1.5 million copies per month. Of these, foreign licensed properties dominated, as they always have (Evdokimova, "History").[1]

No one has done more or worked longer to "normalize" comics for the Russian reader than Zaslavsky, who since the late Soviet era has toiled tirelessly as artist, publisher, editor, historian, translator, and writer to instill a genuine love for comics among the young. ("To build a genuine comics culture, you start with children," he has told me more than once.) With Advance

---

1. Egmont, the most successful foreign publisher operating in Russia at that time, alone held 70 percent of the market, with a combined monthly print run of 1 million (Styshneva, "Samye"). St. Petersburg's Praim-Evroznak published *Hellboy* from 2003 to 2005. Pangloss Books (its eponymous Moscow bookstore served as an important venue for comics sales in the 1990s and early 2000s) specialized in French books and comics. It released Bogdan's (Bogdan Kulikovskikh) Russian manga graphic novel *Nika: The Magic Book* (2002). Komiks Press published *The Simpsons* and, almost uniquely, Marvel titles (including *X-Men*) in the '00s (Kunin, "Komiks industriia": 6). See also Alaniz, *Komiks*: 126–130 and Styshneva, "Samye" for details.

Press he published pioneering monthly children's series such as *Nu, Pogodi!* (*Just You Wait!,* 2004–2010), based on a popular Soviet-era animated TV show, and *Yula* (Whirligig, 2004–2008). *Nu, Pogodi!* fared best against foreign competitors, with a circulation of 35,000 to 40,000, the largest in Russia at the time for a domestic comics periodical. From 2009 to 2013, Zaslavsky as writer, with his fellow KOM veteran Askold Akishin supplying art, produced over fifty issues of *Masha and the Bear,* a series released by the Danish publisher Egmont and based on the enormously popular children's animated series. In 2017, Zaslavsky and a team of artists collaborated with the online science and technology portal Reactor 9 to produce *Re@gen,* a series of webcomics, including the sci-fi story *Prikazano vyzhit'!* (*You Are Ordered to Survive!*), with Akishin. In 2018, Zaslavsky translated Will Eisner's *A Contract with God* (released by Mann, Ivanov and Ferber).

Over the course of Zaslavsky's thirty-plus-year career, the publishing landscape for comics has transformed drastically in Russia, with now over two dozen dedicated comics presses. Other, larger concerns pursue comics projects of their own, such as Amfora Press, which published Moore and Gibbons's *Watchmen* in 2009 to coincide with the film adaptation release,[2] and Corpus, which released the aforementioned *Maus* translation in 2013. As those and other publishing successes show, one can make money in the business much more easily now—though not necessarily as a creator.

With a 2014 law mandating foreign ownership of media companies be limited to 20 percent by 2017, transnational corporations like Egmont had to adjust operations. In a public letter of May 25, 2016, the publisher announced it was selling off its Russian company and publishing rights (including for comics) to the existing management there, though it would maintain a close partnership with the new firm. The upshot: More of the money Russian comics readers spend on foreign titles stays in Russia.

Still, compared to its long-established counterparts elsewhere, the Russian comics market remains "tiny" (*kroshechniy*), in the description of Leonid Shkurovich, head of Azbuki-Attikus—which holds the rights for DC comics properties. He values it at no more than 600 to 700 million rubles (about 10 to 11 million USD) and calls it "highly fragmented." For example, in 2018 over ten publishers held licenses for Marvel comics in Russia, indicating considerable saturation, according to the business newspaper *Kommersant* (Makarova, "Chelovek-Pauk").

---

2. Many Russian comics scholars and fans designate Amfora's unexpected success with *Watchmen* in 2009 as the beginning of the Russian comics boom, which led to the consolidation of a bona fide industry.

Most Russian comics publishers date only to the 2000s or later; of the oldest, not all survived that decade. Major Moscow-based presses include Nitusov (2002), translations of French graphic novels as well as Russian material; RKK (2004–2005), youth-oriented material such as the "pot-head" series *Dimych and Timych*, with art in its latter issues by Andrei "Drew" Tkalenko; Zangavar (2009), US and European classics; and Jellyfish Jam (2015), genre material like Alexei Volkov and Alexei Gorbut's nostalgia-driven *Conquerors of the Impossible* (2017) (discussed further on). Major St. Petersburg publishers are Boomkniga (2008), Western and Russian alternative comics;[3] Live Bubbles (2011), a creative association and small press founded by the alternative artists Vladimir "Pitersky Punk" Lopatin and Ilya Obukhov; Comix-Art (2008, an imprint of Domino), Neil Gaiman's *Sandman*; and White Unicorn (2011), fantasy and adventure, publisher of Filipp Sosedov et al.'s series *Pantheon: Cult of Duplicity* (2012–2016). Other notable actors in the field include Comics Factory (2006, largely manga) and Tien (2015, vintage Russian 1990s works), both based in Ekaterinburg, and Green Cat (2006, Italian comics, including from Sergio Bonelli Editore), in Omsk. Micropresses such as Space Cow Comix, associated with Comic Arts Tyumen, I discuss further on.[4]

With distribution (a huge problem in the '90s) more secure now that major bookstores are willing to carry comics, competition is fierce, as the various publishers carve up a limited number of return customers who buy superhero titles or try to appeal to a larger readership with a *Maus*-like hit.[5] Concerns over saturation are rife, as are fears of the "fickleness" of Russian fans, always eager to move on to the next trend.[6] And always there looms the

---

3. Yakovlev learned an important lesson from KomMissia in its early years: "In 2007 I started the comics festival Boomfest, and quickly understood that it's rather hard to run such a festival, and in general talk about comics, in a country where they don't exist. That's how Boomkniga came about" (Prorokov, "Komiksy").

4. Other outfits include Panini Rus (2012), Marvel titles; Comics Publisher (2015): *To Murmansk and Back* (2019) by Varvara Lednyova; and 42 (2012): *Hellboy*.

5. Examples for the educational market include *Entertaining Physics: Quantum Mechanics* by Ishikawa Kenji et al. (DMK Press, 2016) and *Marx's Capital Illustrated* by David Smith and Phil Evans (Bombora, 2017).

6. Komilfo Press director Mikhail Bogdanov told an interviewer: "We're seeing an oversaturation of the comics market. Once there was this huge shortage and everyone eagerly sought after any new releases, but now Russian readers are spoiled and you always have to find ways to surprise them. In all of this there's really only one thing that upsets me: truly cool comics series that last several volumes are sinking fast. Readers interested in comics today have as their goal not to collect a series that they've started, that they actually like, all the way to the end. Instead, they'd rather go get some new shiny thing. I don't understand at all why, for example, that happened with *Scott Pilgrim*. The print run of the first and second volumes was four times bigger than the print run for the third volume and after" (Ditrih, "Bogdanov"). Similar drop-offs in reader interest routinely occur in Western comics markets as well.

threat of an industry-wide crash at the hands of either alienated fans or the unpredictable Russian economy.

"It's true, I am prophesying the apocalypse of the world of comics," said Mikhail Bogdanov, founder of St. Petersburg-based Komilfo (launched in 2007):

> I prophesy that, indeed, the entire comics industry might collapse, but this very pessimistic approach of mine, along with my view on things, helps me find a solution, so that this does not happen to Komilfo, at least. If you just swim with the current and try to wait it out, and hope everything sorts itself on its own, there's a risk that a wave of difficulties will drown passive players in the market. (Ditrih, "Bogdanov")

As it happened, the year after making those comments, Komilfo tied its fate to the recent movement toward consolidation; Eksmo-AST, the country's largest publishing trade group, bought a 90 percent stake in the company. The 2018 deal demonstrated the conglomerate's confidence in the continued growth of the Russian comics market.[7] It was a shrewd purchase: Komilfo holds the coveted licenses for several Marvel titles, including *Iron Man, Deadpool,* and *Star Wars.* And Bogdanov got the insurance he wanted; if and when any turbulence comes, Komilfo will now likely weather it better than most. Before the purchase, in 2016, the company had reported earnings of 6.1 million rubles (about $933,000 ~~million~~ USD), with a tiny profit of 626,000 rubles (or $10,000 USD). Upon announcement of the deal, Bogdanov—who retained creative control—indicated he would move aggressively to expand his offerings and print runs by at least 30 percent—the opposite of his doom-and-gloom prophecies a year before (Makarova, "Chelovek-Pauk"; Gerden, "Marvel's").

The superhero genre dominates sales for monthly titles, mirroring the US, though formats and marketing differ. As Egmont co-owner Lev Elin explains, "In countries like Russia in which the comic book market isn't developed, projects sold in limited runs with high margins have been the most profitable so far" (Gerden, "Marvel's"). Chernyavsky of Chuk and Geek confirmed this to me, saying Marvel had the superior position because it provided more accessible information, packaged older and newer material in *treidy* (trade paperbacks),[8] in larger print runs and for more affordable prices, while DC

---

7. Eksmo-AST director Oleg Novikov noted that "the comics segment of the Russian market is seeing steady growth and has begun attracting more interest from the wider industry" (Gerden, "Marvel's").

8. Other terms of art in the modern Russian comics market include *singly* (singles/floppies), *khardy* (hardcovers), *krossover* (crossover), and *stend-aloun* (stand-alone). *Stend-alouny,* Chernyavsky told me, sell better than *singly.*

mostly sold singles (Chernyavsky interview, 2017). "The Russian audience is a model of the world's audience and superheroes are very popular all over the world," he said in 2015. "However, the truth is that here in Russia the circulation of comic books is 100–200 times lower, and 'the freshest' issues come out two or three years behind schedule" (Evdokimova, "What").[9] To some extent, the demand for new material has since taken care of that problem; for example, in 2017 Komilfo published the first arc of Jeff Lemire and Dean Ormston's series *Black Hammer* soon after its 2016 US release.

Digital platforms also offer room for growth. In 2015, Bubble became the first Russian publisher to sell its wares on Comixology, including in English translation. The MyBook service, a subsidiary of LitRes (itself owned by Eksmo-AST), moved into the e-book comics market with SplashPage in 2018 (Gerden, "Marvel's").

In 2014, the journal *Mir Fantastiki* (*World of Fantasy*) organized a round-table with leading comics publishers and presses who included comics in their catalogs, to discuss the tremendous changes in the Russian reading public's attitude toward comics as medium and art form. Their comments made for a fascinating snapshot of the scene at the time, as well as of the mentality of those who would most determine the direction of the fledgling industry, at least in the short term.

So why was the boom happening now? The publishers, in brief, had these explanations: Fans' unofficial translations and pirated works circulating online had sustained the scene in its lean years; similarly, the key role of Komiks Press, which virtually alone through the 2000s published US superhero comics and prepared the market for the next decade's breakthrough; readers' desire to follow the latest trends; the new generation does not have their parents' Soviet-era baggage, and welcomes global popular and geek culture; the fantastically popular Hollywood adaptations of superhero comics (though as Komilfo's Bogdanov pointed out, such adaptations had been coming out for many years before the Russian comics boom); the realization on the part of small publishers that licenses for foreign product were not so expensive or complicated to get; and the preparation for the market carried out by manga publishers starting in the late 1990s. Some of their answers manifested along cultural materialist lines, such as that of AST's Sergei Tishkov ("The ordinary paper book is becoming more and more an object of luxury, a beautiful arti-

---

9. He goes on: "My partner, Vasily Shevchenko, has suggested a theory that the Russian reader is stuck in 2008. It's seldom that our readers ask us to order anything that appeared later. I have an explanation for this; at roughly the same time the popular website *SpiderMedia.ru* worked out the rating of 'the 100 Most Recommended Comics.' There's a joke that Russian publishers still use this list when buying the rights to foreign comics" (Evdokimova, "What"). See the Spidermedia.ru list at http://spidermedia.ru/mustread.

fact, a thing to collect, to gift, to lovingly contemplate"), others on the transnational (XL Media's Anna Logunova: "We are today seeing a growth of interest in comics throughout the world. A generation has grown up which does not consider games, fantasy, comics and the like as entertainment exclusively for kids, teenagers or geeks"). Whatever the reason or combination of reasons, Natalya Nesterova of Panini Rus put her finger on what everyone was witnessing: "Whereas before they were first and foremost perceived as little booklets with pictures for small children, today comics are becoming an indispensable part of youth culture." She added that a third of the market was over eighteen years of age (Serebrianskiy, "Izdateli").

The 2009 publication by Amfora Press of the Russian translation of Alan Moore and Dave Gibbons's *Watchmen,* to coincide with the film adaptation release, proved an unexpected success, which helped open the floodgates. Within five years, some of the most celebrated works of recent global comics culture had entered the Russian market at last: Boomkniga released translations of David B.'s *Epileptic* (2011), Marjane Satrapi's *Persepolis* (2013), and Joe Sacco's *Palestine* (2016), and Corpus published Spiegelman's aforementioned *Maus* (2013) (see Birger, "Kupit'"). "There are enough outstanding foreign comics for us to release for several more years, which will create a positive association with this art form," noted Valentin Zavarzin of 42 Press. "And if Russian writers and artists can up their game, then we won't need to worry about the future of the industry here. On the other hand, there is a risk that low-quality products will overwhelm the market to the point that the 'gold reserve' of comics will run out" (Serebrianskiy, "Izdateli"). Zavarzin's description struck me as an odd "resource extraction" reification onto the comics market of the Russian economy's fossil fuel–dependent anxieties. In such a scenario, the 64,000 ruble question becomes: When will the industry reach "peak comics"? Has it already?

The Case of Manga

The experience of manga publishers in Russia offers a cautionary tale for the new mainstream comics industry. Manga had started to make inroads into Russian culture even in the late Soviet and early post-Soviet eras, thanks largely to videocassette circulation of Japanese anime (closely related to manga culture), and the screening of films and series like *Sailor Moon* in theaters and on television. From the late 1990s, a Russian market for manga had taken firm root. Much of the manga on sale at this time, however, was second-rate, according to manga scholars such as Semyon Kostin ("Neizvestnaia"). Despite exceptions, like Sakura Press's 2005 launch of the first licensed Japanese manga series in Russia—Rumiko Takahashi's gender-bending *Ranma ½*—the situation persisted until market saturation, illegal scanlations, piracy, and inferior product led to a partial collapse of the manga market in 2013. Several publishers shut down.[10]

Still, the vibrant scene[11] spawned a number of remarkable Russian manga artists and works. Journals such as *Great Dragon,* catering to computer and video game enthusiasts, also featured manga starting in the mid-1990s, as did *AnimeGid* (2003–2011). In 1999, Bogdan (Bogdan Kulikovskikh) and Vyacheslav Makarov published the serialized version of their *Nika* in *Klassniy Zhurnal* (in 2002 they repackaged it as a graphic novel, *Nika: The Magic Book*). This journal went on to publish another important series, Vladislav Yartsev's *Legend of the Silver Dragon,* starting in 2015. In 2008, Midorikawa Zuyosi (Svetlana Chezhina) won second place in the 2nd International Manga Prize competition. Rosmen published the journal *ruManga,* featuring Russian manga artists, from 2009 to 2011. Manga series such as Olesya Kholodchuk's *Sunsniy Mur: Path of the Spirit* (2010), Sideburn004's (Tatyana Lepikhina) *Once upon a Tale* (2013), and Ksenia Kudo's *The Medallion* (2013) all drew on Slavic mythology and/or Russian fairy tales for inspiration, characters, and plots (Maguro, "Russkaia").[12]

But speaking with me in 2013, some in Russia's comics community declared manga dead. Artyom Gabrelyanov, founder of Bubble Comics, told me with characteristic hyperbole that he had never read manga and had no desire to: "Manga has gone belly up. It was all over two years ago," he said. "All the big manga publishers have closed down. You just see old copies on the shelves. What's left, nobody buys. The market for manga has died. They didn't cultivate a new readership for themselves, the girls who bought it grew up and got tired of it. That's basically it" (Gabrelianov interview, 2013). (What went unspoken: Manga directly competed with Gabrelyanov's company for the rubles and eyeballs of young readers.) Anna Logunova of XL Media put it more measuredly: "The manga crisis happened because publishers overestimated the amount of potential buyers and literally inundated the market

10. Anatoly Dunaev, director of Alt Graph Press, noted that "in 2011 in Russia up to 20 volumes of manga were published in an average monthly print run of 10,000 copies, but in 2015 this was reduced to only 3–5 volumes in a print run taking less than 4,000 copies a month" (quoted in Evdokimova, "What").

11. Manga scholar Natalya Samutina credits the participatory cultures and illegal scanlations as fostering a strong sense of community among those making and consuming manga (Samutina, "Iaponskie").

12. Major Russian manga and manhua publishers include Comics Factory (2006, Ekaterinburg); Istari Comics (Moscow, 2008); Palma Press (Moscow, 2008); XL Media (2005, St. Petersburg); Sakura Press (Moscow, 2003–2016); and Alt Graph (Bryansk, 2010). Neo-Manga (2006) has a reputation as a leading purveyor of unlicensed manga (Lisitsyn, "IMKhO").

with product, a lot of it of poor quality. Many manga series ended up getting dropped, which also reflected badly on the situation—many people now are simply afraid to buy printed manga, worried that they'll never see the conclusion of their favorite series, and they prefer to read manga on the internet" (Serebrianskiy, "Izdateli").

Even those not directly competing for market share sensed a change in the public perception of manga. Kunin told me in 2013: "Manga is not growing in popularity anymore. It was a great stepping stone for Russian comics. Lots of young artists learned to draw through it, but they're making European comics now, regular comics. . . . In Russia, manga has assumed a particular niche in readers' interests, with no further development. *Naruto, Pet Shop of Horrors,* these are steps people take as they develop their taste and craft" (Kunin interview, 2013).

As it happened, though, and *pace* the nay-sayers like Gabrelyanov, the rumors of manga's death in Russia were greatly exaggerated. One sign was a 2017 open letter by major manga publishers against piracy and unlicensed products.[13] "Some were predicting the demise of manga in Russia, but with the years the situation has stabilized," reported Kostin in 2018. "In the last few years Japanese comics have experienced a renaissance, and many famous franchises have received official Russian editions" (Kostin, "Neizvestnaia"). In 2013, Alt Graph Press published a new edition of one of manga's seminal masterpieces: Keiji Nakazawa's anti-war series *Barefoot Gen.* (It was a big improvement on the incomplete and rather shoddy 1995 Russian publication by Japan Today Press.)

A February 2020 announcement from Azbuka, the largest manga publisher in Russia, posted on the popular social media platform VKontakte, declared a new manga boom was indeed underway. This was no mere PR claim; its data showed over 500 licensed volumes of manga currently in print in Russia. Wary of once more saturating the market, publishers were focusing on "quality" product such as Eiichiro Oda's *One Piece* and Hajime Isayama's mega-hit *Attack on Titan.*[14] Around the same time as Azbuka's announcement, Kunin—who had earlier dismissed manga as a mere "stepping stone for Russian comics"—told me it was now "selling at a stable rate" (Kunin personal correspondence, 2020). Manga scholar Natalya Samutina added that, contrary to conventional wisdom in the 2010s, superheroes had not displaced manga among readers: "Superhero comics are very quickly knocking up against their ceiling, because the

---

13. See it at https://vk.com/wall-19731404_38840.

14. Available here: https://vk.com/@azbooka_graphic_novels-manga-ot-azbuki-chto-budet-dalshe?fbclid=IwAR2dnYfLHvZ13dldpvdLzqItF7-3akyntTyTOmEQstfwaabFuoxMbgip-WzI.

groups which are interested in them are few in number. Meanwhile, manga is breaking out to a wider readership," she said. "In Russia right now we're going through another efflorescence of manga publishing: online they are reading it a lot, along with Chinese comics and all sorts of *ranobe* [Japanese illustrated novels]" (Samutina personal correspondence, 2020).

Perhaps most telling of all: In 2015 the manga skeptic Gabrelyanov's Bubble launched a creator-owned imprint, Bubble Visions, which prominently featured Russian manga such as Anna Sergeyeva and Maria Privalova's series *Tagar* (2017). In 2019, Comics Factory released the seventeenth issue of its ongoing *MNG: An Anthology of Russian Manga* (in publication since 2011). March 2020 saw the opening of the country's first Center for Manga and Comics, housed at the Chekhov Library in St. Petersburg (Kuznetsova, "V Peterburge").

Challenges Ahead, or, "A Momentary Upgrade to Their Brains"

Dmitry Yakovlev's St. Petersburg-based Boomkniga, voted by the Comics Boom site as the best Russian comics publisher of 2017, has seen remarkable success within its very specific niche of the market: alternative comics. "We grew by almost 20 percent in 2018, both in the number of books we published and turnover," Yakovlev told an interviewer, though he saw clouds forming on the horizon. "Despite some impressive growth rates demonstrated by the comics sector in recent years, our domestic audience is still rather limited. The number of comic books published in Russia in recent years has significantly increased, but the circulations are getting smaller. So it's unlikely that comics in Russia will be able to achieve the same popularity they enjoy in the United States or France, at least in the short-term." He counted among the structural problems preventing sustained rapid growth:

> A lack of distribution channels; a small number of bookstores; a lack of book journalism which might help push sales with visibility; and an absence of fixed prices and resulting price wars among the largest players. Finally, the situation in the market is complicated by the growing attempts at monopolization by some of the consolidated leading players, such as Eksmo-AST. (Gerden, "Comics")

Russia's political climate might complicate an alternative comics publisher's business model, especially for controversial content. Upon Boomkniga's release of Alison Bechdel's LGBTQ+-themed *Fun Home* in 2018, I asked

Yakovlev if the Russian "anti-gay propaganda" law posed any problem for the book's distribution and sale. "No," he answered, "as long as we wrap it in plastic and put an '18+' label on it."

Content-related troubles of a different sort sometimes visited Vladimir Morozov's Moscow-based Zangavar Press, among the most innovative and ambitious of Russian comics publishers, purveyor of Russian-language versions of Winsor McCay's *Little Nemo in Slumberland,* Hal Foster's *Prince Valiant,* Bill Watterson's *Calvin and Hobbes, The Moomins* by Tove Jansson, *The Leaning Girl* by François Schuiten and Benoît Peeters, and other classics in lush, oversized, and expensive editions. At the 2010 KomMissia Festival, Morozov—among the most "boosterish" apologists for the comics medium in Russia—told me in excited tones about his plans for a Russian edition of George Herriman's seminal *Krazy Kat.* "Isn't that, uh, going to be hard to translate?" I gently asked. Morozov waved away the concern, saying he had "good people" on it. Years later, with the much-delayed project in limbo, he admitted to an interviewer that *Krazy Kat* had confounded three translators, who all quit in despair over Herriman's unique language (Kostenko, "Interv'iu").

Despite such frustrations, Morozov breathlessly promotes the art form of comics through several media, with Khikhus-like élan. Also like Khikhus, he interviews well on television and has a flair for colorful descriptions. He insists on the ancient roots of comics on native soil, arguing that "for us, the modern-day citizens of Russia, this is not some kind of super-novelty." In that same 2018 interview on the state's Channel One, he went on an extended riff regarding the purported salutary effects of comics-reading—quite a contrast to the decades of Soviet vilification of graphic narrative as deleterious to proper learning:

> Comics gives people the possibility of developing both hemispheres of the brain together. This is the most important key to understanding what comics is. Because, as is well-known, left- and right-hemisphere people are divided based on what their brains perceive better. Some perceive text better, others perceive pictures better. . . . And comics in this case acts as a little bridge between these two categories of people, if we may divide them through such a rather crude method. Comics is, as it happens, that happy opportunity for people to experience a momentary upgrade to their brains. That is, people at one and the same time perceive pictures and text together. This is an unheard-of, unprecedented modality for human civilization. (N. Aleksandrov, "Vladimir")

Whether such advocacy will win more converts to the cause of graphic narrative in Russia seems an open question (though in any case rhetoric like this is not unheard of elsewhere; see Widdicks, "Visual" for a recent example). Still, the fact that figures like Morozov now regularly appear on national television to speak about comics in glowing terms points to a fundamental shift in the culture since the turn of the century. The phenomenon also recalls the irreducibly social and "imaginary" nature of what we mean by "comics industry," according to comics and media studies scholar Benjamin Woo:

> As a collective concept, industries are theoretical rather than empirical objects, although they obviously have empirical effects. What we perceive as an industry is itself the result of boundary-drawing practices imposed on a fluid, complex field of social practices. It must be constructed before it can be analyzed, but such processes of construction are never neutral. (Woo, "Is There": 40)

"Never neutral" indeed: The emergence of a comics industry in Russia, once unimaginable or at best taken as the prognosticator of societal decline, today signifies that the country has joined in with twenty-first-century trans-global pop culture—and has something of its own to contribute. In 2009, Kunin posited what he considered the pillars of a modern comics industry: internet resources for creators; exhibits and festivals; dedicated comics publishers and comics sections in larger presses; specialized shops and sections of shops for comics sales; comics sections in libraries; independent print and online publications (Kunin, "Komiks industriia": 7). By 2014, each of those criteria had been filled in Russia.

Introducing his publishers' roundtable that year, Sergei Serebriansky could confidently sum up:

> Dozens of publishers releasing comics in the Russian language. Specialized shops in the major cities. Monthly releases of all kinds of comics, both individual issues and collections, for every taste—from classic superheroes to adaptation of famous books to space operas and fantasy. Just a few years ago all this would have seemed unbelievable, but today it's become reality.[15]

---

15. Such "a few years ago this was impossible" discourse peppers Russian media the way "Bam! Zap! Pow!" headlines infest US media discussions of comics to this day. For example, from 2017: "Five to seven years ago, comics were hard to get in Russia. Practically nothing was published in Russian, and the rare foreign publications were sold either for high prices in the foreign sections of the bookstores, or second-hand at the markets. Few people visited foreign comics shops and large internet stores. Today the situation has changed drastically" (Barkov, "Kak").

We would like to believe that comics have come to Russia for real and for the long haul (Serebrianskiy, "Izdateli").

Where to Buy and Where to Get for Free

In 2010, Vasily Shevchenko and Ivan Chernyavsky borrowed $1,000 USD, called in some favors and in December of that year opened the first comic book store in Russia, Chuk and Geek, on Moscow's Big Palashevsky Lane (not far from the central Tverskaya Street business district). They did so well that the next year they opened a second location in Moscow, in the Novokuznets-kaya district (near the State Tretyakov Gallery). They would eventually add a third store.[16]

By the end of the second post-Soviet decade, Chuk and Geek represented just one of several options Russian fans had to buy comics and related merchandise. In 2017, the RBK news service estimated that some 150 to 200 comics shops were operating in Russia, with more than sixty of them in cities of a million or more (Arkhangel'skaia, "Million"). These included Comic Street in Moscow; Apelsin, Bazinga, and 28th in St. Petersburg;[17] the Karandash chain in Volgograd, Ekaterinburg, Novosibirsk, and Krasnoyarsk;[18] Vault 14 in Vladivostok; Got Comics in Ekaterinburg; Space Cow in Tyumen; Illusion in Tomsk; and Bizarre Book in Ryazan. This in addition to the fact that since the mid-2010s major bookstores such as Biblio-Globus, Moskva, Dom Knigi, and Respublika had sections dedicated to comics. In late 2019, St. Petersburg's world-class Hermitage State Museum's bookstore began selling comics works—the most prominent Russian cultural institution to do so.

Those preferring to shop from home also had plenty of options, from internet stores like Fast Anime Studio and the massive portal Ozon, to publishers' sites and *barakholki* (secondhand sales) via social media and classified ad sites like Avito. Even Mile High Comics in the US would ship free to Russia

16. In 2017, *RBK Gazeta* reported that the first two stores generated a monthly profit of $7,200 USD, with revenues totaling about 3.5 million rubles (about $61,000 USD) per month on about 5,000 transactions. As in the US, Russian comics shops purchase product from publishers on a "no returns" model (Odintsova, "Lavka").

17. As Komilfo's Bogdanov told a reporter: "Sometimes the press feeds the shop, sometimes the shop feeds the press" (Odintsova, "Lavka").

18. Due to the low popularity of comics, the proprietors of the Novosibirsk shop were supplementing sales with art books related to the Avengers films, T-shirts, and other souvenirs, according to store manager Roman Markevich (*Sibnovosti*, "Perviy"). Chernyavsky, co-owner of Chuk and Geek, also credits the superhero figurines of Funko Pop for helping expand sales (Ditrih, "Cherniavskiy").

on orders of $125 USD or more—though customs might prove a hassle. And then there was Comixology, which started featuring Russian comics in 2015.

Visiting Chuk and Geek in summer 2017, I felt a sense of both déjà vu and spatial dislocation. For someone who had been studying (and with some difficulty, seeking out) Russian comics since the early 1990s, the store represented a sort of utopian space—an oasis of comics culture in a nation that had historically shunned the medium. Language aside, there was nothing in Chuk and Geek that would have seemed unfamiliar to a Western comics fan; the modern shelves were crammed full of Marvel and DC product, with some alternative comics here and there. I even saw a translation of Frank M. Young and David Lasky's graphic biography *Don't Forget This Song* (2012) for sale (Lasky is a friend). Though of course I gravitated to the Russian domestic productions, which made up a sizeable minority of the stock. Staff was friendly and helpful. The shop felt welcoming, and not "judgmental" about comics-reading as a legitimate form of leisure. Even the fact that comics boxes, mylar bags, and other collector paraphernalia were on offer struck me as a seismic change compared to twenty, or for that matter ten years prior. Though it dates me to say so, I had to remind myself I was still standing on Russian soil.

In his Bourdieuan analysis of US comics shops as social spaces, Benjamin Woo argues that they serve: "1) as locales providing spaces for interaction among participants; 2) as nodes, interlocks, and regions relating contingent communities of practice; and 3) as both 'sanctuaries' from mainstream hierarchies of taste and status, and arenas of competition for social and subcultural capital" (Woo, "Android's": 125). While Chuk and Geek's first shop has functioned more as an exclusively commercial operation (it proved too much of a challenge to accommodate a large audience there), the second location does fulfill Woo's criteria better, given its monthly social calendar of talks, get-togethers, and signings.

What sort of people open the first comics shop in Russia?

Chernyavsky told me the 1990s *Spider-Man* animated series, with its "rather mature, extended plotlines" and "a hero who didn't always know how to make the right choice," had a profound effect on him as a child. Both he and partner Shevchenko worked as editors for the publisher Komiks in the 2000s (Chernyavsky also spent time at publications such as *Rolling Stone* and *Time Out Moscow*, and played music). Career dissatisfaction ultimately led them to their new venture. For the store's name they made a pun on Arkady Gaidar's classic children's story "Chuk and Gek" (first published in 1939 and adapted into a film in 1953), about a duo of problem-solving boys. To this day they continue to get two responses: Those who don't understand the reference (a majority) say it sounds terrible, while "older people come and tell us our name has a mistake in it," he laughs (Cherniavskiy interview, 2017).

An interview with Chernyavsky yielded a cornucopia of "from the trenches" facts and observations on the burgeoning Russian comics market. Most trade paperbacks and collections have print runs of 5,000 to 6,000, and this is mostly what fans buy. While not necessarily still "stuck in 2008," the Russian comics reader is not reading the latest material; a lag of a few years is common. Publishers like Panini Press and Hachette shrewdly issue double-sized collections that contain older and newer stories with the same character or a related plotline.[19] At the time we talked, the best-selling comics works in Russia were Moore and Gibbons's *Watchmen* and Morrison and McKean's *Arkham Asylum* ("That's had a crazy print run. It's up to its eighth printing, which very rarely happens in Russia"), with Spiegelman's *Maus* and Marvel's *Civil War* line also popular. All those were at least ten years old. And obviously not Russian.

I was mildly surprised to see comics singles (floppies) in the original language, mostly English, in the shop. Chernyavsky said some collectors seek them out, along with back issues, for which the market is developing fast. Online secondhand markets sell old Russian comics, as well as "15-year-old Marvel," which for some are cult items (Cherniavskiy interview, 2017).

For all Chernyavsky's enthusiasm, and the steady stream of customers coming through Chuk and Geek as we talked, comics for most Russians remain a subcultural phenomenon, which even the intelligentsia sometimes still struggles to understand.[20] Elena Avinova, who in 2016 ran a graphic novel

---

19. Kirill Kutuzov, comics author and administrator of the website Old Komix, praised Hachette Press's anthology editions, which combined newer Marvel content with material from the 1980s, for filling gaps and helping fans understand beloved characters' histories better. "Thanks to this collection," he wrote, "a Russian-language reader had access to the works of Chris Claremont and Jim Shooter. We could finally have a look at Frank Miller's superhero work" ("Amerikanskie": 131). Azbuka's publication of "New 52" material from DC, he claimed, fulfilled a dream of Russian geeks "to not lag behind the Western industry and hold in one's hands something, anything, as long as it's new" (Kutuzov, "Amerikanskie": 132). On the other hand, whether a series appears in Russia as *singly* or as *sborniki* (collections) depends on the newness of the series: The more recent *Saga* appeared as *singly* soon after its US launch, while *Walking Dead,* an older series, as *sborniki* (Serebrianskiy, "Izdateli"). *Saga*—not a big franchise, not an adaptation—served as a test for the maturity of the Russian market, which it passed brilliantly, according to XL Media's Logunova (Serebrianskiy, "Izdateli").

20. In 2012, over breakfast at an academic conference, a well-regarded Russian-Jewish Slavist admitted to me that they had tried to read *Maus,* but couldn't get past the first few pages. When I asked what the problem was, they replied that they had never read comics before, and it proved much more complicated than they had assumed it would be: "I didn't know whether I should read the text, then look at the picture, or the other way around." I advised them to give it another try some time. As Litichevsky told an interviewer in 2016, such reluctance is widespread among this demographic: "When our intelligentsia sees comics, they say things like, oh, their eyes go all blurry, and besides if they want to read something, they'll just pick up an actual text, and if they want to look at something, well, there's pictures for that. Even the most progressive people in Russia experience irritation when they encoun-

workshop at Moscow's prestigious School of Creative Writing, could still speak about comics in rather pessimistic tones:

> I don't think comics are unpopular among artists, it's just that this niche still exists underground. If you attend the Moscow and St. Petersburg festivals, you'll see the halls full of people who aren't just "consuming" comics, but also trying to draw something. These people are creating their own closed-off communities, and we simply don't know about them. In the bookstores, comics are pushed off to the far corners, while specialized stores, like Chuk and Geek, have their own audience, and the mass Russian reader just doesn't go to them. (Khanukaeva, "Elena")

Nonetheless—and it did take them a while—the Russian publishing industry as a whole has responded to comics and their rising profile. In 2019, Boris Kupryanov, member of the expert council for Moscow's prestigious Non/Fiction Book Fair, cofounder of the Phalanstery bookstore, and director of the website Gorky (devoted to books and reading), had this exchange with an interviewer:

> KUPRYANOV: In the last two-three years a new reader has appeared, completely different, and in order to satisfy this reader we need to expand. We have to display more books according to classifications that before we didn't have any interest in. For example, we never used to have comics. We were skeptical about this genre. And now it's clear that there are new processes going on in the intellectual segment of the comics scene, really interesting stuff. And we can't not share this with our customers. By the way, our country has more comics shops than independent bookstores.
>
> INTERVIEWER: Really?
>
> KUPRYANOV: Absolutely. In Tyumen there are three comics shops and one No One Sleeps, a classic independent. There's one more: a knock-off of Republic, which they call Democracy there. And that's it. Everything else is chain stores. (Shenkman, "Liudi")[21]

---

ter text and pictures together, as if we were talking about something improper" (Miktum, "Interv'iu"). As noted, such attitudes steadily gave ground, even among intellectuals, over the course of the 2010s.

21. Georgy "Gosha" Elaev, director of the Comic Arts Tyumen festival and a resident of Tyumen, confirmed this account.

For some, of course, print books are so twentieth century, LOL. Luckily, the internet offers even more fabulous diversity and choice than IRL—and often for free. Those seeking out webcomics in Russia may turn to social media portals like VKontakte for Roman Gorbachev's superhero parody *The Keepers* (Blyustiteli, 2013) and the wry stylings of Duran or Martadello; Instagram and Facebook for the Chelyabinsk cartoonist Anastasia "Stushona" Ivanova's *Comicada* (2018), about "a reflective girl falling into different life situations";[22] pornokomiks.com for . . . what one might expect; authors' own sites, like that of Ufa-based Olga Makarova's sci-fi series *Gifts of Wandering Ice*; or the website *Avtorsky Komiks*[23] for the thousands of choices available there.[24]

Today's web-based works[25] stand on the shoulders of a previous generation who pioneered the form in the 2000s, among them Oleg Tishchenkov, whose *Tomcat* book series started as postings on his LiveJournal blog; Linor Goralik, especially her *F—ing Hare and His Imaginary Friends*;[26] and Konstantin Shelikhov (aka Kotka). Special mention in this regard goes to Uno Moralez (Stas Orlov), a sensation beyond Russia, whose unsettling sequential imagery (some of it in animated GIFs) has haunted the internet for over a decade (see Collins, "Uno").[27]

Another way to read and discuss comics for free: informal comics and manga clubs organized by fans, which predated the KomMissia festival. Such clubs were scattered throughout the country—a particularly energetic one was led by komiksist Konstantin Dubkov in Ekaterinburg. Their activities ranged from discussions of particular works to hosting lectures to creating comics

---

22. From her Behance page: https://www.behance.net/gallery/63853247/Comics-about-life-and-not-only.

23. Home of *Gennady the Dove* (*Golub' Gennadiy*), a well-known work about a misanthropic dove by a female Ukrainian artist known as Koro (who writes in Russian). Komfederatsia published a collection under the same title in 2018.

24. According to the site's administrator Nikolai "Swamp Dog" Kovalev: "We see thousands of webcomics authors, the majority of which, however, can barely draw and write. . . . There's a lot of turnover in webcomics; since the majority get no money or real fame for their hard work, their enthusiasm quickly dries up" (Liashchenko, "Kuda").

25. Not all succeed. In 2012, Narr8, an online platform for interactive comics, launched with an investment of $4 million USD; it closed after three years (Arkhangel'skaia, "Million"). Not including illegal scanlations of manga, other online comics reading portals include Uni-Comics, Comics Maniac, Drawn Stories, and Comixbox. Various presses also allow access to digital comics, like Comics Publisher.

26. A 2018 English-language collection of Goralik's work translates this series as "Bunny-puss" (see Goralik, *Found*). A noted author, interviewer, and translator, Goralik's comics work is widely known, particularly among the literati.

27. For creators, the internet might also serve as a source of revenue, through crowdfunding campaigns such as that of Serge Mozhev of Tambov, who went on Planet.ru to finance social activist comics about his hometown (the project apparently failed to meet its goal of 18,000 rubles). See Mozhev's proposal and video pitch here: https://planeta.ru/campaigns/88790.

FIGURE 3.1. Alexander Kunin, first director of the Center for Comics and Visual Culture (TsKVK) in Moscow, 2013. Photo by José Alaniz.

in a supportive environment. Before the boom, especially in the provinces where comics culture was a rarity and comics inaccessible, such clubs could "do a lot of good," Kunin told me in 2013. Cartoonist and KOM veteran Alim Velitov, who with comics scholar Mikhail Khachaturov cofounded the very active Moscow club in 2008, advised groups and those wishing to start them in other cities (Velitov, "Sem'").

Eventually, Russians eager to read comics could visit their local library or comics center—state-sponsored institutions partly built on the foundations of the comics clubs. The first one was established in August 2010, at Moscow's Russian State Library for Youth (RGBM). The Center for Comics and Visual Culture (TsKVK) emerged from the manga roundtable organized by Kunin and Shamarina at that year's KomMissia festival. RGBM director Irina Mikhnova, who participated in the roundtable, saw the tremendous relevance of manga and comics to the library's mission. Kunin became the center's first director (see figure 3.1).

The center rapidly moved to develop a superb comics collection through purchase and donations. For example, collector Vadim Palonin gifted the center over 450 items, while reader Alexei Musatov donated 100 works of comics history and theory (Kunin, "Moskovskii": 108–109). Within three years, the

FIGURE 3.2. Boomkniga founder and director Dmitry Yakovlev and artist Yulia Nikitina at the first Comics Library in St. Petersburg, 2013. Photo by José Alaniz.

TsKVK had amassed over 2,500 items in several languages (Kunin, "Komiks v Rossii": 45). The center organized events, including lectures, exhibits, artist signings, and conferences; published a journal of conference proceedings, *Izotext*; as noted came to host KomMissia; and promoted comics at other libraries throughout the country. In 2017, TsKVK was renamed the Center for Drawn Stories and Imagery (Tsentr risovannykh istoriy i izobrazheniy, or TsRII).

In the 2010s, library- and city-affiliated comics centers sprung up throughout the country.[28] One of them, the Comics Library in St. Petersburg, housed at the Izmailovsky library and part of the Lermontov Interdistrict Centralized Library System, opened in December 2012 under curator Sergei Karandeyev (see figure 3.2). On September 4, 2019, the library's Facebook page posted this reflection, which accounts for the experiences of many such institutions in Russia:

---

28. These include the Urals Comics Center, founded by Konstantin Dubkov in Ekaterinburg in 2015, and the Penza Comics Library, built on the personal holdings of local collector and teacher Rashid Yanov in 2012.

Over the course of these years we've lived through a lot. Indeed: we even encountered misunderstandings, as well as a disdain for comics as an art form. But always we found those willing to open themselves up to the enormous world of drawn stories and meet it halfway. In our history there is more than one incident when librarians and even whole libraries, who were at first inimical to comics, started to become interested in them once they got acquainted with us, and to work with comics themselves. We believe that it is never too late to open your heart to comics.[29]

The Rise of Russian Comics Studies

Concomitant to comics' heightened attention and financial appeal during the Medvedev administration, comics studies began to coalesce as a field in Russia. While it remains a tiny segment of academia, which by and large continues to view graphic narrative with some skepticism—as anything beyond a manifestation of Western-oriented youth culture, rather than, say, a legitimate object of study in its own right—the researching, teaching, and writing on comics and related media represents yet more proof of the form's new viability in a country long known for resisting it on ideological grounds.

We need look no further than the very late Soviet era (1987, to be precise) for evidence of the previous regime's recalcitrance. "Through the Language of Satire," an article in *Tvorchestvo* (*Creativity*), journal of the USSR Union of Artists, discussed the work of the artist Yury Aratovsky, who combined words and sequential imagery in panels, which the unbiased eye would identify as comics. But not the eye of the unnamed Soviet critic who stiltedly wrote:

> The unique [*svoeobraznoe*] combination of disparate meaningfully figural principles in the work that went into this book yield unexpected and interesting results, whose form of elaboration, according to the concrete criteria for the working out of plot, we could define as "comics." However, the given work has nothing in common—with the exception, possibly, of some superficial elements of the structure of the layout and the unfolding of the graphic story—with the purely diverting productions of the Western book market, which serve as it were as the personification of bourgeois mass culture. (*Tvorchestvo*, "Iazikom": n.p.)

---

29. The post was in part a response to minister of culture Vladimir Medinsky's comments on comics earlier that month at the Moscow International Book Exhibit and Fair (discussed in chapter 5). See the full post here: https://www.facebook.com/comics.library/photos/a.30314427 6533283/1588284644685900/?type=3&theater.

It took the implosion of the Soviet Union (which, incidentally, led to the closure of *Tvorchestvo*) before comics got more even-handed treatment from Russian scholars. Chief among them was Viktor Erofeyev, a well-regarded novelist and literary critic, whose 1995 essay "Comics and the Comics Disease" finally gave the medium its due. This does not mean that he wholeheartedly embraced it: "No single art form so precisely conveys the ongoing dumbing-down and debasement of humanity as does comics. . . . Comics is the mirror to man's collapse, the cheery pictures that accompany our own decomposition" (Erofeyev, "Comics": 36).

Despite such pronouncements, meant to provoke as much as edify, Erofeyev has no truck with graphic narrative as an amoral art form one may use to illuminate or "dumb down" the reader. In short—and to mix metaphors—by stripping comics of much of their Soviet-era baggage, Erofeyev's Wild Age essay opened a window to some much-needed fresh air. Critics and educators would continue to debate what they saw as the merits and hazards of the medium, as seen in a 2002 roundtable organized by the journal *Narodnoe Obrazovanie* (*National Education*),[30] but notions of comics as unequivocally injurious, dumb, or "the personification of bourgeois mass culture" steadily ceded ground.

More and more, comics made it into classrooms. Olga Davtyan, a well-known translator from French and a lecturer at St. Petersburg's Smolny College of Free Art and Sciences, started teaching courses on French and Russian comics in the early 2000s (Duncan, "Graphic": ii). In 2011, Khikhus led the first Russian faculty on comics-making at Synergy University (aka Moscow University for Industry and Finance), a private higher learning institution (*Ria Novosti*, "V Moskovskoi").

With the post-2009 boom, things really started picking up. A new generation of scholars built on the work of Erofeyev, Zaslavsky, and others who had for years recognized comics as a worthy object of study. As noted, the essay collection *Russian Comics* appeared in 2010, though its origins date to the "100 Years: Comics in Russia" exhibit in St. Petersburg in 1998.

As in the West, much comics scholarship in Russia was founded on (or reacting to) long-standing fan discourses in boosterish publications (many of them online) such as *Spidermedia* and *Comics Boom*. Many internet forums had also proliferated since the advent of the web, a central node of which was formed by Andrei Ayoshin's database/gallery/community *Komiksolyot* (1999). Kirill Sukhhov's fanzine *Big Name Fan* (launched in 2013), devoted to the Russian comics industry, also deserves mention in this regard, as does

---

30. See Alaniz, *Komiks*: 105–111 for an account of this roundtable and the scandal that swirled around it.

Kunin's *Khroniki Chedrika* (Chedrik's Chronicles) website (2009), which also published a print edition (No. 0) in 2009.[31]

2010 saw the first issue of *Izotext,* TsKVK's annual comics studies journal. Coeditor Kunin proudly announced in its inaugural foreword: "We have no doubt that Russia, today joining itself to global cultural processes, will in time put forth its own unique school of the ninth art. Meanwhile, comics, manga, and other forms of izotext[32] will assume an important place in the reading repertoire of young people in our country" (Kunin, "K chitateliu!": 4). The issue led off with an essay on the comics museum at Angoulême by French scholar and publisher Thierry Groensteen, who had attended Boomfest 2009, and included comics as well as academic articles.

A later article by Kunin, in *Izotext's* second volume (2011), folded graphic narrative into a larger "iconic turn" of late and post-Soviet culture; with reproductions from Scott McCloud's *Understanding Comics* as illustrations.[33] McCloud's seminal and much-argued-over work, which appeared in an official Russia translation only in 2016 (from Beloe Yabloko Press), was taken up as a sort of bible for the aspiring comics artist. It was applied by Alim Velitov in his comics-making courses (Kriukov, "Energiia"), along with Stan Lee and John Buscema's *How to Draw Comics the Marvel Way* (1978).

Izotext also launched the first annual international comics studies conference in Russia, also named Izotext, organized by Kunin as part of KomMissia in May 2016.[34] The two-day conference, whose proceedings appeared later that year in *Izotext* the journal, devoted attention to comics in cultural studies, manga for girls, Jeff Lemire's *Sweet Tooth,* and myriad other topics. In 2020 the conference, now called "The World of Comics," moved to the Institute for Oriental and Classical Studies at the National Research University Higher School of Economics.

A rival conference, Comix Studies, also launched in June 2016, at the Comics Library in St. Petersburg. It was founded by Alexei Pavlovsky (then a history graduate student) and manga scholar Yulia Tarasyuk. Literary critic Vasily Vladimirsky attended the conference and reported:

> In the last half-decade the Russian comics industry has gone through a fantastic upswing. Initial print runs in the tens of thousands are not uncommon,

---

31. The website published a translation of chapter 7 of my book *Komiks: Comic Art in Russia,* while the 2009 print edition included a translation of my essay "Notes from the Inside," on my experience as a jurist for the 2008 KomMissia comics festival.

32. Kunin put forth this umbrella term to account for the different national traditions of graphic narrative going by different names ("K chitateliu!": 3).

33. With translation by Zaslavsky.

34. It was held annually at the RGBM for several years.

second printings are a normal part of business, hundreds of independent comics shops all over the country guarantee lighting-fast sales and a quick return on investment—a performance which publishers engaged in the "traditional" book trade can only dream of. As for readers, things are going well there too: industry-specific festivals attract up to 20–30,000 people over a couple of days, every important release has a thousand comments on the Russian internet. The time has come for introspection, for an apprehension of comics in the context not only of mass culture, but of culture in and of itself. This is precisely what Comix Studies, the first conference of its kind, was devoted to. (Vladimirskiy, "Nauka")

Presenters at the first Comix Studies conference dealt with, among other things, comics in advertising; the representation of the Holocaust in Eric Heuvel, Ruud van der Rol, and Lies Schippers's *The Search*; history in graphic narrative; double identity from Mr. Hyde to the Hulk; and various definitions of the form.

In addition to Kunin and Zaslavsky, prominent twenty-first-century Russian comics scholars include Pavlovsky (founder of the Comix Studies project); Natalya Samutina (Cultural Studies and Manga, National Research University Higher School of Economics); Yulia Magera, aka Yuki Maguro (National Research University Higher School of Economics, founder of the manga research project Mangalectory, editor of the collections *Manga in Russia and Japan*, vol. 1 [Kabinetniy uchenii, 2015] and vol. 2 [Comics Factory, 2018]); Daria Dmitrieva (Cultural Studies, author of *The Age of Superheroes* [*Vek supergeroev*], 2015); Tarasyuk (former curator of the Comics Library, St. Petersburg, founding curator of the Center for Manga and Comics, St. Petersburg); Yevgeny Kharitonov, author of *The Ninth Art: Foreign Fantasy Comics* (*Devyatoe isskustvo: zarubezhnie fantasticheskie komiksy*, 2004); Irina Makoveyeva; and Maria Evdokimova.[35]

Much of the most important work in Russian comics studies verges on the archaeological, that is, the excavation and bringing back to light of works and creators from a national comics tradition little known and less understood (we can't even blame it all on generations of Soviet anti-comics vitriol, either; see below). Zaslavsky provides a model for this type of research in "The Ulyanovsk Comics Journals *Seryozhka* and *Watermelon* (1994–1999): Materials

---

35. Notable foreign scholars of Russian comics include Irina Antanasijević (University of Belgrade Faculty of Philology, Serbia), author of the magisterial *Russian Comics in the Kingdom of Yugoslavia* (Novi Sad: Komiko, 2014); John Etty, author of *Graphic Satire in the Soviet Union: Krokodil's Political Cartoons* (2019); Natalija Majsova (Faculty of Social Sciences, University of Ljubljana, Slovenia); Reeta Kangas (Russian Studies, University of Turku, Finland); Anni Lappela (Russian Studies, University of Helsinki); and Paula Järvilehto (Faculty of Information Technology and Communication Sciences, University of Tampere, Finland).

Towards the Publication of a Complete Electronic Archive in *Komiksolyot*" (2018), published in *Izotext*. As both industry insider and dogged historian, Zaslavsky makes a convincing case for this longest-lived of all 1990s Russian comics journals (it underwent a name change in 1997), founded by publishing magnate Aram Gabrelyanov in Lenin's hometown, as a vital link between the present industry and the so-called Wild Age. This despite the fact, I would venture to guess, that many contemporary Russian comics fans have never heard of it.

The transmedial resonances of comics have also attracted scholarly interest, as seen in Nina Tsirkun's *American Cine-Comics: Evolution of a Genre* (2014). While not a scholarly work per se, and riddled with errors, Andrei Anichkin and Vladimir Osipov's *Comics Collection: 1950–2000* (*Al'manakh komiksov: 1950–2000*) (2019), presents an important overview of the genealogy of Russian comics, still being reconstructed.

In a 2017 interview, Pavlovsky, writer of a graduate thesis devoted to the 1980s and 1990s "Wild Age" and founder of the research project Comix Studies (Nauka o komiksakh), an interdisciplinary society for the study of graphic narrative in Russia, identified the industry's major challenge as financial: "How to go from philanthropy to capitalism—no one knows." Other problems ran the gamut from the need for "fresh blood," especially scriptwriters, to a paucity of works tackling "mature" themes. For Pavlovsky this meant more topical and "meaningful" stories—comics both about the country's troubled history (the Gulags, the WWII siege of Leningrad) as well as about its troubled present (Crimea, the Donbass conflict). "If Russia gave birth to great literature and painting," he concluded, "then great comics is the next step" (Bondareva, "Chto").

The *Raznoobrazie* of Twenty-First-Century Russian Comics

"Great" and "mature," of course, is in the eye of the reader. Perhaps more important than any particular topics, what has characterized the development of the industry since the rise of Putin is its proliferation of subjects, genres, and formats—in short, its *raznoobrazie* (variety). This *raznoobrazie* makes it impossible to identify an "essence" unique to Russian comics (though some keep trying), but it also leads to the production of material that will suit most every taste—in the long run a better barometer for the viability of a mass medium.

Taking in the sweep of history over the last twenty years, we may observe how educators, artists and the state have exploited comics (1) for joke-telling and drama, as seen in the strips and photocomics appearing in the newspaper

Life (due to its enormous print run, likely the publication in which Russians have read comics the most consistently since the early 2000s; see Zaslavskiy, "Ul'ianovskie": 31); (2) for edification, as in psychologist Dmitry Smirnov's *Magnificent Adventures* (with art by, among others, Roman Surzhenko), a notable didactic comics series for young readers, which lasted twenty-two issues, from 1999 to 2003, or the more recent *It's True!: A Devil's Dozen Komiks Stories about Science and Scientists* (Eksmo, 2018), a collaboration of the journal *Schrödinger's Cat*, the Skolkovo Institute of Science and Technology, and several comics artists; and (3) for titillation, as seen in the hardcore hentai porn of Grif and the erotica of Konstantin Komardin. Early twenty-first-century *komiks* ran the gamut from the children's series *Leshiki:*[36] *The Mysterious Abductors* by Sergei Kurchenko and Olga Kozlovskaya (Nitusov, 2004) to *Fairy Tales in Comics* by Stanislav Shchepin (Comics Publisher, 2019), from the ironic playfulness of Andrei Kuznetsov's faux lubok series (2003) to the masculine satire of Zakhar Yashchin's stories about the Dude (*chuvak*, 2005)[37] to the aforementioned Oleg Tishchenkov's internet-to-print success *The Tomcat* (Kot, 2008).

KOM veteran Askold Akishin's 2006 adaptation of the 1939 Tatyana Sikorskaya children's poem "The Gift" embodies, perhaps better than any other comics work of the era, the contradictions of a resurgent Russia under Putin. The two-page story reproduces the original text as it illustrates in twelve panels the story of a little girl wondering aloud to her teddy bear Mishka what she will give "dear Stalin" for his birthday. After rejecting several possibilities ("A tank? . . . For Stalin it's not good enough, either!"), the girl finally settles on Mishka himself, her most prized possession. She holds her stuffed friend up close with a somber or perhaps dreamy expression, congratulating him, saying, "So clap your paws together / Jump up, be happy now!" (Sikorskaia and Akishin, "Podarok": 47) (see figure 3.3).

The dialogue chillingly resonates with the ubiquitous Stalinist slogan of the 1930s, "Life Has Gotten Better, Comrades, Life Has Gotten More Joyous" (*Zhit' Stalo Luchshee, Tovarishchi, Zhit' Stalo Veselee*)—all about compulsory happiness under dictatorship. At her tender age, the child has learned to "speak Bolshevik" (in historian Stephen Kotkin's Foucauldian formulation; see Kotkin, *Magnetic*: 14). In short, "The Gift" risks coming off as a comics version of Soviet propaganda posters like Nina Vatolina et al.'s *Thank You Comrade Stalin for Our Happy Childhood!* (1938).

---

36. A reference to the *leshiy,* a type of Slavic wood spirit.

37. Published online and in two collections, *The Book of the Dude* (2010) and *The Big Book of the Dude* (2012), both from Boomkniga.

FIGURE 3.3. Askold Akishin's adaptation of Tatyana Sikorskaya's
1939 children's poem "The Gift" (2006). Used with permission.

Why exactly would the magazine *The Toy and Presents for Grown-Ups and
Children* publish a pro-Stalin comics story in 2006, long after Stalin's crimes
against millions of his own people had been brought to light? An editorial
note acknowledges the . . . questionability of such a move: "Despite today's
perception about our country's life in those years, these [poetic] lines seem
sincere" (47).

Yet precisely here we find in comics' multimodal proclivity for speaking out of both sides of its mouth a repudiation of any monologic "sincer-

ity." For whatever else they may be, comics are not *sincere*—at least not in the straightforward meaning of that term. Comics, according to Charles Hatfield, "graphically assert truthfulness through the admission of artifice" (Hatfield, *Alternative*: 131). Comics' patent "artifice" in turn leads to what he calls their "ironic authentication" (125), which may among other things destabilize "single-track," unified ideological messages.[38] Similarly, Hillary Chute argues for graphic narrative's "expansive visual-verbal grammar [which] can offer a space for ethical representation without problematic closure" ("Shadow": 352). Through their self-reflexive "fakeness," then, comics communicate like no other medium a sense of the daunting multivoicedness, multivalence, and multiperspectival nature of human perception (whether for truth-telling or to construct elaborate fantasies).

To put it more simply, Akishin's sequential drawings added to Sikorskaya's text in "The Gift" unmoor the poem from its original meaning, imbuing the whole with an unavoidable layer of irony. And this not only because we are a long way off from 1939. "Dear Stalin" in Akishin's renderings looks more malevolent—thuggish, even—than Sikorskaya's words-only encomium might lead one to believe. A doll, which the little girl considers as a gift, lies prone on its back with vacant eyes staring back at the reader, looking just enough like a dead body to suggest the great leader's many victims (46). And so on. A close-up panel of the sacrificial Mishka (the same in which the child tells him, "Jump up, be happy now!") shows not joy on its blank, stitched-together face, but if anything—given the reader's knowledge of twentieth-century national atrocities—a silent scream of terror (47).

"The Gift's" final panel hammers home the subversive subtext. Sikorskaya tells us that the girl's gift will reach the "friend of children" in the "big Kremlin." Akishin dutifully illustrates the indicated location, where we'll find he who is "the strongest, the best, the nicest on Earth!" (47). But savvy readers of course know who works in the "big Kremlin" today, filling Stalin's old seat. And what flag flies over the old fortress? Akishin's black and white ink strokes suggest the banner of the USSR, which makes sense for the period in which the poem was written. But another reading also presents itself: that maybe 1939 is not that far off after all; maybe things haven't changed all that much. That banner's never really come down. After all, "the strongest, the best, the nicest on Earth!" doesn't sound all that different from "A man like Putin, / full of strength" (as Singing Together once crooned).

Russian comics in this era could also assert a more forthright social message along with the irony. The EU-funded Respect project (launched in 2011;

---

38. See also Kuhlman and Alaniz for an elaboration on how comics' "ironic authenticity" may challenge dominant ideological narratives of present and past ("General": 18).

see Alaniz, "Flashy") sought to use drawn stories to instill tolerance for historically othered social groups. The project emerged from Khikhus's repeated experiences with aggression and violence on city streets due to his appearance (he wore dreadlocks) (Voronkova, "Komu": 62). It produced thousands of booklets and took artists to workshop directly with young people in numerous regions of the country.

Once the Russian government launched its own initiatives to support the domestic industry, they were initially met with skepticism from some in the comics community. Kunin and others aired their misgivings about a 2015 presidential grant of 13 million rubles (about $184,000 USD) awarded to Dobroe Slovo ("kind word"), a Moscow-based foundation "for the Support and Development of Artistic and Journalistic Creativity" (which had existed for barely a year), to contribute to the development of Russian comics. Given the high rates of corruption and cronyism in Russia, it did not seem very reassuring that the foundation, which had no connections at all with the comics world, did have links to a "large media holding" (Akhmirova, "Putin").[39] It didn't require great deductive skills to ascertain which "large media holding" that might be, especially when Dobroe Slovo used some of the money to hold several comics-making workshops administered by Bubble, a comics company run by the son of a close associate of the president. In addition to lectures, presentations, and a nationwide competition, the project culminated in 2016 with a 300-page *sbornik, There Shall Be Russian Comics!* (*Rossiyskomu komiksu byt'*), composed of project participants' works. It was distributed free.[40]

Komiks in the Art World

In the twenty-first century, comics also continued to make inroads into Russian contemporary art.[41]

---

39. As Kunin wrote at the time: "I will be happy if these 13 million (or even two or three of them) do in actuality go towards some sort of support of the domestic culture of drawn stories. But I have the suspicion that in the best case we will never know about the fate of this money, and in the worst, that everything will end in the discrediting of the genre on principle, that they will make a bogey out of it. As a result of which, it will become simply disreputable [*pozorno*] to continue to engage in comics and drawn stories in our country" ("13 millionov").

40. Another presidential grant competition was announced in 2018, for the creation of a Comic book on prehistoric peoples. This much smaller grant (the equivalent of about $7,000 USD) was awarded to the Chernozemya Center for the Preservation of Cultural Heritage; a group of young students from the provincial cities of Lipetsk and Voronezh produced the book in 2019.

41. This section supplements and updates Alaniz, *Komiks*: chapter 5.

Artist Georgy "Zhora" Litichevsky, who has been making comics since the 1970s, wrote in his review of an exhibit at KomMissia 2010 on Comics in Contemporary Art, on the peculiar challenges faced by Russian artists working in this area:

> Judging by the works presented at the M'ars Gallery exhibit, we could say that in Russian art too one meets with the "Lichtenstein approach" along with the "Pettibon approach." It's also obvious that both these approaches are impossible here in their pure form. The followers of Lichtenstein in Russia (no matter how ironic and analytical their relation to comics) are compelled as well to (unwillingly) propagandize the object of their irony and analysis, an object which for the Russian viewer is still unusual. Pettibon's Russian brothers-in-arms, meanwhile, who find themselves as it were inside of the comics, developing their own comics language and constructing their own environment, cannot limit themselves only to this, and are compelled (again) to invoke global comics traditions. Both groups are united by a hidden or explicit promotion of comics, which does not at all concern their fellow artists in the US or other countries where the position of comics is obvious and solid. (Litichevskii, "Estetika": 20)

But already as Litichevsky was writing his review, this cautious stance toward comics in the art world (as with so much else relating to comics in 2010s Russia) was changing. Just four years later, the 2014 "After the Comics" exhibit curated by Elizaveta Shagina at St. Petersburg's Erarta Museum (the country's largest private museum of contemporary art) showed the depth of the changes. "The relationship between comics and art in Russia has never been simple," wrote Shagina in the exhibit catalog, "but that makes it all the more interesting to ponder" (10). The exhibit's artists, mostly Russians, included Litichevsky, Nikolai Vasilyev, Nikolai Kopeikin, Alexander Petrelli, Georgy "Gosha" Ostretsov, Yury Alexandrov, Irina Vasilyeva, and others who had largely or wholly embraced a comics sensibility in their work.

For many, this often meant embracing the storytelling capacities of comics—part of what Shagina meant with her "never been simple" remark. For as art historian Alexander Borovsky wrote in *The New Storytellers in Russian Art of the 20th-21st Centuries* (2014):

> Russian fine art has found itself in an eternal love-hate relationship with storytelling and narrative. This is understandable; Russian culture is literature-oriented, while fine art constantly feels what seems like a natural urge to shrug off "literary approaches." . . . The peak of the "state of love" came in the

second half of the 19th century, while "the loveless state" [*nelyubvi*] defini-
tively reigned in the era of the classic Russian avant garde. ("Novye": 5)[42]

Russian art's problem with pictorial narrative seems to extend even to
the term *comics*. Borovsky's descriptions of the works he chooses to discuss
avoid the use of that term, instead talking around it. For example, he refers
to Kopeikin as "a storyteller and at the same time a portrayer [*sochinitel' i
odnovremenno—izobrazitel'*]" (22), when this artist's stylistic roots in particular clearly lie in cartoons.[43] In fact, his *Skirmish in the Boonies* (*Stychka na
kulichkakh*, 2009) and other works were brought to R-rated animated life in
the video for the rock group Leningrad's song "Khimki Forest" (directed by
Andrei Zakirzyanov, 2010). The video graphically depicts a cartoon armaged-
don, with recognizable figures like Spider-Man, Shapoklyak (from the Cheburashka animated films), the Wolf from the *Just You Wait!* cartoon series, and
the Simpsons ripping each other to pieces on a battlefield. Kopeikin's "warring
snowmen" series also recalls Igor Kolgarev's thematically similar graphic novel
War with the Snowmen (1992), one of the last KOM publications.

Other artists featured in the 2015 "New Storytellers" exhibit at St. Petersburg's Russian Museum (the occasion for the book of the same name) likewise
turn to decidedly comics-like touches—if not to outright making comics on
canvas. Vladimir Shinkarev's *Holiday Tree* (1997) recounts a folk song through
text and image, arranged in ten panels and four tiers; Motornina and Alexei
Baranov's *Diafilm No. 1* (2007) tells a very adult story in a Soviet-era film strip
format originally aimed at children; Vasily Golubev's *Partisan District* (2004)
and *Good Film!* (2013) utilize text labels ("We pop up out of the bushes!")
identifying individuals, circumstances, and dialogue; Elena Gubanova and
Ivan Govorkov's *Incident in the Snowstorm* (2009), a series of six paintings,
each smaller than the last, sequentially "zooms in" through a window; Yury
Alexandrov's *An Authentic Picture of a 1930s Political Killing* (1998) repur-
poses Milo Manara-style comics panels. Alexandrov, Kopeikin, and other
artists appeared in both the Erarta and Russian Museum shows, narrowing
the difference still further between "comics" and "storytellers/portrayers" to
effectively zero.

Other contemporary artists working in a similar vein include Lyudmilla
Gorlova, Leonid Tishkov, the PG Group, Konstantin Zvezdochetov, and Maria
Arendt, who executes delicate word and picture combinations on textile. Kras-

---

42. Borovsky sees the recent reemergence of narrative in fine art as part of a larger cultural
"narrative turn"; see Borisenkova, "Narrativniy."

43. A 2009 exhibit of works by Kopeikin, a member of the Mitki group, was titled "Anireal-
ism" (*mul'trealizm*).

noyarsk conceptualist artist Vasily Slonov's 2015 "Imperial Kokoshniki" series (named after a type of traditional woman's headdress) depicts a bear anally violating Mickey Mouse.

Add to the foregoing the increasing presence of works by self-identified comics artists in museums, the most prominent being Viktoria Lomasko.[44]

More unusual are fine artists producing works that most would identify as actual comics, and even embracing the label "komiksist." Litichevsky is the best example here, while in more recent years veteran artist Viktor Goppe has been creating "poetic comics" (*poeticheskie komiksy*) based on other poets' verses. Unusually, even uniquely, Goppe places himself in competition with the mainstream comics industry. "I have some friction with contemporary Moscow comics artists who are trying to position themselves as epigones of Western comics," he told an interviewer. Comics, he claims, "is a model of the capitalist system, which reorganizes itself, eats itself, and rebirths itself" (Semenova, "Doroga"). Like Akishin with his ironic adaptation of a pro-Stalinist poem, Goppe sees in comics a means to evade the "monologism" of an all-text or all-single-image approach.

The Small and Midsize Press

In 2014, an artist from Omsk, a city in central Siberia not far from the border with Kazakhstan, launched a self-published comic book series. Ivan Eshukov's *Borovitsky* deals with an eponymous sleuth in 1919 Omsk, which was then under the control of the anti-communist Russian White forces led by Navy Admiral Alexander Kolchak. Eshukov himself calls his deliberately paced, eight-volume period piece with cosmic sequences a "mystical detective story" (Frazier, "Russia's"), while his art provides a tantalizing glimpse into what Moebius's work might have looked like if that French artist had grown up in Eurasia. *Borovitsky* proved one of the most highly regarded successes of Russian's burgeoning mid-2010s zine and small press culture.

Its partial origins lie in zines like Ilya Kitup's *Propeller* in the 1990s;[45] Volgograd's prolific KOmixSISTERS, made up of siblings Darya "Dasha Ko" and

---

44. Lomasko's art exhibits range from her early shows in Russia, like the 2015 Oxfam-supported "HIV: The Unequal Ones" (devoted to barriers facing HIV+ people) at St. Petersburg's Borey Arts Center, to monumentalist murals in various locals in New York, Germany, London, and elsewhere. Though to complicate matters, she does not consistently identify as a comics artist. See my conclusion.

45. As well as creators like those behind a self-published zine gifted to me in the Moscow metro in 1997 (Alaniz, *Komiks*: 100).

Maria Konopatova, active since 2007 (mutatis mutandis, they are the Hernandez Bros. of Russian comics); and small-print-run anthology series like *ChPKh,* published by Dmitry Yakovlev and SpB Nouvelles Graphiques in St. Petersburg, in the mid-2000s (and later picked up by BoomKniga). Greater access to and lower prices for photocopying equipment, risography and desktop publishing software, the rise of micropresses, and the greater emphasis on a DIY ethic among youth subcultures had led by the third Putin administration to a vibrant independent scene. Established publishers and professional artists also got into the act.

Works range from minicomix like Masha Foot's *Between Two Cities Part I* (n.d.), Lena Uzhinova's graphic medicine *Miracle* (2015), and Artyom Trakhanov's horror story *Slavic Nihilism* (2017); to perfect-bound books such as Pyotr Psymuline and Denis Alekseyev's *Gazelle of Death* (D. Ivanov, Sad Wave & Psymuline Publishing, 2017), based on Alekseyev's experiences driving punk bands on tour in his van. Others in this format are *Flowers on the Earth* (2015), an anthology of adaptations of the Soviet writer Andrei Platonov from alternative micropress Grotesque, in Voronezh, and the painted wordless comics of Yegor Vetlugin and Nikolai Pisarev's series *Objects* (Alt Graph, 2014). *Doctor Lucid* (Lyutsid) by writer Alexei Volkov and various artists (Izoteka, 2014), Daniil Vetluzhskikh and Alexander Andrianov's animal space epic *Dogs: Galaxy Gang* (KomFederatsia, 2017), Sergei Potapov and Kirill Cherkay's *Spidersnake Vs. Everything* (n.d.), and Tyumen artist Alexei Abramov's *Saga of a Clever Dog* (Saga o khitrom sobakene, Komfederatsiya, 2017), all appear in "floppy" format; *Chapiteau* (Brennik Arts, 2017) by Alexei Gordeyev and Eshukov, is minicomix on glossy paper.

The career arc of Danya Udobny, a young artist from Kaliningrad, presents a model many would doubtless like to follow. While in the US in 2010, Udobny grew enamored of Jeffrey Brown's work and soon after produced his own quirky, surrealist minicomix. These drew the attention of Boomfest director and Boomkniga founder Yakovlev, who published them along with new material in the collection *Withme* (Somnoi, 2014/2016).

The micropress Sputnikat, established in 2016 and directed by the Briton Christopher Rainbow (who teaches at Moscow's British Higher School of Art and Design, dubbed the Britanka), released a number of works by students and young komiksisty, like the anthology series *Personazh* (2016). Each volume depicts the life of one character (*perzonazh* in Russian), in chapters separately illustrated by different artists. Sputnikat has also published important work by young female artists, including *Gopnik*[46] *Walk with Me* (2018)

---

46. *Gopnik* means "thug," "crook," or "low-life."

by Kameellah (Kamilla Mamedova) and *Chill Pill* (2019) by Katya Dorokhina. Kisety (founded 2016),[47] an artist collective comprised of graduates from Viktor Melamed's illustration courses at the Britanka, produces an annual anthology in newsprint tabloid format, *Cut away from Yourself* (Rezh'te ot sebya), along with other works on the online platform Behance. *Gasoline: Labyrinth of the City,* a 2019 *sbornik* from the creator's association Dusha Russkoi Komiks Shkoly (The Spirit of the Russian Comics School), bills itself as an entry point for those curious to learn more about what is happening in the "underground" scene.

Festival catalogs have long served as a venue for comics works. These include those of Immersion: Days of World Comics Cultures in Ekaterinburg; Street Vision, devoted to street art, music, and new urban culture (since 2018, including comics) in Tomsk; and KomMissia. *Izotext,* in addition to its academic mission, also publishes short comics and excerpts of domestic and foreign material in translation.

Needless to say, what I have presented here is far from a comprehensive list.[48] But the alternative micropress Space Cow Comix in Tyumen, Siberia, affiliated with the Comic Arts Tyumen festival, does deserve special mention. Space Cow published its first anthology, *Black Milk,* in 2015, and has released a dazzling assortment of minicomix in various sizes and formats, a number of them in English or with English translation for distribution in foreign markets. Standout works include *Comix Book* (n.d.) by Qjay 163 (Alexei Zhulikov, aka Zakharchenko), partly created during the author's stay in a psychiatric hospital;[49] Zhulikov's *Like Everyone Else,* an oddly moving story about the friendship between two misfit boys; and Sasha Mccai's *Confusion* (2019), a coming out narrative (see Alaniz, "We").

Other publications, occupying a different segment of the market, often have larger print runs and higher production values (such as color), cater largely to alternative, nerd, or fan communities, and are sometimes found in bookstores, rather than exclusively in comics shops or at festivals.[50] Chief among these I would name stand-alone anthologies such as the commemorative *Super KOM* (KOM, 2011) and *Gorelovo* (Komilfo, 2015), by writer Vitaly Terletsky and twelve artists; as well as anthology series such as *Comics*

47. *Kisety* is a type of drawstring bag.

48. To see the extraordinary *raznoobrazie* of Russian comics culture, both mainstream and of every other stripe, one need look no further than the artist's alley page of the Comic Con Russia website.

49. Zhulikov spent sixteen days in a psychiatric ward as a way to evade military service (Zhulikov interview, 2019).

50. Caveat lector: These categories are fluid, generalizations impossible.

Republic (Live Bubbles, 2011) and *Parallel Comics* (Parallel, 2016); and graphic novellas such as the surrealist *Products 24* by Terletsky and Artyom Bizayev (Komilfo, 2017).[51] The anthology *Tsunami* (Jellyfish Jam, 2019), made up of works devoted to water disasters, represents the type of themed collection that publishers consider relatively easy to make (less of a commitment for creators) and release. 2019 saw the collected edition of *This Is Komiks*, a satirical four-issue series produced by and starring Stas Davydov and his associates from *This Is Horosho*, a popular Latvian web series. The motley crew traverses different Russian locales and historical eras in stories with art by Dmitry Dubrovin, Dmitry Osipenko, Askold Akishin, and others. The first issue's cover paid tribute to the classic cover of *Action Comics* #1 (1938).

I choose Alexei Volkov and Alexei Gorbut's *Conquerors of the Impossible* (Jellyfish Jam, 2017) as an exemplary object worthy of closer attention for how it lies at the intersection of geek culture, Russian sci-fi, and a form of transnational ironic nostalgia familiar to many comics readers, East and West. Founded in 2015 by former Chuk and Geek employee Beata Kotashevskaya, with investment from the shop's owners, Jellyfish Jam caters to an alternative audience steeped in US and European comics history and visual clichés, which Volkov and Gorbut's retro graphic novel revels in to great effect. The cover prominently features a Kirby-crackled cosmos-scape, while the story bristles with so many allusions and shout-outs to Western and Soviet popular culture as to nearly merit comparison with Alan Moore and Kevin O'Neill's *League of Extraordinary Gentlemen: The Black Dossier* (2007). If, as noted earlier, Oleg Kozhevnikov's *Batman in Russia* (1992) presents a tantalizing "alternate universe" view of how superhero comics might have operated in a Soviet Union with a Western-style comics culture, then *Conquerors of the Impossible* takes that experiment several steps forward in complexity and winking nuance.

In his afterword, comics scholar and author Kirill Kutuzov puts his finger on the matter:

> *Conquerors of the Impossible* is about the love for what developed in our country in that place which in the States was occupied by comics. Bookish fantasy, practical collective farm esoterica, the teachings of totalitarian cults and urban legends—all these cultural phenomena in the Soviet Union and Russia appeared and died out one by one; rarely did it ever occur to anyone

---

51. Terletsky is one of the most inventive of contemporary Russian comics scriptwriters, as seen in his visually arresting *Shafirovsky Avenue*, with art by Artyom Bizayev (Komilfo, 2015); his mind-bender *Georges d'Anthès: Astonishing Traveler through Time*, with art by Askold Akishin (Komilfo, 2016); and the dystopian fable Sobakistan, with art by Katya Chinasky (Terletsky Comics, 2019).

to bring together all these narratival treasures. *Conquerors* is precisely that, it's just such a bringing together, a supposition, a "what if?"

What would have happened if Daniil Kharms had written books about Nat Pinkerton? What if Detective Nick Carter had knocked about some pre-revolutionary Russian provincial towns? What if Jack Kirby had illustrated an Electronic story? (n.p.)[52]

The book's back cover puts it more succinctly: "A comics work uniting the traditions of the Silver Age of US comics with the scifi of the 'Soviet reading circle': Bulgakov meets Jack Kirby, the Strugatsky Brothers in the style of *Strange Adventures,* Kir Bulychev and Karel Čapek under the editorship of Julius Schwartz!"[53] Like Marvel and DC's mid-1990s joint experiment Amalgam Comics, then, Volkov and Gorbut's opus bills itself as the ultimate geek mash-up and labor of love (see figure 3.4).

Conquerors' plot, inspired both by Kirby's 1950s DC series *Challengers of the Unknown* and Yevgeny Veltistov's sci-fi novel *Ressy: An Elusive Friend* (1971), among other sources, features a quartet of super-powered beings: Mor, a living bacteriological transmitter; Proton, a child robot from the former regime, who spouts Soviet phrases; the temperature-altering Vulcanica; and their savant leader Mars, shown in flashback as a child solving the "anti-life equation" (in homage to Kirby's *Fourth World* series) before an annoyed teacher.

While on occasion making pointed critiques of post-Soviet neoliberalism, as when treacherous entrepreneurs seek to demolish a beloved stadium so as to build a trade center, Volkov and Gorbut seem most interested in their narrative as a pretext to play in beloved pop cultural sandboxes. The team's first adventure, for example, takes them to a rural farm where giant snakes hatch from eggs, the result of an experiment gone wrong—and a tribute to Mikhail Bulgakov's 1925 sci-fi novella *The Fatal Eggs.*[54]

Accumulating like snowflakes on your *shapka* fur hat in a Moscow winter flurry, the references come fast and furious: Mod-looking Mars is based on Dylan Moran and Syd Barrett, Vulcanica on Jane Birkin and Modesty Blaise, while the book's paratextual back matter notes that Proton's appearance owes to "Electronic from [Yevgeny] Migunov's illustrations, crossed with Astro

---

52. Yevgeny Veltistov wrote the children's sci-fi novels *Electronic: The Boy from the Suitcase* (1964) and *Ressy: An Elusive Friend* (1971), about a boy robot. These formed the basis for *The Adventures of Electronic,* a 1979 TV miniseries directed by Konstantin Bromberg.

53. Too juicy to resist, this language even makes it into the discourse of comics scholars like Pavlovsky, who calls Volkov and Kutuzov "the dynamic duo of Russian comics," who "cross Bulgakov with Kirby" (Bondareva, "Chto").

54. Dmitry Tkachev had previously adapted this story into comics, in *Mukha* #11 (1993): 20–31.

FIGURE 3.4. The cover of the first *Conquerors of the Impossible* by
Alexei Volkov and Alexei Gorbut (2017). Used with permission.

Boy" (n.p.)—in short, they are all walking quotations. El-Itsa, a girl from the
future, evokes both classic anime and Alisa Seleznyova, familiar to generations of Soviet readers as the young heroine of a Kir Bulychev sci-fi children's
book series; machine designs derive from Dr. Who's Tardis and HAL 9000
from *2001: A Space Odyssey,* some of the costuming from Marcel Allain and
Pierre Souvetre's classic Fantomas. Even *Conquerors'* sound effects are borrowed: When Mor punches a villain, we see the word "POU!," a transliteration of "Pow!" (n.p.) (see the sound effects section in chapter 4). And on and

on. All of this recalls nothing so much as the endlessly allusive play of Viktor Pelevin's 199 novel *Generation "P"* (aka *Homo Zapiens*).

Along with Kirby's, the predominant stylistic influence on the novel is that of Yevgeny Migunov, a renowned Soviet-era cartoonist and illustrator of children's sci-fi. For Chuk and Geek's Ivan Chernyavsky, this fact makes *Conquerors of the Impossible* an important, even patriotic work—rather than a mere collection of Easter eggs. As he told me, "More people will learn about Migunov through this blending of US and Russian styles. Through your art style you can show that you're from Russia" (Chernyavsky interview, 2017). I agree, though would add that Volkov and Gorbunov's exhilarating mash-up of native, Western, and Japanese traditions itself—like a superhero comics version of Vladimir Nabokov's Antiterra—rebukes long-standing notions of Russian comics as having nothing to offer but remixes of preexisting foreign material.[55] Despite the many imported elements, the novel does have very Russian DNA. The fact that Volkov and Gorbut present the story in defamiliarizing black and white, rather than color as the original sources appear, also argues for something beyond slavish epigonism—to a cool distance from the material, even.

Above all, *Conquerors* "chart[s] the ways in which graphic narratives have been shaped by aesthetic, social, political, economic and cultural interactions that reach across national boundaries in an interconnected and globalizing world" (Denson et al., *Transnational*: 1), validating all the more the recent transnational turn in both comics studies[56] and Slavic studies. As Connor Doak, Kevin Platt, and Vlad Strukov write in regard to the latter:

> The prefix *trans* suggests both an emphasis on movement *between* nations, as well as a gesturing *beyond* the nation as an epistemological paradigm, though it does not assume—as some predicted in the 1990s—the demise of the nation as an empirical phenomenon. . . . Moreover, whereas globalization theory assumed the traffic of ideas would flow from West to East, as developed countries exported liberal democracy to the post-socialist world, the past twenty years have proved that multidirectional verbs of motion are

---

55. On notions that Russian comics only combines elements from other traditions, see comments by Konstantin Dubkov, Andrei Snegirov, and Alexei Lukyanchikov, as well as Zaslavsky's response, in Alaniz, *Komiks*: 123.

56. For more on the transnational turn in comics studies, see Denson et al., "Introducing"; Schmitz-Emams, "Graphic"; Brienza, "Manga"; and Kuhlman and Alaniz, "General." On the transnational turn in Slavic studies, see also Connor Doak, Andy Byford, and Stephen Hutchings, eds., *Transnational Russian Studies* (2020); Kevin M. F. Platt, ed., *Global Russian Cultures* (2019); and Vlad Strukov and Sarah Hudspith, eds., *Russian Culture in the Age of Globalization* (2018).

needed to describe the direction of travel. ("Transnational": 3, emphasis in original)

Simply put, the rise of the Russian comics industry since 1991—despite a lot of blood and suffering in the 1990s and early 2000s—is the result of transnational cultural processes that, especially after 2011, have led to remarkable growth and relative stability. That industry's existence is a testament to how "people, cultural artefacts, and ideas move across geographical and political borders" (Doak, Platt, and Strukov, "Transnational": 3)—memic migrations that made possible the emergence of figures like Volkov, Gorbut, and Kutuzov, ultrageeks beholden to popular culture both oceans away and right there at home.

Avid devotees of classic US mainstream comics, Volkov and Kutuzov administrated Old Komix, a *publika* (public page) on the VKontakte social media site, dedicated to Golden, Silver, and Bronze Age material. Volkov and Kutuzov created Dr. Lucid, a sort of Golden Age Sandman knockoff with a Lovecraftian twist. Gorbut, the driving force behind Ekaterinburg's independent studio Slam Comics, has produced and/or collaborated on series like the space opera *Cosmobandits* (2016), the sci-fi romantic comedy parody *Maha* (2016), and the occult horror vehicle *Mutagen* (2019)—all types of storytelling that did not exist in the Soviet era. Volkov and Kutuzov collaborated (with artist Yevgeny Frantsev and others) on *Frontier* (2016), a postapocalyptic meta-Western series, while all three worked on *Thief of Shadows* (2019).

The latter is, like *Conquerors,* another Marvel homage, this one in a more Sikoryak-like vein in that it duplicates the look of older comics, down to a faux four-color palette, benday dots, and a newsprint tone. The covers, modeled on Lee/Kirby-era designs, even come with a seal on the upper right, proclaiming (in English), "Approved by the Old Komix Authority." A work of loving ironic parody, like Alan Moore et al.'s *1963* (1993) and *Supreme* (1997–2002) series, or Ed Piskor's more recent *X-Men: Grand Design* (2018), *Thief of Shadows* is smart-alecky reflective nostalgia[57] for readers who never actually experienced the "real thing." Those who truly "get" it belong to a small sliver even of contemporary Russian comics readers. Volkov's response to an interviewer who asked about his prolific output is telling: "The great scriptwriters of the Golden and Silver Ages, like Gardner Fox and Otto Binder, managed to do a whole lot more than me. I read a lot about the luminaries who worked on the comics of the past, and envy starts to eat at me, so I throw myself into doing more and more" (Vorobeva, "Aleksei"). Outside a tiny coterie of aca-

---

57. In Svetlana Boym's sense of the term; see Boym, *Future*: chapter 5.

demics and superfans—on either side of the pond—how many could identify those hallowed names today?

With their sequel *Conquerors of the Impossible: The Second War with the Amphibians* (2018), Volkov and Gorbut continue the allusive fun with a plot derived in part from Karel Čapek's sci-fi philosophical novel *War with the Newts* (1936). They have promised the series will go on in a similar vein. Though as noted, such works represent a niche interest for the connoisseur.

Others have taken the formulae and clichés of those "luminaries who worked on the comics of the past," and rebranded, Russified, and marketed them for much larger, less nostalgia-driven audiences. Such was the strategy behind the most prominent mainstream example of post-Soviet Russian comics, whose success would be difficult to explain without a transnational outlook.

I have in mind the publisher Bubble, to which we turn in the next chapter.

CHAPTER 4

The Mighty Bubble Marching Society (and Its Discontents)

In 2011, twenty-four-year-old Artyom Gabrelyanov, scion of a publishing and media empire, announced: "I will bend over backwards to do this. I will create a market for comics in Russia" (Martem'ianov, "Gabrelianovy"). The person he was addressing was his father, Aram Gabrelyanov, who had built said empire in the 1990s with his tabloid and online portal *Life* (and from there had moved on to bigger holdings). Along the way he had also founded the journal *Seryozhka* (later *Watermelon*), the longest-lived comics publication of the Wild Age. But this was something larger, much more ambitious. Unsure that anything would come of it, the paterfamilias decided to invest $3 million USD in his son's venture (Arkhangel'skaia, "Million").[1]

The younger Gabrelyanov had grown up in a very different time and place than his parents, and spent the '90s for the most part without comics. As he told me in 2013, he occasionally ran into translated foreign imports featuring Indiana Jones and Mickey Mouse, and knew about his father's publications. But the animated TV shows he saw as a child, like the Spider-Man and X-Men series, made a big impression (as they did on many a future komiksist of that generation). Video games, later the X-Men films, and the internet did the rest (Gabrelianov interview, 2013).

---

1. Mikhail Bogdanov of Komilfo expressed utter stupefaction at that sum. He told a reporter he had put maybe $300,000 USD into his press, which in its entire existence had never recouped anything near the amount of Gabrelyanov's starting capital (Arkhangel'skaia, "Million").

Gabrelyanov founded his comics company Bubble in 2011 (housed in the same building as his father's News Media Holding) and that fall launched a crude humor magazine by that name. It bombed. Maybe its failure had something to do with the fact that many readers did not find it funny, or good. Also, some newsstands refused to carry journals with headlines like the one on the cover of *Bubble* #3 (2012), which announced, "Fairy Tale Sex: The Three Little Pigs Opened a Bordello." Gabrelyanov, a garrulous, ebullient personality, sneered at the scandal: "I saw a *Men's Health* or a *Maxim,* one of those, that had two girls on the cover, and it said, 'How to Teach Sex to Lesbians.' There's no problem selling that, but when it's comics . . . It's a strange irony" (Gabrelianov interview, 2013).

Alexander Kunin of KomMissia and the Center for Comics and Visual Culture pinned the blame elsewhere:

> They started off on the wrong foot, with a big mistake. They made *Bubble* a humor journal because that was the sort of artists they had, people who do caricature. But comics fans didn't want to read that. The comics community related very negatively to Bubble at first. It was immediately clear that Gabrelyanov had a lot of money, that he wanted to make more. But those of the older school, like [*Komiksolyot* founder Andrei] Ayoshin, wanted something like *Veles* or *Mukha,* a continuation of that tradition. But here we had some sort of nonsense. Nobody knew why or what for. They were sharply against. I also approached them with some caution. We didn't organize any meetings or presentations with them. We didn't want to attract fire to ourselves. I didn't want people to think that if we opened up our space to them, that meant we were with them. I didn't want a repeat of the situation at KomMissia 2008. (Kunin interview, 2013)[2]

For his part, Gabrelyanov explained the 2012 cancellation of the first *Bubble* journal after only four issues this way: "Everyone has a different sense of humor" (Cherniavskiy, "Artem"). Agreed: Some like their humor funny.

Act II proved far more auspicious.

Before the year lapsed, in October 2012, Bubble rebranded as a full-on domestic competitor to Marvel and DC, with a line of four monthly interlocked superhero comics series featuring the evil-vanquisher Demonslayer (Besoboi), the time-traveling Friar (Inok), the former thief/adventurer Red Fury, and the super-cop Major Grom. Publisher and idea factory Gabrelyanov and editor-in-chief Roman Kotkov set about creating their own comics universe, along a US mainstream model. This time it worked.

---

2. The KomMissia 2008 festival was riven by discord and scandal. See my insider's account: Alaniz, "Notes."

The business journal *RBC* reported in 2017 that Bubble was consistently publishing about 5,000 copies of each of its titles month in, month out,[3] commanding 80 to 90 percent of the sales for monthly comics periodicals (i.e., singles, or *singly*)—though this may largely owe to the fact that most foreign translated works sell as trade anthologies released on a less than monthly basis. (Bubble's *singly* also sell at a lower price than their foreign counterparts.)[4] Overall Bubble products represented 14 percent of the total comics market, with Azbuka 25 percent, ACT 20 percent, and Komilfo 16 percent, according to Komilfo director Mikhail Bogdanov. Gabrelyanov's company allegedly recouped its investment in 2016, and was by then even making a small profit (Arkhangel'skaia, "Million"). As a young start-up and the sole actor on this scale, Bubble's achievements were impressive—the sort of sustained success against international publishers that was unimaginable in the 1990s.

More than that: Gabrelyanov put Russian superheroes on the map, in a big way. As *GQ Russia,* writing in 2014, described the country's pre-Bubble comics environment:

The Russian market, just like the world market, is literally inundated with every possible product related to—exclusively American—comics and super-heroes: from films to collectible figures of Wolverine to underwear with Cat-woman and sneakers with the Batman logo. But in all those 25 years since comics stopped being a forbidden art, Russia never had its own mass culture heroes coming off the printing presses. (Martem'ianov, "Gabrelianovy")

Kunin now had better things to say about Bubble comics themselves, too:

Gabrelyanov . . . made a good decision. As a scriptwriter he categorized the material according to genres: this is an action series (*Major Grom*), this is a mystical thriller (*Friar*), a more violent mystical thriller (*Demonslayer*), and a typical superhero series (*Red Fury*). And he released them to see what would get noticed and discussed, and then he would develop that. And it all got attention. (Kunin interview, 2013)

---

3. A paltry amount, even by US standards, where print runs for monthly titles have been in decline for decades. By way of comparison: If Bubble were competing in the US market and its title *Friar* had completely sold out its print run in June 2015, that would only have been good enough to make it to 294th place in the monthly sales rankings (displacing that month's issue of *Swords of Sorrow: Vampirella & Jennifer Blood*) (Comichron, "June 2015").

4. Chuk and Geek's Chernyavsky told me Bubble undersold its *singly,* for as little as 75 rubles ($1 USD). (Bubble also repackaged its series into *treidy,* the market standard.) "They're not the best sellers, but they're not the lowest sellers," he said. "They have a certain permanence" (Cherniavskiy interview, 2017).

I pick *Demonslayer* for a closer look due to its obvious continuities with the 1990s—especially in its themes of postapocalypse and social disorder. The inaugural story, "His Name Is Demonslayer: Part I" (*Demonslayer* #1, Oct. 2012), with script by Gabrelyanov and Yevgeny Fedotov, and art by Andrei Vasin, sets the scene with a two-page spread of a nighttime Moscow, in bird's-eye view, beset by leering satanic forces.

Puffs of sulfurous smoke double as textboxes, painting a still grimmer picture:

We live in a nightmarish time.

A time when the most revolting degenerates feel on top of the world, while ordinary people find themselves cast to the winds of fate.

Gangsters.

Junkies.

Killers.

Robbers.

Rapists.

Scum of every kind, running amok in all their cruelty.

Grown used to lawlessness and injustice, little by little they turn the nation into a branch of Hell on Earth. (n.p.)

Danila, a veteran of the 2008 Georgia War, is chosen by occult forces to take on the role of the Demonslayer. (The name and context recalls Danila Bagrov, the ultraviolent nationalist hero and veteran of the first Chechnya war, played by Sergei Bodrov Jr. in Alexei Balabanov's popular films *Brother* [1997] and *Brother-2* [2000].) Powered by mystical living tattoos on his body and accompanied by his "little demon" (*besenok*) sidekick Shmyg (a name that implies "sneaking" or "scurrying"), Danila prowls the nocturnal streets seeking out demons (*besy*) to dispatch. When we first encounter him, our hero finds a nubile young woman, falling out of her ripped dress, as a would-be rapist holds her at knifepoint (see figure 4.1).

The lurid imagery could have come straight out of a 1990s "adult" series like *Novy Komiks* (see chapter 6). Freeing the woman, Danila instructs her, "Take off. And don't be walking down dark alleys by yourself anymore" (n.p.). The not-so-subtle implication: She is at fault for her plight—par for the course in a country as patriarchal as Russia. Danila and Shmyg then draw out Goriman, the gigantic demon hidden inside the rapist (who like many hooligans and drug addicts has sold his soul to satanic powers), for a battle to the death. Thus does Danila "clean up" Russia.

With its mix of metaphysics, humor, nationalism, and pulp, *Demonslayer* evokes the early 2000s *Night Watch* film series by Timur Bekmambetov (based

FIGURE 4.1. *Demonslayer,* part of Bubble's original line
(2012). Art by Andrei Vasin. Used with permission.

on the novels by Sergei Lukyanenko), though it is perhaps a closer cousin to
Russian comics of the Wild Age, like Oleg Kozhevnikov's "Through Blood and
Suffering" (examined earlier). The series makes plain that the fecund "Russia
as accursed land" trope still had purchase in Putin's third term. In fact, I find
Demonslayer remarkable for how it mines *chernukha* archetypes of societal
breakdown dating back to the Perestroika era, literalizing them into its "Hell

on Earth" premise. Furthermore, like Pavlovsky's point about the reparative function of many 1990s comics (including Kozhevnikov's), Gabrelyanov and his collaborators' work here attempts to palliate—if not wish away—the moral vacuity and lawlessness of so much contemporary Russian culture (as many perceive it), at the same time as it wallows in same. Even as Danila rescues the woman from the clutches of her near-rapist, Shmyg leers after her as she walks away, saying, "Hey, hot stuff, call me up sometime, eh?" (n.p.). *Demonslayer* "palliates" collective guilt for the nation's woes in another way: The idea that desperate, benighted people have sold their immortal souls to demons, leading them to ever-more-odious crimes, largely absolves them of responsibility. After all, the *besy* made them do it.

In other words, Russia is clean but for malign external forces led by the Antichrist (literally), which a strong hero can vanquish—in essence, Dostoevsky's Christian prescription by way of superheroics. Even Danila's order to the woman is basically an updated macho version of "Go and sin no more." Such rather bland pseudo-religious nationalism pervades the original Bubble series,[5] especially *Demonslayer* and *Friar*, in which a super-powered Orthodox believer travels through time, visiting important events in the country's history (the 988 CE Christianization of Kievan Rus, the Russian-Turkish War of 1877–78, the WWII Battle of Stalingrad) to fend off Russia's spiritual and physical foes.

Bubble debuted two new series in 2014, *Exlibrium* (on a secret order guarding the border between reality and fiction)[6] and *Meteora* (space opera). In 2014, Gabrelyanov boasted that Bubble's VKontakte page had 115,000 followers (Serebrianskiy, "Izdateli"). In 2015, Bubble became the first Russian comics publisher to sell its wares in translation (not always good) on Comixology. That same year Gabrelyanov founded Bubble Studios, a branch of the company tasked with developing film adaptations of the comics. Its first project, the short film *Major Grom* (directed by Vladimir Besedin), debuted on YouTube in February 2017. Within a few months it had accumulated 4.5 million views and about a 7.0 rating on Kinopoisk, the biggest online movie portal in Russia. "*John Wick 2* has the same rating," Gabrelyanov bragged to a

5. As Gabrelyanov told me, "There's a lot of [good, honest citizens], it's just that people write more about the bad ones, the killers, because that sells better" (Gabrelianov interview, 2013). On the other hand, some readers accused Bubble of acting like a pro-Kremlin mouthpiece when, in the first *Major Grom* story arc, the murderous supervillain Plague Doctor leaves a white ribbon—the symbol of the 2011–2012 anti-Putin protest movement—as his calling card. Gabrelyanov waved away the criticism by saying he included the ribbon for a laugh, and of course as provocation (Martem'ianov, "Gabrelianovy").

6. In 2016, Bubble financed an English-language hardcover edition of *Exlibrium* through a successful Kickstarter campaign; see Parker, "Russia."

US journalist at that year's San Diego Comic Con (Parker, "Russia"; see also Alaniz, "Sarik").

In January 2017, after the original four titles had reached their fiftieth issues, Bubble revamped its comics line as part of its "Second Breath" initiative. It replaced four of the series with new titles: *Red Fury* led to *Allies* (Soyuzniki); *Realmwalkers* (Mirokhodtsy) spun off from *Friar*; *Major Grom* became *Igor Grom,* as the character left the police force; and the now more family-friendly *Demonslayer Vol. 2* replaced *Demonslayer*. It also added *Ziggy the Space Hamster,* an all-ages spin-off from *Meteora* (and a blatant knockoff of Rocket Raccoon).[7]

In their art styles, "narrative compression" storytelling, production values, Comico fonts, lack of thought balloons, cinematic effects, often garish palette, glossy paper, crossovers, mega-crossovers, and mediocre scripts, these comics greatly resemble contemporary mainstream US product.[8] If not for the Cyrillic alphabet . . .[9]

This is not to besmirch the work of Bubble writers and artists. These include stars of the independent scene lured by Gabrelyanov's deep pockets, like scripters Alexei Volkov (of *Conquerors of the Impossible* fame) and Alex Khatchett, as well as those artists whose careers the company launched: Artyom Bizayev, Eduard Petrovich (*Red Fury*), Vyacheslav Doronin (*Friar*), Konstantin Tarasov (*Major Grom*), and breakout star Anastasia Kim.[10] As Kim's example shows, Bubble has done exceptionally well in opening doors for women in the industry, like editor Irina Mikhailina and artists Anastasia Katerinich and Anna Rud (creator of *The Club,* 2016), among several others. The "Second Breath" series *Allies*—like *Red Fury,* fronted by a heroine—was at first produced by an all-female creative team: writer Natalya Devova, artist

---

7. When a reporter pointed out that Bubble's Plague Doctor looks a lot like the villain from Ohba and Obata's *Death Note,* Gabrelyanov answered, "It's stupid to say in one's defense that there's only seven notes on the musical scale. Heck, everything had already been done before we got here. . . . We look a little bit like everyone else and we don't look like anyone" (Cherniavskiy, "Artem").

8. Gabrelyanov has expressed admiration for Stuart Immonen, Scott Campbell, and other contemporary stars of US mainstream comics, upon whose work Bubble modeled its house style (Cherniavskiy, "Artem").

9. In the late 2010s, Bubble added a slate of new komiks and imprints like Bubble Visions, melding the worlds of mainstream and independent in ways not unfamiliar to readers of Image comics. Titles included *Igor the Eel* by diverse hands, *Wolf Helsing* by Yevgeny Yakovlev, and the publisher's first manga series, *Tagara* by Marina Privalova and Anna Sergeyeva. The new imprint Bubble Legends featured a *Demonslayer* spin-off, *Black Dog,* by Alexei Volkov and Andrei Vasin, and *Anna* by Maxim Karganov and Ekaterina Ovchinnikova.

10. Other artists in Bubble's expanding operation include Natalya Zaidova, Oleg Okunev, and Yevgeny Tonchilov.

Alina Erofeyeva, and colorist Viktoria Vinogradova (I discuss this series in chapter 7). And all these creatives, it should be noted, toiled under a work-for-hire contract that allows Bubble to retain all rights to the characters.[11] In short, Gabrelyanov's staff delivered exactly what he paid for: run-of-the-mill mainstream comics for the nondiscriminating consumer (see below), which he could then exploit in other media (board games, trading cards, merch, music, a planned cinematic universe).

In any case, given all we've seen since the Yeltsin era, it's safe to say the emergence and decade-long survival of Bubble signals a genuine shift in Russian popular culture. Not unlike Stan Lee (to whom he likes to compare himself), the publisher and impresario Gabrelyanov brought comics to the masses like no one in Russia ever had before. The foregoing prompts a number of follow-up questions (along with some answers, drawn from a spectrum of opinion).

Are these comics any good, and does it matter? What does Bubble mean for Russian comics?

> KUNIN: The first issues were horrible. Unbelievably bad scripts, unbeliev-
> ably bad art, but when you compare the first issues with the 10th or 11th
> issues, you can see that the series are starting to come together, they're
> taking on life. New artists were brought on board who stepped up to the
> task, who knew this world, who tailored their work to the style. That was
> very good. It's also very good that all the characters belong to the press.
> That way we can have reassurance that as long as the press is around, the
> characters will be around. (Kunin interview, 2013)
> CHERNYAVSKY: In the Russian mainstream, artists who work for Bubble
> definitely have their own style. It looks like that because their artists are
> oriented towards manga and even more towards Western comics, which
> they adapt, and you wind up with a hybrid of East and West. Russia has
> a lot of hybrids of East and West. (Cherniavskiy interview, 2017)
> MAX MASLOV, GENERAL MANAGER OF COMIC CON RUSSIA: I think the
> most important thing that Bubble does for us right now is they are show-
> ing everybody in the country that a comics company can be a mature
> business, which can be expanded not only to comics, but also to movies,
> books, shows, and so on. (Longo, "Bubble")
> KUNIN AGAIN: I don't believe they are [aping Western superheroes]. I
> believe they took onto themselves the role of sacrificial victim—and

---

11. Gabrelyanov confirmed Bubble's work-for-hire practices to Ivan Chernyavsky (Cherniavskiy, "Artem") and to me in our 2013 sit-down.

good for them—so as to create a normal market. Not a mainstream. It's not clear what mainstream means in Russia. This is because we have underground and cliques (*tusovki*). Those who love European comics, those who love American comics, etc. We need to have enough publications so that the ordinary comics reader will have a choice. Like now when you go to a bookstore and you want to buy a work of literature, you have a look and say, uh-huh, here's erotica, here's memoir, thrillers, romance novels, whatever you want. And so you choose. When we have a choice like that in comics, then we'll know what's mainstream and what isn't. When a reader has free access. That's why right now it's important that all approaches to comics be represented. What Bubble did is one approach. And if two or three other publishers appear who do something similar, that's great. If we see more things like Askold Akishin's *My Comics Biography*,[12] that's great, too. (Kunin interview, 2013)[13]

PAVLOVSKY: There's precious little money sloshing around in that part of the comics industry that turns out only the work of Russian creators. Bubble doesn't count. In their case a big corporation showed up, poured in and to this day continues to pour in a lot money into six monthly lines—seemingly without hope of financial success, but with faith in a symbolic success. Therefore Bubble will exist as long as News Media stays healthy. But I hope that one day people in Gazprom Media Holding[14] will wake up, and a second Bubble will appear. But how to go from charity to capitalism—no one knows, (Bondareva, "Chto")

Publisher, writer, and scholar Mikhail "Misha" Zaslavsky, whose considered judgment I tend to value highly, and whose children's comics journal *Just You Wait!* had the largest domestic print run for a monthly in the 2000s, told me in this regard:

Bubble is a real phenomenon, because they are working in real time, in the context of real production conditions, which are much more complicated than for *Just You Wait!* They're producing a lot more pages per month. . . . The stories one may like or not like, but they are creating a professional environment. (Zaslavskiy interview, 2017)

---

12. Discussed in the conclusion to this study.

13. In the years since Kunin's comments, the industry has indeed grown to answer that call for market *raznoobrazie.*

14. Gazprom Media Holding, a subsidiary of the natural gas and energy corporation Gazprom, is the largest of all such concerns in Russia.

Other questions present themselves: What kind of comics does the most successful monthly comics publisher in Russia think his country needs? How does he see his audience?

> GABRELYANOV: You just can't not take the demands of the market into account. Right now the market needs American comics and that's exactly what we're making: *American comics*. . . .
>
> We're talking about a mass product here. It has to be accessible, it has to be based on elementary ideas, ideas understandable by anyone, ideas about good and evil, revenge, love. Something that everyone knows [my emphasis]. . . .
>
> Our audience are those who are just opening themselves up to the world of comics, with their clichéd explosions, melodramatic dialogue and so on. We could have made comics for those who know all the Marvel crossovers going back 15 years—but what for? We want to work for a wide audience. This audience doesn't know anything about comics. . . . I want to establish a market, a comics industry, to write our staff's names into history as the founders of commercial comics in Russia. Maybe it sounds overly self-confident, but until we came along no one had even tried to take a shot at that. (Cherniavskiy, "Artem")

It does in fact sound a tad overly self-confident, to say nothing of dismissive of those who strove—against much stronger cultural and financial headwinds—to build a bona fide Russian comics industry: KOM starting in the late Soviet era; journals like *Blaster, Veles, Mukha, Magnificent Adventures, Komikser,* and a host of others in the ruinous 1990s and beyond. I would also find it easier to excuse Gabrelyanov's evident disdain for his "comics beginner" readers if he didn't infantilize them so much. And I mean that literally: "Look, I have a baby. He's eight months old. I don't give him roasted meat, or bloody steak to eat. I give him milk, then porridge, then apples. You have to train readers, step by step. You have to develop them, gradually" (Cherniavskiy, "Artem").

But Gabrelyanov saves his most jaundiced views for those who today produce the kind of work he thinks the country *doesn't* need. In particular his opinions on auteur or *avtorsky* comics make for quite the contrast with those of Boomkniga's Yakovlev or Zangavar's Morozov. No mumbo-jumbo from him about comics as a "temporary upgrade for your brain":

> Look, our failed artists love to say that Russia will be saved by *avtorsky* comics. That's a bunch of crap. Russia will be saved by commercial comics with good drawings, not by *avtorsky* comics that some guy drew for himself and

12 of his friends. People are just consoling themselves with some sort of hopes. [I'm talking solely about] mass market comics with clear character motivation. But comics that you can only understand if you've first read Joyce's *Ulysses* or whatever—that's just bad comics. We need something designed for a mass audience. Let me tell you something else. In the first issue of *Demonslayer* we had this line of dialogue: the little demon says, "You did great, Stanislavsky would give you an A." My brother[15] told me, "What's the matter with you? You living under a rock? What's this 'Stanislavsky'? Who's gonna know these days who Stanislavsky is?" So we went and asked a couple of kids. They said, "Uh, is that a soccer player, maybe?" So we put in "Spielberg" instead. (Cherniavskiy, "Artem")[16]

Gabrelyanov put it similarly to me, though a bit more diplomatically (perhaps because he was talking to a foreigner):

To get a grant and make comics for your friends as long as the grant lasts, this doesn't lead to anything. Akishin's *My Comics Biography*, that's fine. Fine art-house comics. It had a print run of 1,000. It's Boomkniga, right? About 1,000.[17] But again, as far as I know, this book went out primarily to friends of Akishin, those same KOM people, right? That's fine. It's an important step, to show the history of Russian comics, right? This book is made for those who seek it out. For his *tusovka*. (Gabrelianov interview, 2013)

In interviews and media appearances throughout the 2010s, Gabrelyanov returned again and again to his mantra, that Russian comics needs an industry based on mainstream, commercial, common-denominator product, like every other country. "Even the alternative comics we make, we should make them so they'll be understood by more than ten of the artist's friends," he told me. "It's a business," he kept repeating. "I think that any activity is first and foremost conditioned on the basis that it returns its investment" (Gabrelianov interview, 2013).

To that end, even when discussing highly regarded auteurs with large audiences, he still tended to see them in terms of dollars and cents (or rubles and kopecks). At one point David Lynch came up. Gabrelyanov conceded that this US director had a unique, even opaque artistic vision, but he seemed much more impressed by the fact that Lynch's films and TV shows got financ-

---

15. Artyom Gabrelyanov's younger brother, Ashot Gabrelyanov, is a noted journalist, blogger, and media manager.

16. The line, which appears in *Demonslayer* #1, reads, "Spielberg would personally give you an Oscar!" (n.p.).

17. Gabrelyanov was close: Akishin's *My Comics Biography* had an initial print run of 1,100.

ing and made a profit. Later in the conversation, he seemed pleased when I told him the Bubble line reminded me of Image comics from the 1990s—not necessarily a compliment, though he took it as such.

Bubble did have a DC of sorts to its Marvel: the rival comics publisher White Unicorn (Bely Edinorog), led by Alexander Korotov, which published the postapocalyptic series *Pantheon: Cult of Duplicity* (Panteon: Kult Dvulichia) by writer Filipp Sosedov and artist Roman Onishchenko (mostly) from 2012 to 2016. The dense plot involves an alternate Earth in which Barabas rather than Jesus is crucified, leading to innumerable repercussions throughout history; for one thing, Western Europeans never "discover" America, while a power vacuum leads several factions, imperial states, and their hired muscle to vie for dominance of the globe.[18] The fan site Geekster called *Pantheon* "the Russian *Game of Thrones*" (Anokhin, "Panteon"), though one might also describe it as "Through Blood and Suffering" on steroids. The series serves up graphic violence, nudity, and *nenormativnaya leksika* (swearing) in liberal dollops, far beyond anything seen in a Bubble comic.

Pantheon comes off as an above-average ultraviolent Vertigo or Image comic; a scene in the third issue, in which a man is decapitated while eating sushi, even reminded me of Anthony Bourdain and Langdon Foss's *Get Jiro!* (2012). Onishchenko's art,[19] reminiscent of Stuart Immonen's, has a dynamic flair in action scenes; he does less well in long sequences of characters sitting around talking. At times the art looks rushed and/or done by various hands, or else the quality drops markedly, recalling *Novy Komiks* of the 1990s and early 2000s (with a lot of computer effects trying to cover for flaws in the line work).

The writing, too, has its ups and downs. Though Pavlovsky calls Sosedov "our future Alan Moore, Warren Ellis and Scott Snyder all in one" (Bondareva, "Chto")—as if that were a good thing—the series suffers from an excess of dry, expository narration and world-building at the expense of character. The verbosity most threatens to interfere with genre pleasures during battle scenes. For example, when the mercenary Yat' is engaging a monstrous ram-headed creature while on a mission, textboxes recount his thoughts:

> Gemogs are Genetically Modified Humanoids [*geneticheskie modifitsirovannye gumanoidy*]. Among the people they're known as "the emperor's bastards."
>
> My professional killer's consciousness automatically served up encyclopedic background info.

---

18. *Pantheon: Cult of Duplicity* has much in common with the dystopian alternate histories of Ukrainian comics artist Igor Baranko, especially *Jihad* (2004/2012); see Alaniz, "Igor."

19. Onishchenko relinquished the art reins to other artists for the later issues.

Gemogs are the result of failed cloning experiments. The first generation of clones was identical to humans, but they quickly went insane.

By testing the faulty individuals, Professor Alexander Kitos put forward the theory that the human mind cannot withstand insertion into an artificial body.

The church supported the professor's conclusions, declaring that scientific evidence for the soul had been found.

It was decided to cross the second clone generation with animals. As a result, they wound up with humanoid creatures suitable only for combat purposes. With a low intellect, but a stable psyche.

That's how Gemogs emerged. Some of these individuals are long-lived. Those like my victim here had survived since the world war.

Gemogs were one of the military factors which allowed for the destruction of the Asiatic Triumvirate . . . (Sosedov and Onishchenko, n.p.)

And so on, and so on—an awful lot of words for six panels depicting a ferocious battle to the death (see figure 4.2). Though on the one hand, one could read the scene as a subtle parody of superhero conventions, along the lines of writer Steve Gerber's arch running commentary in the 1970s Marvel series *Omega the Unknown* (see Alaniz, "Omega": 40–42 and 47–49), the text-heavy approach strikes me as belabored and distracting, as if Sosedov has simply cut and pasted subtext from his series bible, if not from the D&D *Monster Manual*.

We can imagine Gabrelyanov brutally reducing the word count by two-thirds to move things along quicker. To protestations that *Pantheon* has its dedicated fans, who appreciate its artful fusion of steampunk, futureshock, and religious allegory, "Russia's Stan Lee" would coldly reply that comics need to be "understood by more than ten of the artist's friends" and that "we need a mass product."[20] To its credit, Bubble's comics may come off as average (almost by design), but at least they let the art tell more of the story, that art tends to be mediocre but consistent, and they come out mostly on time. *Pantheon*, meanwhile, was beset by months-long delays between issues, and severed its ties with White Unicorn in 2013. Bubble aims lower, and often scores.

Let the man who made comics cool (or at least cool enough) for mass Russian consumption have the last word:

---

20. Of *Pantheon*, Gabrelyanov said that they didn't world-build well, but he wouldn't mind poaching their artist (Cherniavskiy, "Artem").

FIGURE 4.2. *Pantheon: Cult of Duplicity* by Filipp Sosedov and
Roman Onishchenko (2013). Used with permission.

Yevgeny Fedotov, you can compare him to Stan Lee. Andrei Vasin, he's our Jack Kirby, our Jim Lee. None of us are worse than Stan Lee. Let Stan Lee be the American Artyom Gabrelyanov! This was the perspective of our creative team, when we started out. . . .

Journalists, people online, my friends ask me, "How much money did you invest in this? $2 million? Are you crazy? You could have put that in a bank and gotten a percentage." I don't need the money, I don't need material things. . . .

We want to create commercial, mainstream comics. Now no one can say that if you're, like, involved in the comics business, you're an idiot. (Gabrelianov interview, 2013)

Vababai!: The Politics of Sound Effects

Like the 2015 uproar with *Maus,* media interest in comics flares up on occasion, throwing open a widow onto the national psyche. What follows recounts another such incident, prompting the query: Can comic book sound effects be patriotic?

On August 10, 2015, the newspaper *Izvestia* reported that representatives of Moscow's Center for Comics and Visual Culture (TsKVK) had sent a letter to the Vinogradov Institute for the Russian Language proposing the creation of a dictionary of Russian comics sound effects. The letter read, in part:

As is well-known, in comics one may encounter an enormous quantity of onomatopoeic sound effects [*zvukopodrazhanii*]. How does one translate the sound of a telephone, the squeak of a door, the opening of a soda can, the rustle of a plastic ice cream wrapper, the sound made by a motorcyclist's feet dragging along the ground? Most often translators simply replace the English letters with Cyrillic ones, as a result of which emerge the *unpatriotic* "beng," "kresh," "bems" "vau," etc. (Korobkova, "Perevodchiki"; my emphasis)

As is clear from this passage, the TsKVK letter stressed the nationalistic implications of such "derivative" linguistic borrowings, proposing instead to construct a list of new, "patriotic" sound effects based on the languages of the various ethnic groups of the former Soviet Union. Some of the possibilities offered: "chorkh" for scratching and "khurt-khurt" for swallowing water (from Lezgin); "ssurch" for the sipping of liquid (from Armenian); "galdyr-dyms" for a large object falling, "duberdyms" for something medium-sized, "ingeldyms" for something small or made of glass (from Mari); and "vababai" (from Avaric) to replace "vau" (wow). "In our opinion," TsKVK director Alexander Kunin told a reporter, "utilizing the linguistic richness of the peoples of Russia is not only a beautiful solution to the problem, but also a splendid means of bringing our peoples together" (Korobkova, "Perevodchiki").

The center's mission to "nationalize" Russian comics sound effects, with its echoes of Soviet-era practices to "bring the peoples together," was met with some approbation by the Vinogradov institute—but widely ridiculed by the Russian comics industry and fans, who uploaded numerous mocking memes. These replaced the sound effects in various US comics (including *Deadpool*) with the proposed variants "galdyrdyms," "chorkh," and "vababai," to cutting comic effect.

Online comments were no less sardonic, such as: "Vababai, Kapiton! I almost duberdyms from my chair. Now I'm afraid to ssurchat' tea" (Molot, "Importozameshchenie"). Artyom Gabrelyanov, of the mainstream publisher Bubble, drily opined: "Onomatopoeic sound effects and interjections can't be patriotic or unpatriotic. You won't be taken seriously if you talk about using the exclamation 'vababai' instead of 'vau'" (Korobkova, "Perevodchiki"). (Gabrelyanov may also have felt peeved that *Izvestia* chose to illustrate its story with a panel from Bubble's *Demonslayer* #1.) In short, the campaign proved little more than a laughingstock.

As these reactions show, the nationalist-tinged "Vababaigate" not only demonstrates how geopolitics filters into the aesthetic and the pop cultural. The incident represents an almost farcical reification of Russia's vexed contemporary engagement with the West in the Putin era, as seen through the marginalized practice of comics. The fact that much of the original reported story—which appeared in August, a notoriously slow month for news in Russia, when many take their annual vacations—was, according to Kunin, cooked up by *Izvestia*,[21] does not alter the fact that these very real ideological fault lines exist (as evidenced by the extensive and many-splendored online responses).

Non-manga-related studies of onomatopoeia in comics remain rare, while translation studies scholars have only in the last decade or so begun to explore the complexities and specificity of comics translation.

As Klaus Kaindl, among the first to assay the topic, noted in 2010:

Whether onomatopoeia are translated or not depends on the retouching effort, the genre and the target group. Translation strategies range from

---

21. Kunin, personal correspondence, 2019. However, an August 11, 2015, article on *Spidermedia*, with screenshots between the *Izvestia* reporter and Kunin, cast doubt on the latter's assertions that the TSKVK had had nothing to do with the debacle (Admin, "Ekskliuziv").

direct borrowing (sometimes with graphemic or phonological adaptation) to literal translations and category changes as well as to new creations of onomatopoeia. ("Comics": 39)

He goes on to offer this warning, of sorts: "The font, for example, can express the nationality or political attitude" ("Comics": 39). As seen in the very particular setting of twenty-first-century Russia: Can it ever.

New Frontiers: Comic Arts Tyumen

Georgy "Gosha" Elaev was born in 1988, when his country was slowly collapsing, and Russians had nothing Westerners would recognize as a comics culture. The KOM studio had just barely formed, in far-off Moscow. But Elaev grew up about 2,900 kilometers (1,800 miles) away, in Tobolsk, Siberia.

Despite that remoteness, comics reached him as a child. Some of his first reading material was *Teenage Mutant Ninja Turtles* (*TMNT*; then published in translation by Makhaon). "I didn't have that Soviet understanding of comics as some kind of American propaganda. That is, for me comics reading was completely normal," he told me. "My parents didn't mind. My mother got them for me." Soon he was making his own comics adventures about the amphibian quartet. For Elaev, *TMNT* became "like the patterns on the wallpaper in your room, that you look at and they imprint themselves on your memory forever." He even confided that seeing comics about the Phantom, with the domino mask and the whole masculine superhero aesthetic thing, was "probably my first homoerotic experience." Later came the comics he saw in *SPID-info*, a racy tabloid that typified the 1990s yellow press. As a young man, seeing the work of R. Crumb and Jim Woodring (which he read in English) showed him graphic narrative could be real, serious art (Elaev interview, 2019).

Elaev moved to Tyumen, an oil industry town sixty miles north of the border with Kazakhstan. He studied journalism at Tyumen State University, worked for several years in online and print media and television. He tried art school and gave up after a couple of years.[22] Inspired by Yegor Letov, legendary frontman of Civil Defense (a seminal band of the 1980s Siberian punk movement), Elaev dreamed of starting up something similar—but not with music.

By now comics were finally starting to get some respect in Russia, so in 2014 Elaev and friend Vitaly Lazarenko organized a pop-up comics store,

---

22. Though in art school he did discover the work of the Kukryniksy (Kresling, "On prosto").

Space Cow, inside the No One Sleeps bookstore's coffee shop. It served not only as a commercial venue, but as a community hub and artist hangout. They held a weekly *"risovach"* (drink and draw). Lots of people were making minicomix, like the graffiti and street artist Alexei Zhulikov, who walked in one day.[23] They founded the Space Cow Comix micropress. As noted, the first volume of its anthology *Black Milk* appeared in 2015; solo artist books followed in 2017. That same year they organized a summer comics camp for twenty-five young students. Elaev, subscribed to the Instagram pages of Comic Arts Brooklyn and other small press/indy comics festivals in the States, was working toward the next step: "I wanted a festival like that, devoted to independently published comics, to art, not to the industry mainstream. Here, in Tyumen" (Elaev interview, 2019).

In 2016, Elaev and his group applied for a city grant, "My Idea," designed to support social activist projects. They received 90,000 rubles (about $1,500 USD), enough to invite guests, make more comics, and print up posters. The first Comic Arts Tyumen (CAT) took place in March 2018, inside the cavernous, multistory SibSab skate park ("They gave us the space for free"). They held a comics market, panels, a concert, workshops, and various events. Attendees came from all over, including Krasnoyarsk and Ekaterinburg. A number of independent Russian comics artist made the journey, including Olga Lavrenteva and Yulia Nikitina, as well as Boomkniga's Dmitry Yakovlev and Komfederatsiya editor Stepan Shmytinsky. The guest of honor was David Schilter of *Kuš*, the legendary Latvian comix anthology.[24] Entry was free. More than 2,000 attended (Rovbut, "Prikliucheniia").

CAT represents the leading edge of Russia's new independent comics culture: egalitarian, youth-driven, inclusive, and DIY, as exemplified by Zhulikov. In 2013, Kunin had told me that it was too early to tell what mainstream versus alternative looked like in the country, because there was not enough product and not enough diversity of expression: "When we have a choice like that in comics, then we'll know what's mainstream and what isn't" (Kunin interview, 2013). That statement today belongs to a different era, thanks to people like Elaev, who help define a mainstream by all the things about it they reject. As he wrote: "New comic shops and exhibitions like Comic Con emerged in

---

23. One of those artists, Alexei Abramov, drew the attention of the St. Petersburg collective Komfederatsia, which published his *Saga of a Clever Dog* in 2017.

24. Schilter wrote me in 2020: "I was very impressed by the organization and the enthusiasm of Gosha, his co-organizer and all the volunteers. Very great start for a brand new festival in a place where comics aren't very popular yet. [I] think they do a great job in promoting alternative comics there. It's nice to see that not everything is based in Moscow and St. Petersburg and [to] get new voices out from Siberia, which indeed is a very different place. Sure, it's a great addition to the Russian comics scene" (Schilter, personal correspondence).

the 2000s, finally opening spaces dedicated to creators and fans. But many of these institutions were largely focused on mainstream comics, [they] also became gatekeepers. It was hard to engage with them if, for example, you lived way out in Siberia and drew weird stuff that was nothing like Spider-Man (Elaev, "Against").

Lower prices and greater access to publishing technology has also made a difference:

> The average price for a zine is 120 rubles [about $1.50 USD]. Unlike 10 years ago, when beautiful comics editions cost too much, now there are more pos-sibilities for printing. You can find a good printer at a university, or even at home. They're not expensive, and people know desktop publishing. . . .
>
> There's now a generation of people who don't begrudge 120 rubles for a well-made zine or book, because they want to support the artist. It's not just a consumer relationship. There's an element of fellow feeling and sup-port. An understanding emerged among us that you're not just coming to buy a book from someone, you're not just securing a material transaction, you're exchanging emotions and feelings, and you're making each other bet-ter people. This is what I think helps us in our work. (Elaev interview, 2019)

Furthermore, while social media and digital platforms play an important role in the community (especially for promotion and connecting with others abroad), this scene remains committed to a physical, print-on-paper format. In this they are anticipating future developments for the culture as a whole, Elaev believes:

> I've started noticing the emergence of a group of people especially interested in works on paper, in print, the materiality and texture of the printed work. They like to feel it in their hands. This is coming back, I think, because peo-ple are already so accustomed to scrolling, they're used to something empty and flat, that if you show them a book, even if it's the same content as what they have available on the internet, it's different all the same. This personal contact also plays a big role. (Elaev interview, 2019)

Finally, the Tyumen scene's abjuration of sleek, professional production values, transactional relationships between creator and consumer, and all-digital formats finds its correlate in the "ugly" aesthetics of the comics and zines themselves:[25]

---

25. All this bears more than a passing resemblance to the contemporary punk-inflected comics scene in former Yugoslavia, especially Serbia; see Sekulić, "Reality."

We try to get our authors not to look at mainstream comics, where everything is pretty. This matters less in comics than in film, for example. Instead of that, we show them examples of US underground comix and European avant garde, so they won't feel that they have any limits within which they have to work, that they have to conform to anything. (Kresling, "On prosto")[26]

This makes sense for a punk komiksist who has declared, "I don't want comics to be beautiful" (Mikhailov, "Ia ne"), though something deeper—even existential—seems to lie behind Elaev's teaching philosophy: what he sees as a near-crisis of individualism, if not a national inferiority complex, among the young. As he told an interviewer:

One of the biggest problems which you run into is people not really believing in themselves—like, catastrophically. Everyone thinks that they're too weird, that they can't draw, that nothing will come of it, that they don't have time to make comics or something like that. We try to show them, so they'll understand that comics can be diverse: weird, horrifying, unusual, whatever you want. And that their comics can be interesting not only for us in Tyumen, but for anyone, that they can and must show them to others. It might turn out that people you don't know will see in these strange, incomprehensible comics something interesting and unique. (Maas, "Sozdatel'")

Or else this might just be another case of making "comics only you and your ten friends will understand," as Gabrelyanov might jeer. Indeed, we're not talking about "a mass product" here. Still, in his teaching and in discussing his own work, Elaev approaches comics as a form of therapy, suitable for treating many a spiritual malaise. In other words, as transcendent. He has his models in Russian culture; in fact, Elaev's prescription again comes off as an update of Dostoevsky: Not beauty will save the world,[27] but boundless self-expression in that most "humble" of art forms, minicomix, whose "democratic" ease of access helps the underconfident step out beyond the roles they feel society has set for them.

---

26. Elaev insists: "The important thing in comics is the story. It doesn't matter how well you draw—that's just a matter of time. If you have a story—and I believe that everyone has a story—and a desire to tell it, then you can do it even with just little circles and squares" (Kresling, "On prosto"). In other words, Elaev sees comics primarily through the lens of literature, returning us to Russian logocentrism and Borisenkova's "narrative turn."

27. The most familiar and much-mocked line from Dostoevsky's novel *The Idiot* (1869).

On the other hand, the society in question has historically punished those who cross arbitrary lines set by power. (Dostoevsky did spend a decade as a political prisoner, after all, much of it in Siberia.) Elaev calls CAT "the first truly inclusive indie comics show in Russia" (Elaev, "Against")—therein lies the rub. Problems erupted for the festival in the lead-up to its second iteration, in 2019. Organizers invited artists from the LGBTQ community, as well as avowed feminists like illustrator Nika Vodvud and the rock band Pozory. As a result, one of the sponsors, the University of Tyumen, demanded that Elaev remove a Facebook invitation, and one of the organizers was even questioned by the FSB (the Federal Security Service, successor to the KGB) (Elaev, "Against"). As he explained it to me,

> Even though the universities we work with are telling their students that they must think critically, all the same when I post on our festival group page (not a public page) that we're inviting artists from the LGBT community to take part in the festival, that we're creating a safe space for everyone, all the same the university powers-that-be contact me to ask that I delete that post, because they don't want to have problems with the law. This is strange, because they're hosting conferences on all sorts of things. They invite foreign instructors who teach Queer Theory and Feminist Theory, so that's odd.[28] (Elaev interview, 2019)

When I asked if he personally feels in danger, he replied, "No, I'm not afraid. But it's just weird. You don't understand why it's going on." I suggested, "All the same this is Russia we're talking about." "Yes," he said. "This is Russia. You can do what you want, just keep quiet about it" (Elaev interview, 2019).

For Elaev, the modern Tyumen comics movement is carrying on an age-old antiauthoritarian tradition. He points to Mikhail Znamensky, a writer, ethnographer, and artist who lived his whole life in the region, as an ancestor of the scene. He knew a number of the Decembrists, former officers who had revolted against the tsar in 1825, many of whom were exiled to Siberia. He was mentored by the Decembrist Ivan Yakushkin and wrote a novel about them, *The Vanished Men* (1872). Despite his remote location, Znamensky published over 300 cartoons in the important St. Petersburg satirical journal *The Spark* (*Iskra*). Some consider his 1875 book *My Journey to Kumys: Clubby Daydreams* (*Moya poezdka na Kumys: klubnye sonnye grezi*) the first Russian comics, akin to Töppfer's *Adventures of Obadiah Olbuck* (an English version of his 1837 *Les Amours de Mr. Vieux Bois*).

---

28. Perhaps not so odd after all; some have described this institution as an "academic sweatshop" (Savelyeva, "How").

Taking inspiration from such examples, Elaev has published his own work, including the autobiographical *Sex Issues* (Sputnikat, 2020), originally posted to Instagram, and the superhero parody *Tyuman* (Space Cow, 2016), featuring a character whose powers derive from oil (discussed in chapter 6). He partly financed the latter through a crowdfunding campaign (*Komsmol'skaia Pravda*, "Avtor").[29] He also travels widely (Omsk, Tula, Moscow, St. Petersburg, and other Russian cities) and has attended, among others, the Hamburg Comics Festival, Comic Arts Brooklyn, Seattle's Short Run, and Chicago's CAKE, always with a heavy bag of Space Cow books to hand out, trade, and sell. As Yakovlev told me, "He travels the world, for the sake of Russian comics."[30] Everywhere he spreads the comics gospel—though given the independent-mindedness of his home region, you might do better to call it the Siberian comics gospel.[31]

I've come to think of Elaev as a sort of Khikhus 2.0 (or, if you will, the anti-Gabrelyanov). A tireless advocate for comics as an art form, not necessarily as an industry. As someone familiar with both the Western and Russian comics scenes, he seemed a logical person to ask something I had been pondering for almost thirty years. Why did it take the Russians so long to get to this point? Why didn't a viable comics industry take hold in Tyumen (or the country as a whole) in, say, 1993 (when I was living in Moscow)? He answered:

> I think this depends on a lot of social and economic factors. Because, for example, this city program which gave us the grant for the festival, they introduced it very recently. This was because the local government started tackling the problem of young people [in Tyumen] just leaving. . . . They're leaving because there's nothing to do in the city, they have no opportunities. Even though this is a fairly large city, and it has a lot of money, a big oil and gas industry. But it was like nobody had any interest in living there, it was boring. For me, too.
>
> And it seems to me that only now has a generation of people arisen who grew up reading comics. (Elaev interview, 2019)

Listening to Elaev, I could just see Misha Zaslavsky smiling—Zaslavsky, who as noted always told me, "If you want to build a comics culture, start

---

29. The report notes the campaign was endorsed by Andrei Venediktov, chief editor and co-owner of the radio station Echo of Moscow and longtime comics fan.

30. Yakovlev, personal correspondence, 2019.

31. We may say the same of projects like the *Kras Comics Zine,* an anthology series of Siberian comics cofounded by Denis Denisov of Krasnoyarsk. Denisov also writes for the news portal *ComicsBoom!*

with the children." It seems that all those *Teenage Mutant Ninja Turtles* and other foreign licensed product, as well as the occasional domestic kids' series like *Keshka, Yula,* and *Just You Wait!,* had an effect. Elaev is the living proof.

Small press and indie scenes like those in Tyumen also represent a sort of do-over, a rewriting of troubled origins. This is more or less what I expected the beginnings of modern Russian comics to look like back in the early 2000s: small-scale, supportive, enthusiastic, grass-roots. Instead, the early KomMissia era was marked by internecine wars that periodically ripped apart the Moscow comics community (as I've documented).

I told Elaev about the case of Nikolai Maslov, who in the mid-2000s was ostracized by that community for the crimes of (1) being middle-aged, (2) getting his autobiographical comics successfully published in France, (3) "not being able to draw" (though he graduated from an art institute), and (4) painting a dour picture of the USSR during the Stagnation era—what Khikhus had called, charmingly, "that old shit." (Elaev hadn't heard of Maslov; more on that below.) He told me:

This is proof that the scene was not mature. People were behaving immaturely. Because today, for example, me, I'm traveling to the USA, and for one thing I'm not just bringing my own comics. I'm not, like, you know, "Publish me, please, I'm good! I'm really talented!" I'm bringing with me 50 kilos of comics by other people. We're translating them into English. . . . They don't look at me like some sort of self-promoting break-out star who left to conquer America. On the contrary, they are happy for me, that I'm able to do this, and they see what's valuable about this. . . . We understand this is a collective labor. It's not just me going off somewhere, it's like we're all of us together a part of me being here. (Elaev interview, 2019)

He added:

I've traveled a lot, I've held workshops, met artists from various cities and regions, and I like that in Moscow and St. Petersburg, compared to more remote places, practically nothing is going on. In our two biggest cities, there is no close-knit community of people who support each other and help each other to do interesting work.[32] . . . The farther away from Moscow I go, the more surprising work and the better artists I see. . . .

We [in Tyumen] help each other, we have enthusiasm, a real culture. This is not just a financial undertaking. These are people truly drawn to art

---

32. Yakovlev and his cohort at St. Petersburg's Boomkniga might differ.

and immersed in it. They know what's going on in US comics, with *Spider-Man,* but also with Crumb, Woodring, young German comics artists, Latvian artists. And they understand that they're not just some little mice that live far, far away, that no one has any reason to know, but that in fact they are participating in this large world . . . this greater process. (Elaev interview, 2019)

I very much liked that image Elaev used, for its evocation of one of the most popular *lubki* of all: the seventeenth-century "Burial of the Cat by the Mice." As in that authority-flouting work, released in different versions as a coded rebuke of Tsar Peter the Great and his Westernizing reforms,[33] the "little mice" of post-Soviet indie comics scenes like Tyumen's carry the "dead cat" of the Russian comics industry's tortured history (with its failures, false starts, and squandered potential) to its final rest—the better to move forward. *Pust' zemlya tebe budet pukhem.*[34]

All the same, something else he said, about "this greater process" contemporary Russian comics artists are involved in—even ones as noncommercial as he—brings up another issue. For in many cases this "greater process," I've observed, entails connection with what's going on now and far away (a, so to speak, "lateral" process), but not with what happened here and (not even that) long ago—that is, a sense of history. Elaev's ignorance of Maslov and of the mid-century Ivan Semenov character Petya Ryzhik ("the Russian Tintin")[35] seemed a symptom of that stance, his mention of an even more obscure figure like Znamensky notwithstanding.

What I'm getting at is this: Russian comics' roots, as understood by Elaev, Gabrelyanov, and other young stalwarts of the contemporary scene, run wide—but not deep.

Is that a problem?

On Not Caring about Your Own History

At the end of the day the genre of comics was not invented in Russia, and therefore, naturally, many of our artists fell under the spell of foreign models.

—Andrei Erofeyev (Kravtsova, "Marginal'niy": 91)

33. See Alaniz, *Komiks:* 22–25.

34. "Rest in peace" (more literally "May the earth be your resting place"). The Russian is derived from classical Latin: *Sit tibi terra levis.*

35. The adventures of Ivan Semenov's Petya Ryzhik and his dog companions Mik and Muk first appeared in 1956, within the pages of *Veselie Kartinki.* See Alaniz, *Komiks:* 65.

At KomMissia 2015, a new publisher from Ekaterinburg made its debut with an original art exhibit and presentation. It wasn't quite new, actually: Tien Press, represented in Moscow by artist Oleg Kozhevnikov and director Radik Sadykov, was republishing in handsome crowdfunded collections material (including "Through Blood and Suffering") that had appeared in their landmark journal *Veles* over twenty years before, during the Wild Age.

The reception, while respectful, proved less than overwhelming[36]—as have other such exhibits and publications devoted to the first generation of late and post-Soviet Russian comics. Members of KOM, the first Russian comics studio (1988–1993), and *Mukha,* the Ufa-based journal (1991–1995), have also struggled to connect with the kids these days. It's just more product in a sea of product.[37] These veterans seem to be facing the opposite of what drove them out of comics in the 1990s: If then there was no possibility of reaching people due to a hostile undeveloped market, today the trouble lies in trying to break through the widespread indifference of a presentist developed market. To many in the younger generations, these creators—who produced remarkable and stupendous work before many modern fans were born—are anachronisms. If they've even heard of them.

These harsh conclusions come from years of noting an ahistorical strain in much of the contemporary scene. I base them on statements like this:

> No one knew about KOM and things like that. . . . They drew practically for themselves. I don't deny that they were pioneers, but unfortunately they had no effect on what's going on now. . . .
>
> [Misha] Zaslavsky wrote an article about someone who 80 years ago drew comics for a journal that would later become *Veselie Kartinki.* It turns out this was probably the first Soviet comics work. And they call this artist the father of Russian comics. But he can't be the father of Russian comics because we're only finding out about him now.[38]
>
> Pardon me, yes, he was a pioneer, but he didn't influence anything going forward. From the Russian side, of course, we have lubok. . . . Bilibin, who illustrated children's folk tales, he seems to me super-important. He could be the super-important source of inspiration for new comics artists. There's the

36. In 2018, Tien announced that it was going on indefinite hiatus, adding, "Of course it's sad that we haven't managed to develop [the press] as we would like, but that's the way it is for now." See their VKontakte announcement at https://vk.com/tien_print?w=wall-82537945_2082.

37. That said, presses have had success reprinting comics and children's picture book classics of the Soviet era, like the aforementioned Petya Ryzhik stories (published by both Melik Pashaev and Eksmo). See also Zaslavskiy, "Den.'"

38. Chernyavsky seems to have in mind Zaslavsky's 2017 article "The Birthday of Russian Comics" (Zaslavskiy, "Den'"). A documentary on Russian émigré cartoonist Yury Lobachev was also titled *The Father of Russian Comics* (directed by Pavel Fetisov, 2011).

American comics series *Fables,* from Vertigo, and it has a whole story drawn in Bilibin's style. (Cherniavskiy interview, 2017)

When I asked about *Veles* and *Mukha,* Chernyavsky gave me more of the same:

These people talk about how great those things were, but I take this with the American expression, "with a grain of salt." I really doubt the stories about how *Veles* was published with a print run of a million. To be honest, that's really hard to believe. In the second-hand comics markets [*komiks-barakholki*] you can find old comics. People held on to these, comics about Mickey Mouse, *Elfquest,* which was published here at one time. But *Veles,* that you practically don't see. It's hard to understand where all those issues of *Veles* went, if that's the case. (Cherniavskiy interview, 2017)

Elaev, who otherwise talked effusively about the exciting things happening in Russian comics, became more subdued, and took longer to think about what to say, when I turned the subject to the younger generation's knowledge of Russian comics history:

They don't know and don't care to know. In Russia we had our own history of comics, even if it was a small one: icons, lubok, the Kukryniksy, the early Soviet Perestroika journals . . . Of course, we had our own "dark age" [*proval*], that generation that didn't discover those old journals, like *Krokodil, Merry Pictures,* things like that. . . .

As for KOM, [Askold] Akishin is known as a professional, he's a big name. But in general, no one knew about them. As for me, for example, I have that gap in history. I know nothing about that because none of that made it to me. At the beginning of the 90s, I was reading other things. I hadn't seen *Veles.* (Elaev interview, 2019)

I asked if he felt the "gap in history" was an important matter to bring up:

For some reason, I'm more interested in what's going on now. Because I feel that what's most important is what's happening right now. I agree that both are important. It's just that I have this perception when I look at these old journals—like KOM's stuff, *Mukha,* etc.—it's interesting to me, that first burst of enthusiasm in that era, but I don't feel any, how do I put it, any *priazn'* [fellow feeling, affection, closeness]. I have a sense that this is something completely different. That is, I have the sense that this was a certain despairing attempt in a very difficult time, like the early and mid-90s were. This was such a flash in the pan [*blesk*], an explosion which moved things forward, thanks to which everything later on continued, and spread around a bit and continues to spread. But the connection between what happened then and what's happening today is very, very thin. . . .

It's strange for, say, an 18-year-old. It's a lot easier for me to explain to people the value of comics by showing them, for example, stuff Crumb was drawing in the 1960s and 1970s, or Lynda Barry, or Alison Bechdel's work, than to show them Russian material from the 80s and 90s. For some reason. (Elaev interview, 2019)

That "for some reason" (*pochemy-to*) was doing a lot of work, I felt. On its shoulders it was holding up a tangled snarl of . . . what, exactly? Embarrassment? Contempt? Apathy about family origins? Oedipal dismissal? Russophobia? This was different from the revulsion and mixed emotions US readers might experience toward, say, Richard Outcault's casual ethnic stereotypes in *Hogan's Alley*, or Will Eisner's Ebony White, or Crumb's misogynist work.[39] This had to do with a contemporary identity formation that wanted (needed?) to look forward, not back, and abroad, not domestically, for its inspirational models.

To be "good" was to do what they do in the West (I include Japan), and to really excel was to beat the West at its own game. As usual, Bubble's Gabrelyanov voiced the matter in the crudest, most bracing terms—though his directness only made things more clear:

> I don't like the KOM group. They would just show up, get together, eat shish kebabs, get drunk, and draw some stuff.[40] It wasn't a real studio. There was no real motivation to [take it to the fullest]. And now I read Akishin's *My Comics Biography*. It doesn't talk about sitting around for hours and hours working hard. People in our team come in the morning and don't leave 'til late. We're more professional. I leave work at 11pm. . . . We give 100 percent to the work. We work harder even than US people, people at Top Cow, at Dynamite. (Gabrelyanov interview, 2013)

---

39. Though in the US generational and other polarizations have certainly emerged in the assessment of those figures, especially the latter; see Leblanc's account of the contretemps over Crumb at the 2018 Small Press Expo ("Rounding").

40. If by this statement, heavy on Russian stereotypes, Gabrelyanov means that the KOM artists enjoyed each other's company as they worked, then he's right.

The man who considers himself more Stan Lee than Stan Lee—what greater success could a Russian comics figure have? Was there a contradiction there, even a small one?

I posed these and other questions to Alexander Kunin, of KomMissia and the TsKVK, who I discovered had long pondered this phenomenon. He answered, unusually, in less than diplomatic terms:

> KOM was self-sufficient. They were people who could forge their own path . . . like [Alexei] Kapninsky. He was a whole new school just on his own. It's sad that it didn't continue. All these young people today, those between 20 and 30, they rely on the internet, which gives you the sense that all information is accessible, and they are losing respect for authority. They think they are on the same level as others, that they can do everything themselves, that they already know everything.
>
> It's a problem [that they don't know the history of Russian comics]. . . . This generation from 20 to 30, they're troubled people [*slozhnie lyudi*]. They don't know their roots, in the first place. Secondly, they don't know how to find them out. Thirdly, this is a crisis generation. They are either realizing or will soon come to realize that everything they are doing has been done already. This is not know-how. . . . They don't realize that the style they found for themselves is Watterson, it's Crumb. Or Will Eisner. (Kunin interview, 2017)

Kunin's point—that many of the young today don't know what they don't know—struck me as more than just thirty-something grousing (and I certainly hope my concerns don't sound like mere fifty-something grousing); such knowledge gaps might affect how one (mis)perceives one's own art, one's country, and the world. At any rate, such a view resonates with what others have written about this demographic. The journalist Georgy Bovt, for example, noted in 2006 that

> for the younger generation, Soviet history is as distant as the history of ancient Greece. For them, Stalin is as relevant to today's reality as Alexander the Great. When they see this fellow Lenin—who is, in their personal experience and world view . . . something like Tutankhamen—they honestly wonder what he did to get mummified and laid out in the center of the capital. ("Playing": 36)

Of course I do not argue that young comics artists should close themselves off to foreign influences; many a US comics artist could benefit from exposure to more works from abroad, after all. Presumably, educating oneself about the history of the form and opening up to as many influences as possible can only benefit one's art. I see no benefit, though, in simply jettisoning a decades-old legacy of fascinating comics works, often made under difficult circumstances, and blithely casting it off to some purgatory of the unseen, inferior, and unworthy—just because it's Russian. It's not an either/or. You can have both. Knowing your own national tradition precludes nothing. Acknowledging your past can only enrich your present and future. Or so I would think. All of this, naturally, doesn't mean you have to *like* the old stuff. Maybe you think Petya Ryzhik sucks; that's okay. But to never bother to learn about Petya Ryzhik, and then to make presumptions about the backwardness of your country's comics culture based on your ignorance—that's what I find a bit disturbing.

At one point, my conversation with Elaev turned to Viktoria Lomasko, the most well-known Russian comics artist in the West, who openly embraces her style's origins in Soviet graphics and book design; she doesn't even like to be called a *komiksist* (see Alaniz, "Flashy" and my conclusion). "For me she's a great example of a 'here and there' way of thinking," Elaev said. "She's her own thing. For her, there is there [i.e., the West] and here is here. But I feel myself at home everywhere. I find it interesting to blur this boundary" (Elaev interview, 2019). Their difference in outlook is as much generational as anything else: Lomasko is about ten years older than Elaev—which may not seem like much, but in Russia ten years can make a huge difference, especially in matters of culture. Lomasko, for one thing, belongs to what anthropologist Alexei Yurchak calls "the last Soviet generation"; Elaev does not.[41]

The strong foreign, especially American, influence on Russian comics—even the indie small press—manifests sometimes in unexpected ways, such as language. Space Cow produces both English and Russian versions of its books, to make them accessible to international readers.[42] Much of their comics teaching involves English-language material:

> You can work out a good idea of the mechanics of comics by reading a lot, but a lot of works are not published in Russian. There's a huge part of the culture that those who don't know English can't access. But you need to know Crumb, and others. Knowing English, I could read Lynda Barry's *What It Is*. It's an extremely important work, but it's hard to translate. (Elaev interview, 2019)

---

41. See also Pavlovsky's comments on the different generations of Russian comics artists, framed in terms of anthropologist Alexei Yurchak's last Soviet generation model (Bondareva, "Chto").

42. This strategy is not uncommon among Eastern European comics artists and others seeking exposure in the anglophone world. See, for example, the minicomix and online postings of Anna Krztoń (Poland) and Lucie Lomová (Czech Republic), discussed in Kuhlman and Alaniz, "General": 15–18.

Some artists, like Elaev and Zhulikov, go further: They make their comics in English *ab ovo* (see figure 4.3). For Elaev, writing in a foreign tongue helps him break through a psychological barrier:

> You don't feel constrained when you write in English. Because in Russia we have a lot of taboo topics, a lot of sensitivity to different kinds of content, because it's connected to sex or . . . profanity. We have very strong patriarchal values, and when you write in English it's like you're freeing yourself from that. Somehow that's what happens. I don't fully understand this or how it works, but it seems to me a very powerful and very important factor. When I started drawing comics in English, I did it completely unconsciously. I just felt that it was right to make them in English. *And automatically they became very personal.*
>
> At first these were just experiments. I didn't think I would try to publish them, but then I managed to make such personal stories, which, had I tried to do them in Russian, I couldn't have pulled them off. Simply because the language itself in which I was setting down my thoughts was pushing me to go deeper and deeper into myself. (Elaev interview, 2019; my emphasis)[43]

Artistic processes never happen in a vacuum. It should come as no surprise that in Putin's Russia, the notion that to write in English rather than your mother tongue somehow puts you more in touch with yourself—is not exactly a truth universally acknowledged. I asked Elaev if his flouting of Turgenev's "great, powerful, righteous and free" Russian language[44] has ever led to accusations that he is a traitor to his people. "I think that conservative people who see in the English language a betrayal of the motherland," he said with a smile, "are just happy that this material is not in Russian, so their children can't read it!" (Elaev interview, 2019).

In other words, writing in English makes you more of an outsider—a time-tested posture for an artist. Yet that too is under assault from many quarters in contemporary Russian life; witness rock mega-star Sergei Shnurov, front-man of Leningrad, who said in 2017: "I tried to destroy this fucking romanticism as an outdated genre. But this bitch keeps on coming back" (Ostrovsky, "Rocking").

---

43. For more on the penetration of foreign languages, especially English, into post-Soviet Russian culture, see Ustinova, "English."

44. Ivan Turgenev's much-mocked sentimentalist 1883 prose poem "The Russian Language" (*Russky yazik*) reads, in part, "oh great, powerful, righteous and free Russian language!" (Turgenev, "Russian": 883).

FIGURE 4.3. *Sex Issues* by Georgy "Gosha" Elaev, from
Sputnikat Press (2020). Used with permission.

The alternatives to such nihilism, it seems, come down to either chau-
vinist Slavophilism or a total embrace of other cultures as preferable to one's
own. That's not what transnationalism is about, ideally. In sum, Chernyavsky's,
Elaev's, and Gabrelyanov's attitudes toward institutions like KOM, ranging
from indifference to outright scorn, reminded me of nothing so much as
the words of Pyotr Chaadaev,[45] the classic go-to Russian thinker on national
self-sabotage:

45. Philosopher Pyotr Chaadaev (1794–1856), in his *Philosophical Letters* (first edition
1836), denounced what he saw as a backward Russian culture vis-à-vis Western Europe's.

We Russians, like illegitimate children, come to this world without patri-mony, without any links with people who lived on the earth before us; we have in our hearts none of those lessons which have preceded our own exis-tence. Each one of us must himself once again tie the broken thread of the family. What is habit, instinct among other peoples, we must get into our heads by hammer-strokes. Our memories go no further back than yesterday; we are, as it were, strangers to ourselves. We walk through time so singly that as we advance the past escapes us forever. This is a natural result of a culture based wholly on borrowing and imitation. There is among us no inward development, no natural progress; new ideas throw out the old ones because they do not arise from the latter, but come among us from Heaven knows where. Since we accept only ready-made ideas, the indelible traces which a progressive movement engraves on the mind and which give ideas their forcefulness make no furrow on our intellect. We grow, but we do not mature; we advance, but obliquely, that is in a direction which does not lead to the goal . . . Isolated in the world, we have given nothing to the world, we have taken nothing from the world; we have not added a single idea to the mass of human ideas; we have contributed nothing to the progress of the human spirit. And we have disfigured everything we have touched of that progress. (quoted in Walicki, *History*: 86)

I do hope Russian comics have moved past this point, at least.

CHAPTER 5

Post-Soviet Graphic Narrative in the Mirror, or *Komiks* That Matter

Whether everyone in Russia appreciates it or not, Russian comics has traversed an enormous distance since the collapse of the Soviet Union. From almost nothing thirty years ago, today it comprises both a nation-spanning industry and its wide-ranging discontents. It is an employer of thousands, a colorful mainstay of the cultural calendar, a vibrant means of expression for professional and amateur, veteran and beginner, and has grown into an object of intense scholarly study—all notions that most Russians would have laughed off as recently as Putin's return to the presidency in 2012. It is still a raucous community, online and off. But as a marker of its stability, the industry established its own prize, the Malevich Award, in 2017 (an analogue to the Eisner in the US).[1]

For all that, comics remains a fairly specialized and segmented corner of the Russian publishing market, a scattered and fringe subculture, its public image a Spider-Man cosplayer or bespectacled nerd. It retains a whiff (maybe more than a whiff) of foreignness—which to some, makes it all the more attractive and cool. Above all, it forms a branch of a vast empire of comics

---

1. The award is named after Kazimir Malevich, the Soviet-era Suprematist painter and art professor at VKhUTEMAS, the Higher Art and Technical Studios (Vysshiye Khudozhestvenno-Tekhnicheskiye Masterskiye), an important art and technical institute founded in 1920 by the Soviet government (comparable to Germany's Bauhaus). Before the 1917 revolution he also produced lubki. The news portal ComicsBoom! had established its own comics awards in 2015.

and geek culture that operates transglobally, 24/7, irrespective of time zones, borders, and (more and more often) national sensibilities.[2]

The industry has its troubles; warning lights have been blinking red for some time, as noted. In 2019, the journalist Dmitry Liashchenko, author of *How to Make a Living in the Comics Industry* (Eksmo, 2019), surveyed the major players and got back some sobering assessments. Boomkniga's Dmitry Yakovlev reported:

> The market continues to develop: the number of publishers is growing, but this has led to a certain amount of oversaturation. Inventory turnover [*skorost' prodazh*] is going down. This is especially noticeable in comics shops. At the end of last year [2018], there took place an event which very seriously affected the market: the publisher Komilfo was sold to Ast-Eksmo, which has a monopoly on the Russian book market. After this, the specialized comics shops lost their pricing advantage for popular Komilfo series, and they are losing their customers.
>
> In the area of auteur [*avtorsky*] comics, in which Boomkniga operates, things are more stable. I even sense a growth in sales in traditional book stores, especially online. And I very much hope that the huge publishers do not ruin what has been created over the last five to seven years. (Liashchenko, "Kuda")

Igor Smirnov, of St. Petersburg's Bazinga comics shop, saw the situation even more darkly, with signs of a slowdown and market correction evident to all but those with the most rose-colored glasses:

> If a few years ago there was a so-called boom, and many people tried to publish something, buy up licenses, open up comic shop after comic shop, then now the situation in the market is closer to oversaturation. Many of my colleagues will probably not agree with me, but even by just looking at the sales figures, people have stopped just straight-up buying everything, like they did a few years ago. People have choices now, which in actuality is not

2. As part of a true transnational phenomenon, Russian comics travels in both directions. Having spilled the banks of the Russian scene, some achieved success in comics industries abroad. These include the KOM veteran Yury Zhigunov (aka Iouri Jigounov), who moved to Belgium in the 1990s and drew the series *Alpha* (Le Lombard) and other works; Andréi Arinushkin, a Belarussian emigre who now works in France and has illustrated several books for Casterman; Alexander Utkin, published by the UK's Nobrow; the Russian-Canadian artist Svetlana Chmakova (author of *Dramacon,* 2005), the best-known mangaka of Russian origin, who emigrated in 1995; Artyom Trakhanov, who illustrated the series *Undertow* (Image, 2014); Gleb Melnikov, artist on DC's *Wonder Woman* (2020); Anna Rud, cover artist for Marvel since 2018; and Julia Alekseyeva, Russian Jewish-American author of the memoir *Soviet Daughter* (2017).

a bad thing. But that customer which you wouldn't exactly call a "comics guru," they to some extent have had their fill of product. On the one hand, competition should push low-quality or uninteresting product out of the market. But at the same time, in Russia it's hard to sell the coolest series like *Sex Criminals* or *Locke & Key,* because people are interested for the most part in Deadpool and Spider-Man. (Liashchenko, "Kuda")

Russian comics have matured in another sense: They've achieved a sophisticated self-awareness, as evidenced by the works of two contemporary komiksisty. The first, Dmitry Narozhny, graduated in the mid-'90s from the Diagilev Art Lyceum in Ekaterinburg, and today works chiefly as an illustrator. His delightful collection of philosophical strips and short pieces, *Vitaly, The Unfashionable Illustrator* (Komilfo/Live Bubbles, 2015), emerged from semi-autobiographical dabblings and online postings of his "Strips about Vitaly." The antihero protagonist, a middle-aged artist, frets over his career choices and indulges in outsized fantasies (like his drawing talent earning him fellatio at a sex club), all with an undercurrent of cynicism and hints of despair. Humorous, with a dark, adult edge, these vignettes hold no illusions about the world's recognition of comics as a great art; on the contrary, our komiksist comes off as a pathetic if likeable enough man-child.

Narozhny's clear renderings, reminiscent of Jacques Tardi or Craig Thompson, have a labile facility that makes the sometimes sudden shifts between fantastic and humdrum scenarios go smooth as silk. This quality serves him well in stories that, even if they involve transdimensional travel, all basically boil down to navel-gazing (in this they recall the Russian comics hit of the 2000s, Oleg Tishchenkov's *Tomcat*). The two-pager "Drawing of Norms" (*Risovka norm*) makes for Narozhny's most piquant commentary on comics. The title, a pun, could also be translated as "Mansplaining Norms" or "Showing Off of Norms"—and indeed, it is a virtuoso piece of cartooning. Over a series of two tiers of three panels each and a bottom tier of two panels, the bearded Vitaly has a conversation with his young daughter, who has brought home some books from a comics festival. Examining the material, Vitaly starts to complain about the art, to which his daughter replies, "Well, the main thing here is the plot, the story itself. The presentation [*podacha*] is not the main thing. Plus, that's just the style of the author" (n.p.).[3]

"Style . . ." Vitaly says. "Now style is a thing by which you can tell right away how much time the artist spent on the work, and before that, on his training." With that very panel, the drawing style changes to more detailed

---

3. Note how this echoes Elaev's contention that in comics the story is paramount, with the art merely a means to an end.

linework with a pen (the previous panels evidently were drawn more quickly, with a brush). Over the rest of the story, as Vitaly obnoxiously lectures on the different styles available to an artist, each succeeding panel visually transforms its depiction of the characters to mirror his comments, for example, from a Posey Simmonds–type color rendering with lowercase computer font without word balloons, to a scratchy black line with almost illegible dialogue, as Vitaly opines, "And then BAM!—everything's in ballpoint pen, with a ton of text which you would gladly have read in a book!" Even more uproariously, the characters readily perceive the changes. In the same "ballpoint" panel, the daughter marvels, "Everything looks more . . . prickly!" "Yeah, but it's faster," he replies.

A story mischievously blurring formal and diegetic boundaries, in which the style keeps radically shifting from panel to panel, with self-reflexive characters who keep looking different yet remain the "same," points to profound questions of aesthetics, epistemology, subjectivity—something like that.[4] But Narozhny explicitly aims his quivers at a more mundane target: vapid comics fads. In a panel resembling something Tom Gauld would draw, the daughter muses, "Maybe in all this there's some kind of gimmick [*fishka*]." "There must be," he answers in the next panel, "since people draw it like that, publishers publish it, and people read it." The Vitaly who says this is a naïve minimalist cartoon, the sort that would not look out of place in a Space Cow publication. "Papa, you look horrible!" the girl says. "Not at all," he quips. "Right now I'm more fashionable than I've ever been!" (see figure 5.1).

As the reader has surmised, with each panel "Drawing of Norms" removes more and more detail from the characters, making them increasingly "simplistic," until they reach the stage of stick figures—and then, perversely, "mad face" internet memes. Yet these comics' "successive selves" (Hatfield, *Alternative*: 117; Køhlert, *Serial*) never lose a sense of who they are—even if the daughter sometimes seems less than happy about her representation. In the final tier, Narozhny reverts to the original style (his), for Vitaly's verdict:

> What, did I offend you? I was just kidding . . .
>   Though I really don't understand why, if it's drawn badly, they say, "Well, the story's the main thing." And if it's drawn really well, but the plot's lame,[5]

---

4. See, for example, Charles Hatfield's discussion of Daniel Clowes's "Just Another Day," a story that uses similar devices and makes somewhat similar points about identity (though not necessarily style) in autobiographical comics (*Alternative*: 117–120).

5. I translated *khromaet* as "lame" under protest. *Lame* in the sense of "uncool" or "boring" is an ableist term, which one nonetheless does often hear in English. I hope this note helps in some small way to sensitize to that fact those of my readers who need reminding.

FIGURE 5.1. Dmitry Narozhny's "Drawing of Norms" (2015)

right away they'll scream, "No, no, no! This isn't a drawings exhibit! Without an awesome story, you might as well toss it all out!"

But if anything, if it's a "graphic novel" or a "drawn story"—then that's telling you you should draw the story and write the script equally well.

Those last two panels, with Vitaly expounding upon his dubious aesthetic calculus, break the fourth wall yet again: The artist's photographed hand appears, illustrating the characters—about as bared as the device can get. But maybe not: Paradoxically, the hand stays within the boundaries of the panels (not bleeding out of them as one might expect), betraying the photorealistic "persona" as no less fictional than anything else on the page. At any rate, by story's close our characters' conversation has moved on to why Vitaly divorced his daughter's mother; disquisitions on comics' formal properties and faddish trends were just another way to chew the fat. Vitaly delivers his belabored diatribes in a fish bowl: Nobody cares.

"Drawing of Norms" merits comparison with works like Matt Madden's "A History of American Comic Books in Six Panels" (2012), in which the historically determined style also fluctuates from panel to panel (Golden Age superhero, *Mad* parody, etc.), though I would say Madden's piece is as much about genre as anything else. Yet unlike that or, say, the Kirbyish pastiche homage of *Conquerors of the Impossible*, Narozhny's sly excursus explores matters more ineffable: artistic style (and how this correlates with market demands), literary merit, medium specificities, even the tools of the trade—ballpoint pen, flomasters, clip art, Neopiko brush pen. It also manages to channel quite a bit about post-Soviet attitudes toward graphic narrative's place (if any) in the Russian canon, even working in a dig at literary adaptations: "You should read *War and Peace,* not turn it into comics!"

All this, as mentioned, with the underlying presumption that comics don't matter.[6] This oft-repeated theme appears again in "Family Matters" (Semeynoe), a six-panel strip in which Vitaly interrogates his ex-wife Natalya as to why they divorced. "Because," she answers, "when we met, you told me you were an artist. . . . Well, I thought you'd draw some crap or other that you'd sell for megabucks. . . . But it turned out you're a komiksist." That last line is delivered in a separate word balloon, in its own panel, like a boom coming down. Vitaly objects, saying, "But I'm an illustrator! I've never drawn a single comic

---

6. For Vitaly, comics in Russia would fall into the fourth quadrant of Bart Beaty and Benjamin Woo's Bourdieu-derived "structural fields of cultural production" diagram (*Greatest*: 12). This quadrant denotes "those works poorest in symbolic capital, which have enjoyed neither commercial success nor the esteem of influential cultural intermediaries" (13). That was more true in 2015 than now.

in my life." His ex rejoins, with crushing finality, her dialogue again delivered in its own panel: "All the more reason." The end.

Through such put-downs, *Vitaly, The Unfashionable Illustrator* conflates its hero's professional failures with his inadequate masculinity and clueless-ness—reflecting all the more unkindly on the career of comics artist itself. The stunted little boys who try to make comics for a living will never quite grow up, these pieces seem to say.

The other artist I want to briefly examine does not put things so bluntly, and only rarely does she resort to Narozhny's avant garde hijinks. Olga Lavr-enteva instead reflects on how comics uniquely represent Russian history, popular memory, and trauma—and what that says about Russian comics themselves. A 2009 graduate of the Art Department of St. Petersburg State university with a degree in graphic design, Lavrenteva was welcomed into the ranks of St. Petersburg's Artists Union in 2013. She has released several long-form works of graphic narrative; the harrowing biography *Survilo* (2019), based on her ninety-three-year-old grandmother's experiences during the 1930s Stalinist repressions and the WWII siege of Leningrad, deserves to be called "the Russian *Maus*" (see Alaniz, "*Survilo*").[7]

Lavrenteva's "gothic detective" graphic novel *ShUV* (Boomkniga, 2016) recollects and reexamines a much more recent national trauma: the 1990s. The plot involves a brother and sister of tender age at their dacha late in the decade, who fill their days with imaginative and horribly sadistic games: They role-play Chechen terrorists, Russian dictators, prostitutes, and dead-ender soldiers, subjecting their stuffed toy bears and Barbie dolls to mock torture and executions (in cringingly hilarious scenes that evoke a gory, R-rated *Calvin and Hobbes*).[8] Clearly the unnamed young siblings are reacting to a Rus-sia as brought to them by television and newspapers: a world full of sexual violence, *mafiya* hits, and war. As discussed previously, this was the lurid mediated reality for Pelevin's "Generation Pizdets" in the 1990s, whether on the news; in popular fiction genres like the *boevik* (action story) and *detektiv* (crime novel);[9] or in the movies (where *chernukha* ruled the roost). For the kids, though, all this *bespredel* merely serves as raw material for their fanciful, blood-curdling play.

---

7. She also lettered the Russian translation of Dominic Goblet's *Pretending Is Lying* (Boomkniga, 2019).

8. Like the kids in Phoebe Gloeckner's *A Child's Life and Other Stories* or David B.'s *Epileptic,* the siblings' casual brutality explodes any sentimental notions of children as tender-hearted innocents.

9. Author Alexandra Marinina, for example, ruled the 1990s with corpse-strewn novels partly based on her own experiences in law enforcement, while Polina Dashkova featured a Chikatilo-like serial killer in her 1998 novel *Madness Treads Lightly.*

But nothing fuels their imaginations like the real-life suicide by gunshot of their dacha neighbor Vasya, a pathetic schlub whom they later learn was a drug addict. And their stuffed toys can't compete with another medium—comics—as vehicle for their expressive élan. The boy and girl start making picture stories about Vasya's death, which soon take on a whole new cast when they come to suspect the young man was actually killed by his wastrel parents, who have covered up the crime. Their "super secret" comics in a cheap green notebook take on the significance of a "holy manuscript" (124) as they wildly speculate about how the killing occurred.

Equal parts transgressive, funny, and tragic, these comics within the comic are also, as Alexei Pavlovsky puts it, "comics *about* comics" ("Russkaia gotika"; my emphasis). Our young authors endlessly debate the form and content of their ever-evolving opus, which redounds to the construction of *ShUV* itself—making for an intensively self-reflexive reading experience: "Here's the blackest panel" (148), a textbox announces, over just that. And like Narozhny, Lavrenteva's kids also have a keen eye for style: When one of them objects, "I think the characters look too ugly," the other replies, "That's how it's done: this is in 'hard realism' style" (58). At another point, one of them demands, "That's it, stop! That's enough snakes. Otherwise the comic'll turn out too gross" (141). This is Cortázar or Borges by way of *The Gashlycrumb Tinies*. And, of course, the more mayhem the better. A panel of Vasya with his brains spilled onto the floor prompts one of the siblings to cry out, "Whoa! This comic is cooler than the last one" (93). Variations of the sound effect *BA-BAKH* (*KABOOM!*) repeat throughout the work, as the kids depict different versions of the supposed murder over and over, escalating the gore with every pass.

Lavrenteva heightens the mood of impropriety by conveying to the reader a sense of being inducted into the children's private world: their intimacies, *verboten* pleasures, and hiding places, concealed even from their parents (especially from their parents). The "sacred text" of their comics is a box with many locks. Even the title *ShUV* functions as a code that needs to be deciphered; it's an abbreviation for the kids' hypothesis, made up of the letters *Sh, U,* and *V*: "*Shlomov Ubil Vasyu*" ("Shlomov Killed Vasya") (88). The reader, perhaps discomfitingly, enters an unseemly secret society, a puppet theater of cruelty.

As noted, the author here is primarily targeting the 1990s, a disastrous decade most Russians would rather forget (and also as noted, a decade many in the modern Russian comics industry dismiss outright). She lays the references on thick: Apart from the mentions of Chechnya and the mafiya, we see Yeltsin on TV, while Lenin's portrait still hangs on the wall (143); *Criminal Russia* (191), a blood-and-guts-filled true crime show of the era; a bookshelf well stocked with Stephen King horror novels, whose translations won over many fans in that decade, and which Galina (Vasya's mother) reads obsessively (114). It's no surprise that the siblings label their third comics story "*soversh-enno sekretno*" ("top secret")—plausible, but also the name of a sensationalistic '90s tabloid (106).[10]

Ultimately, *ShUV's* references, devices, and transgressions come to implicate the reader in the excesses and dehumanization of so much Russian media of the Yeltsin era, when the country was veering from the state control of the USSR to the raucous "freedom" of first-stage capitalism. Here, "Through Blood and Suffering" is sick fun—but at what cost? The graphic novel forces a confrontation with the legacy of a terrible time and its unacknowledged psychic scars, with how the survivors of the '90s (failed to) process the horrors of their age, carrying them forward through life.

Lavrenteva is further asking: Why do comics excel at thrilling impressionable young people with Grand Guignol–type fare? Could there be anything redemptive in all the carnage? (We should hope so.) I would say yes: We could read *ShUV* as we do the EC horror comics of the 1950s—grisly, yet steeped in a brand of socially conscious political critique. Others have argued for the psychologically beneficial effects on children of comics violence and "monstrous" representations.[11] But *ShUV's* own answers to the questions it poses are both more profound and more disturbing.

As Pavlovsky perceptibly argues, through their endless production of words and pictures, the kids themselves become Vasya's symbolic killers ("Russkaia gotika"), tormenting his image over and over, just like they do their hapless stuffed toys. But in the process, somehow, through art and imagination, "Vasya" takes on a bizarre afterlife—as indeed do the 1990s themselves within *ShUV's* pages, with all their humiliation and horror. This makes *ShUV*, in part through its mise-en-abyme structure, a graphic novel that insistently interrogates its own medium's Baudrillardian representation of death, its simulacral capacities to both take "life" and to give it back.[12] The kids' version of Vasya is always dying—another way of saying he's always alive, ready to die again. This in turn leads us to consider how graphic narrative, among the most interactive of arts, allows readers to mentally inhabit imaginary characters (perpetrators as well as victims) up to and past the point of death; in other words, how identification functions in comics. Finally, the novel asks us

---

10. Founded in 1989, *Sovershenno Sekretno* was the first truly independent investigative newspaper in Russia, but in the 1990s it suffered a reputation as a corrupt media holding that wrote articles "to order" (see Sloane, "Mafia").

11. See Jones, *Killing*.

12. On comics' engagement with death and the simulacrum, see also Alaniz, *Death*.

FIGURE 5.2. Olga Lavrenteva's *ShUV* (Boomkniga, 2016)

to mull how comics participate in the enjoyment that, however guiltily, comes from the secondhand consumption of human misery. In Lavrenteva's remarkable book, as in any black and white comic, spilled ink looks just like blood (59) (see figure 5.2).

Through such ambitious aims, which earned it the 2017 Malevich Award for Best Script and its author comparisons to Nikolai Gogol (Bondareva, "Chto"), *ShUV* blazes a trail for graphic narrative in Russia even as it looks back at a traumatic period of recent Russian history. Its plot, about the exposure of children to adult material they cannot really understand, which they then sublimate into scandalous art, allegorizes the journey of Russian comics themselves in the troubled post-Soviet era.

A Summation

We may outline post-Soviet Russian comics' first three decades or so like this:

1990s

- Economic uncertainty, loss of state publishing subsidies, collapse of tiny domestic comics market
- Domination by foreign licensed product
- Widespread rejection by readers; comics considered "low" sub-literature, not Russian
- Emergence of internet communities

2000s

- Rise of festivals: KomMissia (Moscow), Boomfest (St. Petersburg)
- Domination by foreign licensed product
- Limited success for children's comics journals (e.g., *Just You Wait!*)
- Putinism's chilling effect on expression

2010s

- Rise of comics centers; comics sections in bookstores and libraries; comics shops
- Stronger domestic competition against foreign licensed product
- Proliferation of festivals, publishers; hardening (and mixing) of genres
- Bona fide emergence of mainstream Western-style comics industry (e.g., Bubble)
- Bona fide emergence of Western-style comics culture, including indie small press
- Rise of comics studies
- The Nonfiction Turn
- Threat of market oversaturation—complicated further by 2020 coronavirus pandemic

In short, a comics reader in Russia today has an extraordinary array of choices, from the US-mainstream flash of Bubble to the indie pleasures of Space Cow, and everything in between. She has a variety of means to access said products: bookstore, comics shop, library, comics center, festivals, artist's fairs, thirdhand markets, online shops both foreign and domestic. Should she decide she wants to make and distribute her own comics, she may do so using traditional or digital methods; finance them through numerous online crowdfunding sites; and post them via social media, print them up herself, or try to sell them to any of several publishers.

All of this, if not unimaginable (many, achingly, did imagine it), was certainly impossible when the Soviet Union collapsed and Russia went through ten years of economic hell. The Russian comics industry as it has blossomed in the last decade or so is an extraordinary testament to native talents, drive, and determination—as well as to the border-dissolving power of a late capitalist transnational popular youth culture that leaves little in its wake untouched.

What remains undone? A lot.

Scholars and historians are slowly reclaiming the past, namely Russia's centuries-old heritage of pictorial narrative, for the present and future, though that process is still only beginning. (As noted, it might help if more Russian comics figures and readers themselves showed greater interest in that heritage.) The year 2020 witnessed a homecoming of sorts, and a good omen: Zaslavsky and Akishin's 1990s opus *The Master and Margarita* was finally published in Russia by Boomkniga, a quarter-century after its completion.[13]

But other problems loom. Far too few people outside Russia know about its vibrant comics culture; fewer still can engage with the vast majority of its works. There exists a critical need for more translations (a problem that besets Eastern European comics as a whole; see Kuhlman and Alaniz, "General"). And as publisher after publisher frets, the domestic industry could come crashing down at any time (though Spider-Man and Superman will doubtless stick around regardless).

Readership is expanding, perhaps the best remedy of all. What may ultimately put Russian comics on a long-term stable footing is not a niche nerd culture, but Kunin's "culturological line" in the guise of the general-interest consumer. Such a reader, browsing in the bookstore, may feel unmoved by *Demonslayer,* but might pick up (and swipe their credit card for) a title dealing with topical real-life questions in sophisticated, artistically compelling graphic narrative.[14] Coinciding with the third Putin administration (2012 and after), there emerged just such an informed, politically conscious if not socially activist type of Russian comics practice, what I call the Nonfiction Turn—a movement led primarily by women. I discuss this phenomenon at length in my book's conclusion.

By way of bringing this section to an end, let us return to Lavrenteva's grand metaphor in *ShUV*: the Russian comics industry as a feral child reared in the "Wild Age" '90s, only let us imagine him somewhat older—on the cusp of adulthood, mental scars and all. How far might he go? Elena Avinova, who

---

13. In 2012 Astrel Press had published the Russian translation of Andrzej Klimowski and Danusia Schejbal's adaptation of *The Master and Margarita* (Selfmade Hero, 2008).

14. Something like this has already happened in the Czech Republic, for example. See Alaniz, "Czech."

taught a comics-making workshop at Moscow's Creative Writing School, pictures him this way:

> For now Russian comics is a juvenile. He's looking around, imitating everybody who's made an impression, and is learning from others' mistakes. This orientation towards the manga, BD and US industries is very marked. But text with pictures, even without being called comics, is getting more and more popular both on the internet and in advertising. They're soaking up the entirety of Russian visual culture, especially the traditions of icon-painting, the lubok, Soviet posters, the art of the Mitki group. I think that comics have a future. We're surrounded by pictures and icons, we make presentations that combine words and visual images, we are thinking like this already. That means that soon we'll learn to talk that way too. (Khanukaeva, "Elena")

#Iachitaiukomiks-Gate

Let us close this chapter with another scandal.

Speaking at the opening of the Moscow International Book Fair on September 4, 2019, Russia's minister of culture, Vladimir Medinsky, surmised,

> Comics are for people who have trouble reading. I do not like comics at all. Comics are like chewing gum. How do I put it, they're not food. But for a grown person to read comics is an admission that "I am a moron [*debil*], I read comics." Comics should be aimed at children who are just starting to read, children up to seven or eight years old. But for an adult to be reading comics, this seems to me pathetic [*ubozhestvom*]. (Anokhin, "#iachitaiukomiksy")[15]

The, ahem, response from Russian comics land proved swift and brutal.

Vasily Kistyakovsky, co-owner of Chuk and Geek and Jellyfish Jam: "Medinsky said something idiotic, which feels especially shameful to read in the 21st century." Ruslan Khubiev, director of Ramona Press: "This is a sign of the deepest incompetence and lack of education." Beata Kotashevskaya

---

15. Medinsky was responding to a reporter's question about whether history could or should be taught in comics format (Agentstvo gorodskikh novostei Moskva, "V. Medinskiy"). Some outlets reported more of his comments, such as the line, "You can maybe collect [comics], that's fun, but not read them" (Sidorov, "Pochemu"). Further context: The Moscow International Book Fair, for the first time in its history, had in 2019 set aside a large section for comics publishers to hawk their wares.

of Jellyfish Jam: "The inability to understand something is an occasion not for pride, but for reflection. And to offhandedly brush off an entire cultural medium, with its enormous palette of hues and subgenres—that's the best way to demonstrate the narrowness of your thinking." Ivan Chernyavsky of Chuk and Geek: "Medinsky is a person whose level of education is under great doubt, and a person who declared war on history as a discipline when he contrived the scandal over *Panfilov's 28 Men*.[16] . . . [R]ussian culture of the last few years has been developing not because of Medinsky, but in spite of him" (Anokhin, "#iachitaiukomiksy").

Apart from the scorn heaped on the minister from the online comics community, the mainstream print and broadcast media treated the incident as laughable, devoting far more time to the backlash than to the igniting spark (for example, KOM veteran Alim Velitov appeared on the Moscow 24 evening broadcast to air his thoughts and to draw comics in the studio, while a reporter interviewed Andrei Drozdov, head of the comics center at the Anna Akhmatova Library). The hashtag #iachitaiukomiksy (#IReadComics) trended on Twitter.

One aspect of the reaction in particular would have stood out to anyone who had been following Russian comics over the years: Everyone rebutting the minister had a ready example (usually several) of comics' cultural worth and/or official approbation. Khubiev mentioned Nick Drnaso's graphic novel *Sabrina* (2018) making it onto the long list for the Booker prize; Kunin pointed to the Nick Sousanis exhibit at the Non/Fiction book fair in 2017 (Anokhin, "#iachitaiukomiksy"). Even as he sighed over Medinsky's characterization, which he called "the most wide-spread stereotype about comics," Yakovlev of Boomkniga cited a 2019 exhibit, "Three Stories: New Comics from Russia," at the Hermitage Berlin art gallery; the show was opened by Mikhail Piotrovsky, renowned director of the Hermitage Museum (Neliubin, "Vystavki"). Medinsky was outclassed.

In other words, comics' value as an art form had taken firm root; it really was a nonissue. Given that most Russians would not consider a politician saying something unlearned a matter worth dwelling on, this minor skirmish

---

16. Chernyavsky refers to a 2016 public contretemps involving the newly released *Panfilov's 28 Men* (*28 Panfilovtsy*), a World War II film directed by Andrei Shalopa and Kim Druzhinin, and financed by the state. It deals with the heroic defense of Moscow against the German onslaught early in the war. When Russian State Archive director Sergei Mironenko questioned the historical accuracy of the events depicted, he was denounced by Medinsky, who remarked, in part, "This is a sacred legend that shouldn't be interfered with. People that do that are filthy scum." World War II mythology remains a central plank of Putinism, with its canonization of a particular version of history. Revisionism is excoriated and often punished. Mironenko eventually lost his post (Bone, "Putin").

in the culture wars would doubtless flame out by the next news cycle. And it did—except for a short opinion piece published over two weeks later in a provincial newspaper, *Nashe Vremya* (*Our Time*) of Rostov.

Alexander Sidorov's "Why Are Comics Hateful to Me?" checks all the boxes of age-old Russo-Soviet comicsophobia. It rehearses many tired arguments familiar to generations of comics readers (some deployed by anti-comics crusader Natalya Markova in the early 2000s),[17] on the deleterious effects of our friendly neighborhood medium on reading ability (check), intellectual development (check), and morality (check). Recalling Viktor Erofeyev's much more sophisticated Marcusian critique in his 1990s essay "Comics and the Comics Disease" (though Erofeyev also praises the artistry of graphic narrative), Sidorov lays down every modern sin at the foot of comics, from illiteracy to dumbed-down internet culture to civilization's fall. Some key excerpts: "Drawn pictures don't even take into account [*ne predusmatrivayut*] full-fledged dialogues, to say nothing of authorial speeches. The basis of comics is action"; "[Comics] are built upon the primitive, on a 'clip' consciousness . . . [They] are readily taken up by the new generation which grew up on socializing on the internet—there there's no need for literacy, the exchange of opinions takes place through short phrases"; "A devotion to comics is a return to cave painting, to regression and degradation" (Sidorov, "Pochemu").[18]

Part of what makes this essay so disheartening is that, unlike legions of other comics haters, Sidorov does not speak from ignorance: He demonstrates a knowledge of the history of pictorial narrative, and expresses an appreciation for its development in his own country, from icons to lubok to early-Soviet ROSTA windows to *Merry Pictures*. He even, movingly, describes his affection for a prized object in his own book collection, an edition of the Strugatsky Brothers' 1965 sci-fi novel *Monday Begins on Saturday* illustrated by Yevgeny Migunov—the very artist (along with Jack Kirby) to whom Alexei Volkov and Alexei Gorbut pay extended tribute in *Conquerors of the Impossible*. None of that stops Sidorov from delivering this verdict:

---

17. Known in the early 2000s Russian comics community by her touching nickname, "the wet rat." See Alaniz, *Komiks*: 108–111.

18. Another choice quote: "And the most horrifying thing: through comics, with their monosyllabic, primitive speeches, preponderance of simplistic imagery to the detriment of words, of the stylistics of a language and of representation, a person develops a clip mentality. It accustoms one to measured-out information on an elementary level, not conducive to a many-sided perception of the world or to a deep conceptualization of events. Batman, Spider-Man, Hulk, Superman, the X-Men (or as they say in Russia, people of the letter X) and such 'heroes' are all cut from the same cloth: conflicts primitive in the extreme, plots so stupid as to border on the grotesque" (Sidorov, "Pochemu"). "People of the letter X" is an untranslatable, scatological pun, sort of like saying "People of the letter F" in English.

Today a generation has arisen which rushes to fiercely defend these "merry pictures."

A dangerous symptom. It bears witness to the fact that in Russia the experiments to raise not a "rational man," but an "imbecilic" man, have nearly been crowned with success. After all, comics are one of the instruments for the formation of a dim-witted people who are easily manipulated. In the USA, according to the latest research, more than 43.5 million citizens experience difficulties with reading and writing. We're talking here not only about immigrants, but about people who have spoken English since birth. Many of them, incidentally, don't live badly at all. But they are easily governed. You can fill their heads with whatever idea you want, and lead them in any direction. (Sidorov, "Pochemu")

In short, "Why Are Comics Hateful to Me?" reeks of a rear-guard action, if not of anachronism. Its apocalyptic warnings, its shaky reasoning, its paranoid conclusions, its very clichés[19] long ago wore out their welcome. The author also does himself no favors by ending the essay with "Lord, save me from popcorn, gay parades and Spider-Man!" (Sidorov, "Pochemu").

Sidorov gets one thing right: Today's popular defense of comics as a medium of expression does indeed serve as a barometer for the vast sociocultural changes that have swept Russia since the USSR's demise. The fact that this rather sniveling little hit piece appeared not in a major newspaper in Moscow or St. Petersburg, nor on the primetime news, but in Rostov, also reflects the growing economic power of the comics industry in this era. Comics' enemies have been driven from the center to the periphery—literally. Medinsky's remarks and Sidorov's harangue would have widely resonated in 1989, in 1999, and likely even in 2009—but could not any longer in 2019.

One more thing. Why is this essay hateful to me? Maybe because like so many Russians before him—and not a few now—Sidorov, an educated man, sells short a rich patrimony (as Kotashevskaya puts it, an "enormous palette of hues and subgenres") for the most closed-minded, dogmatic reasons. Maybe also because it opens up a time portal back to the Stalinist USSR, when another Russian thinker (this one considerably better known than Sidorov) inveighed against graphic narrative in equally misguided fashion.

---

19. For example, Sidorov echoes Medinsky's remarks in his use of the word *debil* (*moron* or *imbecile*) to describe comics readers. Given its ubiquity, the association between *debil* and *komiks* in the modern Russian language suggests an unexamined implicit bias. If only I had a kopeck for every time I've heard the phrase "*Komiks, eto dlya debilov*" ("Comics are for morons") over the last thirty years . . .

Kornei Chukovsky, beloved children's poet and someone who should really have known better, bemoaned in his Cold War–era essay "The Defilement of Children's Souls" ("Rastlenie detskikh dush," 1948) the easy availability (on every corner, at only ten or five cents per!) of those "bloody little booklets, which in America, by some evil game of language, bear the name of 'comics.'" To read Chukovsky today is to be reminded of how deep the roots of Sidorov's reflexive comicsophobia run. The overlaps with his famous predecessor's discourse are eerie: "[Comics] have only one moral basis: man is beast to man"; "the literary formal properties of all the comics are readily grasped by children: the exposition always takes place with the help only of sequential pictures, accompanied by a minimal amount of text: the plot, for all its idiotic vulgarity, is charged with a maximal dynamism"; "Leading educators anxiously point out that American schoolchildren today are reading not Mark Twain, not Dickens, but 'The Adventures of Catwoman,' who steals diamonds with the aid of sleeping gas" (Chukovskiy, "Rastlenie"). And so on.

Juxtaposing the poet and the pundit reveals perhaps the major reason why the younger generations have jettisoned speech like this: It sounds so drearily, backwardly Soviet. ("OK, Bolshevik.")[20] Never was a more on-point statement uttered than when Benjamin Sutcliffe observed: "In the post-Soviet context, distinctions between elite and mass culture relied on inherited arguments" (*Prose*: 132).

To get to the punchline, then: The net effect of the 2019 #iachitaiukomiks kerfuffle was a boost in comics sales in Russia, according to Yakovlev and others (Cuttle, "Russian"). Meanwhile, Medinsky stepped down as minister of culture later that year (for unrelated reasons).[21]

I would leave it there, excerpt for—well—the voices. They don't stop. They are, frankly, quite lovely to hear.

They sound out from all over the country, these voices. For example, from Polina Postavina, a schoolgirl from Sergiev Posad who won third place in a national comics competition, "#Summer of Your Victories," with a naïve story about Asinastra, who strives to overcome her fears and loneliness and find just one friend in the whole world (*Sergiev Grad*, "Shkol'nitsa"); or from Yelena Osipova, a seventy-year-old from St. Petersburg who frequents anti-

---

20. For more on Soviet comicsophobia, see Alaniz, *Komiks*: 69–73 and Pavlovskiy, "Strakh."

21. Olga Lyubimova, who succeeded him as minister of culture in 2020, started the job with a fresh scandal of her own: decade-old social media postings exposed her as a proud philistine who hates opera, museums, classical music, art films, and pretty much everything else that falls into the bailiwick of a minister of culture. "No fucking way am I a cultured person," she wrote on her *Live Journal* page (*Otkrytye Media*, "Ia"). Initial reports led some to believe she might feel better predisposed to comics.

government rallies holding her elaborate posters that strikingly combine words and images in the best traditions of protest art, insisting, "Russia is a bird, not a bear" (Vol'tskaia, "Rossiia");[22] and even from someone long dead: Olga Ranitskaya, who composed a palm-sized comics diary, "Work and Days," while incarcerated in a Stalinist labor camp in 1941–42, a work that languished in obscurity for decades and was at last featured in a landmark 2017 exhibit at Moscow's Gulag History Museum (Eroshok, "Nam"; Sohlman and MacFarquhar, "A Diary").

There are others, many others. And though silent, these voices thunder forth in a chorus, loud and clear. What are they saying?

Artur Safarov, owner of Comicz Era, a comics shop in Novosibirsk, Siberia, captures it well:

> Sometimes parents come out against their kids reading comics, because this is Western and we shouldn't have that here. But in fact it's not like that. Comics don't belong to any one country. Comics is art, and art should belong to everyone. And everyone finds in it something of their own. (*Sibnovosti,* "V Novosibirske")

Did you hear that, former minister Medinsky?
In today's Russia, comics matter.

---

22. An English-language version, "Yelena Osipova: 'Russia Is a Bird, Not a Bear,'" was published online by *The Russian Reader*: https://therussianreader.com/2015/11/23/yelena-osipova-petersburg-artist-interview-protest-posters/.

CHAPTER 6

Post-Soviet Masculinity and the Superhero

No single art form so precisely conveys the ongoing dumbing-
down and debasement of humanity as does comics. . . .
Comics simply reflected—to recite Herbert Marcuse—the
demolition of multi-dimensional man and his transition to
one-dimensional man, his psychological diminution to a few
simple desires. Comics is the mirror to man's collapse, the
cheery pictures that accompany our own decomposition.

—Erofeyev, "Comics": 36

The Russian novelist and critic Viktor Erofeyev's 1995 essay "Comics and the Comics Disease" sought to spark interest in graphic narrative as a legitimate medium of expression (the so-called Ninth Art) and the study of Russian comics art practice (komiks) itself. Yet, as evident from this quote, Erofeyev sees comics—a spawn of the "garbage dump" of the other arts—first and foremost as evidence for the "dumbing down" of human experience; like the Russian joke or *anekdot,* television or other popular media, comics relies on and perpetuates *unidimensional* representations of such social constructs as gender. Unlike those other media, however, comics spent the twentieth century mostly exiled to the margins of Russo-Soviet culture; the official policy of Socialist Realism in the arts relegated komiksisty mostly to light duty at children's journals, while Western expressions of the medium were largely condemned as bourgeois pseudo-literature.[1]

In the post-Soviet era, comics' depiction of the Russian male, with its reliance on such crude stereotypes as the brainless mafiya *byk* (hired muscle, literally "bull") and "stoner" teenagers (e.g., *Dymich and Tymich*)[2] did the form no favors in gaining further acceptance from "sophisticated" readers.

---

1. Though see Alaniz, *Komiks* for a much more complex and detailed picture.

2. An early-2000s series by Vladimir Komarov, Elena Voronovich, Andrei "Drew" Tkalenko, et al.; see Alaniz, *Komiks*: 104.

On the other hand, the imagined male readers of such publications as the spectacularly coarse early 2000s series *Novy Komiks* bore no pretensions to sophistication in the aforementioned sense; for them, komiks held precisely this simplistic, graspable, dumbed-down appeal—an appeal predicated on an image of masculinity painted in very broad strokes indeed. (This of course only affirms Erofeyev's thesis.) Similarly, post-Soviet komiksists' ironic appropriations of American superhero iconography (long seen by the Soviets as a bastion of pseudo-fascist male idealization)[3] directly critiqued dandified foreign models of "being a man," pointing out their absurdity, even as—in some cases—they embraced and translated them into a Russian idiom.

This chapter examines the comics representation of the Russian male in the Yeltsin and Putin eras, through a consideration of how, at a time of extreme economic and social change, the "comics-esque" (to use Erofeyev's term) seeped into media depictions of gender and "the superheroic."

The Real Russian Man

The release of Alexei Balabanov's *Brother* (*Brat,* 1997) and *Brother 2* (*Brat-2,* 2000) took Russian film viewers, hungry for screen visions of a real man, by storm. They found him in the ruthless, baby-faced killer Danila, who guns down criminals like a hay mower but always remains true to family. Like the Rambo film series in the US, which preceded them by almost two decades, the populist *Brother* films meld a fierce, straight-faced hypermasculinity with an equally deadpan patriotism, even chauvinism, inscribing on the armed male body the fervor and frustrations of a humiliated national psyche.

Not unlike Rambo, a scarred Vietnam vet, Danila (as played by the late actor Sergei Bodrov Jr.) cuts his teeth in the Chechnya conflict, and comes home to practice what he learned on a uniformly odious civilian criminal populace. Also like Rambo, Danila lives by a strict moral code, placing personal and familial loyalty above all else. He despises the West, and in the second, wildly successful film, he reluctantly visits Chicago on a mission of mayhem. In the process, he rescues a Russian prostitute, convincing her to return to the motherland—a far better place than the square, hypocritical, politically correct America—and blowing away her Blaxploitationesque pimp for good measure.

---

3. See my discussion of poet Kornei Chukovsky's commentary on US superhero comics in chapter 5.

Though embraced by the public, *Brother 2*'s critical reception was mixed, at times scathing. A 2000 *Iskusstvo Kino* review by Mark Lipovetsky typified the discomfiture:

> In modern Russia, which no one respects or fears, [the film's] ideology seems shockingly in demand, by boys and girls of 16, bursting with a need for national pride; by the new masters of the universe, who don't want any competitors in the Russian market and to whom the idea of a hostile West is economically vital for the flowering of their businesses according to their rules; and by those who feel cheated by the West, which beckoned them with democratic prosperity, but who in fact crowned with riches only its brothers in the Mercedes and "them thieving pricks in the government cars." (Lipovetskiy, "Vsekh": 58)

The "in-demand" nativist ideology Lipovetsky identifies rests squarely on the reified, manly shoulders of the films' hero. Brazen, merciless, and powerful, Danila presents a picture of the Russian male brimming with sexuality and explosive violence, always at the service of a nationalist project. He is "brother" to all true Russians and fearsome foe to those who threaten his extended "family," the Russian nation. *Brother 2*, widely hailed as the most successful domestic film of 2000, especially pleased Russian viewers in that it proved a bigger hit than the Western fare that had dominated the country's market since the early 1990s.[4]

We can attribute the *Brat* series' success, first and foremost, to its reconstruction of Russian masculinity, which had suffered countless severe blows at least since the Soviets' Afghanistan campaign (1979–1989), the Gorbachev era, and the Chechnya Wars. In such a context of reaction, watching the *Brother* films proved cathartic; to follow Susan Jeffords, who termed the right-wing Vietnam films of the 1980s a cultural project to undertake the "remasculinization of America" (quoted in Hatty, *Masculinities*: 171), *Brother* and *Brother 2* served to "remasculinize" Russia.

Yet this project presupposed (necessitated) a thoroughly simplistic—one might say caricaturistic—vision of the Russian male. Danila, in fact (like Rambo before him), can best be described as a sort of comic book superhero,

---

4. All of which only made the psychic blow suffered as a result of Bodrov's 2002 accidental death in a mudslide all the more grievous. Since then, he has achieved a posthumous near-mystical fame as a sort of Russian James Dean figure, a "man's man" that the younger generation could take as a role model.

a (recalling Erofeyev) *unidimensional* pop culture icon.[5] Perhaps more blatantly than myriad other examples from the post-Soviet era, the *Brother* films present a *cartoon* of Russian masculinity.

All of which rehearses Judith Butler's fundamental point about the performativity of gender: It entails a perpetual (often manic) repetition and rearticulation of a given, "chosen"—but always narrowly delimited—role. Yet this "convincing act of repetition" itself can bring about its own crises. As Lynn Segal notes: "The closer we come to uncovering some form of exemplary masculinity, a masculinity which is solid and sure of itself, the clearer it becomes that masculinity is structured through contradiction: the more it asserts itself, the more it calls itself into question" (quoted in Messner, *Politics*: 1).

We see here a downside to the Butlerian performativity of gender: One can protest too much.[6] Following anthropologists such as Margaret Mead and feminist critics like Nancy Chodorow, Eliot Borenstein goes on to note that masculinity must constantly be reaffirmed, through tests, initiation rites, the completion of some task. Only then can the subject say, "Now I'm a man"

---

5. We find a similar cartoon in Sergei Ushakin's examination of discourses in the men's magazine *Medved'* (*Bear*). This too provides a strategically reductive figure aimed solely at stiffening the Russian man's resolve. Ushakin offers this quotation from the periodical, a telling description of the ideal twenty-first-century businessman—a capitalist, more worldly counterpart to the violent, provincial Danila, though no less of a "real Russian man":

> Picture him. A famous man, known (and in some cases loved) by the entire country. Maybe not that attractive, but damned charming. Because being charming is his business. . . . Picture him, at 25–30–35–40 years of age running a large company or even—we're not afraid of the word—a holding company. Capable of making a decision and taking responsibility for it. Not always well-, but almost always expensively-, dressed. Often able to speak in some unintelligible foreign language. Preferring high-priced cigarettes to cheap ones, expensive brandies to vodka, Hugo Boss to "Shiper," Grand Cherokee to Zhiguli, and Paris and Dakar to a vacation on the beach of the Ryabinsk water reservoir. And the *coup de grace*: not only does he prefer these things, he can afford them. And without any ulterior motive we can assert: this is outstanding—a nearly extinct breed of real man, it turns out, has not died out completely. ("Vidimost'": 482)

Despite its sarcasm and irony (which in any case we cannot be sure would be picked up by all readers), the *Medved'* passage, Ushakin notes, identifies the various "road signs" (down to actual brands) that an early 2000s real Russian man must follow to array himself in the armor of a certain unquestioned masculinity. Yet, aside from a Bret Easton Ellis novel, this obsessive laundry list (props, skills, languages, jet-setting locales) reminds me of nothing so much as the heroes of pulp fiction and the comics (millionaire Bruce Wayne, aka Batman, James Bond, Agent 007; the globe-trotting Doc Savage; billionaire industrialist Tony Stark, alias Iron Man).

6. As Elizabeth Badinter writes: "Being a man implies labor. . . . Manhood is not bestowed at the outset; it must be constructed or . . . 'manufactured.' A man is therefore a sort of *artifact*, and as such he always runs the risk of being found defective" (quoted in Borenstein, *Men*: 123).

(*Men*: 123).[7] It goes without saying that the project of erecting a man involves the demolition of a structuring, alien feminine other.

Kaja Silverman recasts that formula in Lacanian terms, centering male subjectivity on the disavowal of a fundamental and ever-present lack, propped up by culture-based "dominant fictions":

> Thus the male subject does not just spontaneously happen to believe that he is not castrated. That belief is instilled in him through the unceasing flow of paternal images and sounds within which he is encouraged to "find" himself; through the externalizing displacement onto the feminine subject of the losses that afflict him; and last, but by no means least, through his subordination to the dominant fiction by means of which his social formation coordinates its diverse discourses. Since this final operation generally necessitates a series of additional castrations, phallic male subjectivity might also be said to be predicated upon a massive cultural disavowal of the lack upon which it rests. . . .
>
> Not only does a loss of belief in the dominant fiction generally lead to loss of belief in male adequacy, but the spectacle of male castration may very well result in a destructive questioning of the dominant fiction. Male subjectivity is a kind of stress point, the juncture at which social crisis and turmoil frequently find most dramatic expression. ("Historical": 113–114)[8]

Certainly we need not recite here the radical shift in "dominant fictions" of all sorts that has taken place in Russia since the collapse of the USSR. But I do wish to emphasize the characterization of this shift in the various post-Soviet discourses as a largely "masculine" crisis, be it the plummeting of male life expectancy, the rise in alcoholism and criminality, or the loss of agency in a "free" market for men raised in a moribund Soviet economy. Moreover, as sexologist Igor Kon noted, it is precisely in such historical periods of precipitous change, when forms of gender relations grow inadequate, that nostalgia for those forms asserts itself the most powerfully, prompting calls to reverse the feminization of "real masculinity [*nostayashchaya muzhestvennost'*]" (*Muzhkie*: 563), as the *Brother* example shows.

Yet this "return to basic principles" as a response to a crisis of Russian masculinity had already made itself evident much earlier, in the Stagnation (*zastoi*) period;[9] one particularly pertinent manifestation for Russian comics is the return of the so-called *kulachny boi* (literally, "fist fight"). As noted

---

7. Borenstein relates this idea directly to the hero Lyutov in Isaak Babel's *Red Cavalry*.

8. Silverman develops these ideas further, through, among other things, Freudian and Althusserian notions of masochism, in her 1992 book *Male Subjectivity at the Margins*.

9. Zdravomyslova and Temkina ("Krisis") trace it to at least the 1970s.

by historians of the Middle Ages, masses of village men would assemble in vast (dis)organized mobs to stomp and beat on each other with sticks, fists, or anything handy. Such outbursts of mass disorder became a normal part of observing various holidays, with the "merriest debauchery" taking place during *Maslenitsa* (Shrovetide), wrote A. Gruntovsky. He cites the ethnographer I. P. Sakharov's 1836–95 folklore collection, *Legends of the Russian People* (*Skazania russkogo naroda*):

> The *kulachniy boi* in Russian family life was considered an act of impetuousness [*udalstvo*], at times leading whole villages and towns to pride and discord. To subject oneself willingly to fights, to beat others without mercy was a luxurious merriment for our fathers and grandfathers. (Gruntovskiy, *Russkiy*: 127)

While Gruntovsky hails the kulachniy boi as the origin of Russian martial arts, and points out that Alexander Pushkin (among other nineteenth-century writers) had great affection for it, other observers held the practice in the lowest esteem, branding it a form of barbarity that confirmed Russia's backwardness.[10]

In the late Soviet era, precisely such behavior bore a political critique. Starting in the late 1970s, the underground art group the Necrorealists engaged in such mass brawls in the outskirts of Leningrad. They would later transfer these "anarchic" Russian antics from the woods to the stage in underground performance pieces with Sergei Kuryokhin's arts ensemble Pop Mechanics, in which they essentially carried on violent, liquor-driven fights onstage, to the hoots and laughter of audiences. By committing these free-for-alls to celluloid, in combination with elements from horror films (like comics, a marginalized "Western" genre), the Necrorealists enacted an ironic, hypermasculinized version of the kulachniy boi tradition. They resurrected a discredited form of "low" social behavior, casting themselves as modern "hooligans" to achieve a kind of masculine "release."[11]

---

10. V. I. Royev, writing in 1914, blamed this behavior on everything from vodka to ill-educated youths to the malign influence of industrialization: "This strange social sickness, appearing in the press under the term 'hooliganism,' has penetrated everywhere, even into the most remote corners of our fatherland" (quoted in Gruntovskiy, *Russkiy*: 199).

11. At least two Russian films in the 1990s also utilized the kulachniy boi for different ends. Tamas Toth's 1993 *Children of Cast-Iron Gods* resets the fights in a factory, putting an industrialized sheen over the violence (the film was cowritten by Pyotr Lutsik, whose 1998 film *Okraina* enacts a similarly riotous hypermasculine parody). Nikita Mikhalkov's more baldly nationalistic 1999 film *The Barber of Siberia*, meanwhile, recreates a nineteenth-century kulachniy boi as an example of "authentic" Russian culture.

These revived representations of the crude, violent Russian male would dovetail with the newly reemerged medium of comics in late and post-Soviet Russian culture. In search of sales strategies to survive a cutthroat market, one turn-of-the-century publisher chose the most lurid and hypermasculine depictions for its male-oriented product.

Novy Komiks and Male Chernukha

The journal *Novy Komiks* (published by Kanton-Flesh, Ltd.) emerged in the early 2000s as entertainment for New Russian[12] men. It was distributed free in casinos, strip clubs, and similar locales, which advertised within its pages. With stories based on coarse jokes, sexist gags, parodies of American films, and ultraviolence, *Novy Komiks* targeted the post-Soviet male eager for sensation. Intriguingly, the journal's creators[13] figured their work as a response to imported Western comics, which they claimed many Russians still found unpalatable.

A sampling of four issues from 2001 and 2002 reveals a mix of pop culture, soft-core pornography, and narratives devoted to living fast in the new Moscow. *Novy Komiks* often reads like an American teen sexploitation flick mixed with *Pulp Fiction*, then rendered into comics by a Benny Hill fan who has read *Mad* magazine and crude British strips, who cannot draw very well but has great coloring software. The men in these stories typically appear as trigger-happy mafiosi or randy ogres, or both, while the women unfailingly are half-naked prostitutes, strippers, or busty molls. Old Russian dirty jokes and erotic vignettes get played out in endless variations; in these stories what cannot be bought can always be stolen at gunpoint.

A casual cynicism fills the pages of *Novy Komiks*: decay and anarchy, sudden bloodshed, men with guns preying on the weak. It was Russia as seen nightly on television screens throughout the Yeltsin era: a country in chaos, ruled by rich thugs who buy women, drugs, and good times at casinos and restaurants, shooting up the city with uzis in between.

To this end, the journal trafficked in two chief aesthetic and narrative strategies popular in the 1990s. The first was *chernukha*, a term derived from *cherny* or "black," signifying a fixation with senseless horror and despair,

12. In the 1990s and early 2000s, the term *New Russian* (*novy russky*) denoted a kind of dullard arriviste, a vulgar, vaguely criminal type who had traded culture for money in the predatory new market economy. See Graham, "Wages" for a fuller treatment. For a longer discussion of *Novy Komiks,* see Alaniz, *Komiks:* chapter 6.

13. All the writers and artists on the *Novy Komiks* staff were male. The journal apparently folded sometime in 2002, after publishing between five and ten issues.

which came to be applied to much film and prose of the period.[14] The second term, *bespredel,* connoting chaos or mayhem, literally means "without limits," and adhered to the most excessive popular literature of the time. As described by Borenstein: "Bespredel takes chernukha to its logical extreme, presenting violence, crime and collapse as phenomena that defy all logic, perpetrated by criminals whose amorality is so shocking that they are often rendered as inhuman" (*Overkill:* 23).[15] Bespredel: chernukha as ontology, as metaphysics, as way of life.

My chat in 2002 with the *Novy Komiks* staff confirmed such an approach to the material. As chief editor Mikhail Terentyev told me:

> Our people are raised on black humor, on chernukha. Violence, horror, that's just part of daily life. Children getting killed, grandmothers run over. We get that all the time. So violence, horror, a dog's life . . . that's what we know. So that's what goes into the comics. (Terent'ev interview, 2002)

"Besides," added Pavel Burko, the director of Kanton-Flesh, "chernukha isn't just horrible—it's also funny!"

It would seem that the komiksist Vladimir Volegov crafted the 2001 story "Black Star" ("Chernaya zvezda") specifically to prove Burko's point; it foregrounds bespredel in an especially bald-faced, unapologetic mode, all while dispensing a heady brew of sexist, racist, and xenophobic humor. "Black Star" opens with a big city skyline at night, skyscrapers glowing an infernal red. A pair of thugs dressed like the Blues Brothers break into the "Bold Ass" strip club (written in English), muttering, "That fat-ass owes us something" (6). The two burst into the manager's back office, and find him having sex with a woman (possibly one of the strippers), on his desk. "Santa Madonna!" says the woman, recognizing one of the gangsters. "Vincenzo, darling!" "Vincenzo" responds by calling her a "black sheep" (*parshivaya ovtsa*)—then thrusts a revolver into her vagina and pulls the trigger, resulting in an eruption of blood and gore.

While Vincenzo ties up the manager, his mustachioed partner produces a Gatling gun out of a music case and "takes care" of several security guards in a splatterfest of flying brains, eyeballs and assorted body parts. This symphony

---

14. On the use of the term in cinema and literature of the late and post-Soviet era, see Graham's seminal "Chernukha."

15. Borenstein's discussion of such 1990s pulp fiction as Sergei Pugachev's *You're Just a Slut, My Dear!,* whose cover depicts a woman forced to fellate a gun, resonates with my reading of *Novy Komiks'* misogyny and casual attitude to sexual violence. See Borenstein's *Overkill:* chapter 7 for the origins of bespredel in Russian prison and gang culture.

FIGURE 6.1. *Black Star* by Vladimir Volegov,
published in *Novy Komiks* (2001)

of mayhem crescendos with a pack of dynamite plunged into the bound manager's mouth ("You'll like this show!") and a huge explosion that destroys the
club, sending nubile strippers flying (10) (see figure 6.1).

We may gather that "Black Star" will win plaudits neither from Natalya
Markova, a Russian anti-comics crusader and director of the pro-family
research institute Barrier,[16] nor from Russian feminists. In many ways the
early-Putin-era story reflects the bespredel ethos of its time, first and foremost
through its sordid content. But Volegov's violence extends to the aesthetic
realm as well; what seems to me the story's "bipolar" artwork appears at war
with itself. The artist cultivates a deliberately "ugly" pen style that clashes with

---

16. See Alaniz, *Komiks*: 108–111.

the careful digital processing and coloring done on computer. Often he will only suggest a woman's breast or other feature with a line, and fill in the figure through warm flesh tones and light shadows with coloring software. (Women's bodies receive by far the most detailed attention in *Novy Komiks'* art.) In the large panel depicting the explosion at the club, Volegov does not bother to draw a stripper's panties all the way to the curve of her hip; instead, he (or the staff colorist) colors that detail in on computer, complete with shadows on her buttocks.

This underscores an important point about the difference between bespredel in komiks versus other media. Even the most transgressive novel or film of this stripe will still maintain a clear narrative flow and adhere to the rules of literary realism; outright experimentation and audience alienation is rare in these works.[17] "Black Star," in contrast, puts forth a contradictory vision of crudely sketched-out layouts lovingly worked over to produce beautiful, delicate effects; it is both shoddy and refined at once.

I can point to no better example than the panel depicting the mustachioed, black-suited intruder firing the Gatling gun directly "at" the reader (as in the conclusions of Edwin S. Porter's 1903 *The Great Train Robbery* or Martin Scorsese's 1990 *Goodfellas,* itself an homage to Porter). Volegov only scratchily suggests the outlines of his face and mouth, hardly bothering with the background—but the erupting gunfire appears in several hues of orange, red, yellow, and white, for an almost psychedelic look. There are sparks, smoke, stars, spent shells, all rendered through the colors, and Volegov even throws in the cinematic effect of lens flare (an option on many computer painting programs). It comes off as a low-budget movie with an unlimited special effects budget (9).

And while the storyline of "Black Star" seems clear enough (even if the two intruders look so much alike they're hard to tell apart), Volegov gives the pages an amateurish design that connotes a crudity beyond the script: Panels crowd against each other with only a thin black line for a gutter, driving the narrative faster; they overlap, seeming to get in each other's way in their eagerness to arrive at the next obscene thrill—for example, the "Gatling gun" panel just discussed is partially blocked by the preceding frame showing the victims breaking down the door (obscuring the mustachioed gunman's hat). The story pages' background is an ugly greenish-brown, which colors a reading as well.

---

17. Kira Muratova's *The Asthenic Syndrome* (1990) is the best example of an experimental chernukha film (see Graham: "Chernukha" for a discussion). Another possible candidate is Alexander Sokurov's *The Second Circle* (1990). Neither of these arthouse films were popular successes, and critics debate whether they should be considered chernukha at all. One does not see such doubts expressed over *You're Just a Slut, My Dear!*

Volegov dispenses one last "transgression": numbered panels. These are mock-ingly "cynical" in that they are not needed to follow the story's progression. Rather, I submit, he includes them for only one reason: their association with diafilms, the Soviet-era slide-projected shows for kids (these had numbered panels). Thus, Volegov represents very adult subject matter through a child-hood device he knows his readers (who were children under the Soviets) will recognize. Part of the sick fun of "Black Star" involves thinking of it as an X-rated diafilm.

All these tricks—intentionally sloppy design, numbered panels, "dia-lectical" artwork—could not be duplicated in film or prose without calling attention to themselves in ways that would alter the work's register.[18] They represent, in addition to the racy content, the *Novy Komiks* brand of aesthetic bespredel.

Returning to the depiction of men in these stories, the reader observes a resolute avoidance not only of morally "upstanding" or heroic figures, but of classically attractive ones as well. Volegov's male characters (little more than types) tend to have absurdly proportioned or dwarfish bodies: the loudly dressed, balding mafioso from "The Tie" (*Galstuk*, 2001), the barrel-shaped muzhik from "The Refueling" (*Zaryadka*, 2001), the "muscle-men" (all upper torso) of "Versace" (2001). In the latter story, even the nymphomaniac's dream man (glimpsed in a thought balloon) seems little more than two huge biceps balanced on a tiny waist. If women in *Novy Komiks* exist only as eroticized playthings with Barbie-doll figures, the journal reflects back to its male read-ers an equally unidimensional vision of Russian masculinity: flat-headed thugs, sweating boors and louts, unappealing fat men. These beer-swilling oafs understand money as their only sex appeal and violence as their sole means of expressing an empowered "manhood" (as in "Black Star").[19] There is no Danila, the upright man's man of the *Brother* films. There is only his churlish bald brother, Viktor. (Or, in the terms of US superheroes: There is no Super-man or Clark Kent in *Novy Komiks*; there is not even a Lex Luthor. Patheti-cally, there are only Bizarros.)[20]

---

18. In this regard, Robert Rodríguez and Quentin Tarantino's *Sin City* (2005) has an exper-imental and stylistic flair that calls attention to itself much more insistently than does its comics source material by Frank Miller.

19. Compare these male figures to those of the KOM artist V. Spiridov: They are ordinary "everyman" types—not superheroes, but not dehumanized ogres either. Even the unappealing taxi driver in "The Golden Lie" has an "average" appearance ("Zolotaia": 15).

20. Overly muscled but heroic figures appeared in the 2000s fantasy series *Ten': The Hero and Death* from Progulka press. These were highly derivative of 1990s Image Comics and had very little that was Russian about them.

"Classically beautiful" male bodies did appear in the journal—but only in the ads. And even then, only in those that contained photographs rather than artwork. A two-page "reportage" from the women's club Little Red Riding Hood featured snapshots of half-nude men cavorting with customers, including one apparently receiving a buttock massage. Significantly, these pictures seem arranged along a roughly sequential line, as if to convey through comics' grammatical juxtaposition of images the pleasures and excesses of a night on the town—with the cream of Russian manhood. But the ads with drawn illustrations (produced by the same team of artists as the stories) reinforce an image of off-kilter manhood similar to that of the comics. One for the pub L'vinnoe serdtse (Lion's Heart) features two topless women flanking a man in a suit of medieval armor, his longsword hanging precisely between his legs (a later variation of this ad lifts the visor to show the man's white-bearded face). Another, for the strip club Amazonia, displays three grinning, oiled-up male dancers (one Black, two with long Fabian-like tresses) who seem less sexy than grotesque. Their facial features are exaggerated to the point of caricature, while the Black man in particular is given a oafish expression. The ads often avoid depicting actual men altogether, preferring an allegorical approach. For the Kirpich (Brick) night bar, Volegov draws an anthropomorphized brick giving the thumbs-up sign, surrounded by a bevy of strippers. Another ad shows a strip bar in which polar bears are the patrons, smoking cigars, talking on cell phones, inserting bills in thongs.

The artists of *Novy Komiks* clearly find theirs an inadequate medium for representing "normal" or average masculinity; unable to countenance comics as anything serious, they turn to extreme, "funny" depictions of sex and violence. The presumed male reader is both receiver and butt of the joke. Like the British toilet humor mag *Viz* or the Spanish magazine *Jueves* (minus the politics), *Novy Komiks* traffics in depictions of a severely compromised manhood for laughs—at the same time enforcing some minimum standard for the gender: A single-panel cartoon by Shamil shows a bloated, balding bloke sporting udders instead of testicles, with the caption: "This is what happens to those who drink milk instead of beer!"[21]

I find it instructive to compare *Novy Komiks*' vision of the "authentic" Russian male to that of more uplifting fare such as writer Dmitry Smirnov and artist Andrei Ross's coeval *Magnificent Adventures,* comics designed to promote positive values among Russian youth. In the 2002 story "Maxim's Holiday: Part 1," Maxim, a "metrosexual" given to daydreaming about romantic love, is accosted by drunken louts in a Bryansk[22] park. "Ey, skinny boy! You still scribblin' away at yer little poems and growin' flowers? C'mere, let's have us some fisticuffs! What're you, scared, you botanist?" (Smirnov and Ross, "Kanikuly": 5). (Smirnov does not have much of an ear for trash talk; no *Novy Komiks* "muzhik" would be caught dead speaking like this!) Maxim (relatively effeminate with his shoulder-length hair and current fashion) walks on, leaving the men (paunchy, casually dressed) to drink beer on a bench— even though they have shattered his reverie of saving a damsel in distress. One can imagine Terentyev's readers snorting at this pacifist, "girly" depiction of manhood.

The comics representation of the "Russian male as neanderthal" type reflects the change in dominant fictions elaborated by Silverman—with the proviso that in Russia the change was much faster, more catastrophic and demasculating than anything experienced in the West. The reaction, as Kon reminds, proved equally drastic: an upsurge not only in male-driven depictions like the *Brother* films but increased militarism, homophobia, and misogyny as well.[23] Of course, comics, especially those such as *Novy Komiks,* could only partially contribute to the Putin era's reconstruction of manhood, due to the medium's perceived lack of seriousness. Not for them the "heavy lifting" representational work of late Soviet-era TV and cinematic stalwarts Stirlitz (hero of the TV series *Seventeen Moments of Spring,* played by Vyacheslav Tikhonov); the strong but gentlemanly Gosha from *Moscow Does Not Believe in Tears,* played by Alexei Batalov; or the bard and actor Vladimir Vysotsky—the sort of real Russian men a nostalgic nation turned to in need. But the loutish, sexist, violent part—*that* comics could handle.

"I'll pay $1,000. I need a superman!" declares the blonde nymphomaniac in Volegov's "Versace." When her pick proves disappointing, she exclaims, "Three hours isn't enough for me! He's a weakling! I'll pay any price! I need a real he-man [*samets*]!"[24] The male specimen who answers her call with the triumphant cry, "By the time I cum, Versace will be out of fashion!" is no Greek god: stubby hands, torso too large for his legs, head much too big for his torso, nose enormous. But he *is* a *samets*; he gets the job done.

---

22. Smirnov here equates toxic masculinity with the "backward" provinces. Maxim is on his way to cosmopolitan Moscow, where he can settle into a more broad-minded version of his gender.

23. See Stanley, "Sexual" and Blomfield, "Sexual" for two sadly consistent portraits, nearly fifteen years apart, of sexual harassment in post-Soviet Russia.

24. The word *samets* denotes a buck, macho, or strong male. In this context, we could translate it as *cocksman,* one "capable of getting the job done."

Recalling Ushakin's *Medved'* caricature, the "real Russian man" is an uncomplicated total package: He dresses well (even if he rips off his clothes when needed); drives the right car (even if he crashes it through walls in the heat of passion);[25] he's a superman in the bedroom (even if he's ugly as sin). Despite its highly problematic image of men, then, *Novy Komiks* appealed to the New Russian male's desire to embody a sexually potent, untamable essence, an uncivilizable id, which "foreigners will never understand." *Novy Komiks'* vision matches the post-Soviet reader's wish not for Superman, not even for Clark Kent, but for the Russian man in the same old dominant fiction: the incorrigible *samets*.

Russia versus the Superhero

The foregoing provides some sense of the superhero genre's uphill struggle, once it formally arrived in Russia in the early 1990s, to provide an alternative vision of masculinity. This in spite of the fact that the hero Makar the Fierce (from the 1930s journal *Hedgehog*), as well as the handsome, manly soldiers of Russian World War II posters, displayed many characteristics and functions similar to superheroes.[26]

Now, in the new free market with comics and films flooding in from abroad, the superhero was hard to miss. But whereas Terentyev, Volegov, and the creative team of *Novy Komiks* ignored the genre, seeking a violent, recidivist depiction of the real Russian man based on some irreducible national essence, several artists from the younger generation of komiks' post-2000 Second Wave would appropriate the conventions and iconography of American superheroes for a more recognizably cosmopolitan, ironic—and self-deprecating—vision of masculinity.

Perhaps no event better crystallized the arrival of this tongue-in-cheek stance vis-à-vis the superhero than the conceptualist, goateed author Vladi-

---

25. Of course, foreign fashions, cars, guns, drugs, women, all serve as mere status markers; he can consume them freely without in the least compromising his identity as a true Russian. (Counterexamples like the udder-sporting milk drinker are there for cheap laughs, nothing more.)

26. Oleg Semenyuk makes this point about WWII propaganda posters: "The positive heroes (mainly Red Army soldiers) in these drawn narratives were as a rule depicted in accordance with the demands of the typical superhero comic book, namely, they impressed the reader with their idealized physiques and super-powers" ("Comics": 61). Pranksters in Sofia, Bulgaria, made the linkage explicit when, in 2011, they repainted a socialist realist WWII monument, transforming Red Army soldiers into Captain America, Wonder Woman, Wolverine, and other superheroes (*Novinite*, "Sofia").

mir Sorokin's mid-1990s appearance on the cover of *Ptyutch* magazine—in a Batman costume. Russian visual culture was still absorbing the superhero through films, ads, and other specifically American cultural productions (and soundly rejecting its foreign representation of dandyish, fantasist male agency as a stand-in for US imperialism).[27] In this Russia shared much of the world's jaundiced view of the superhero, a genre originated in the 1930s US through a fusion of pulp adventures, adolescent male power fantasies, and a pseudo-fascist cult of the body.

At the turn of the twenty-first century, the superhero received long over-due attention from scholars. These studies ranged from echoing Roland Barthes and Umberto Eco's semiotic approaches to mining the genre for clues to the American psyche, to revisionist feminist and queer studies approaches.[28] These showed the superhero as an alluring figure both for the reimagining/re-presentation of selves and for a critique of such rhetorical and tropologi-cal modes. As Charles Hatfield puts it, with admirable brevity: "Superhero comic books have always been about the spectacle of bodies on the page, and the spectacle of Othering: heightened and fantastical displays of difference—gendered, racialized, ethnocentrist, ableist—the graphic clash of bodies both idealized and grotesque" ("Fearsome": 217). Superheroes also proved a very big, easy, and compelling target for those of an anti-American bent.

My own reading here hinges on an interpretation of the superhero as a site of elaborate, overdetermined signification coupled with living flesh.[29] More than anything else, this protean body signifies power, that is, a unified and self-contained corpus or narrative, its meaning as clear and legible as the bright primary colors of many a superhero costume. In fact, as Richard Reyn-olds argues, the obligatory costume, a marker of new identity to the exclu-

27. In the 1990s and later, such presses as Ded Moroz, Praim Evroznak, and Makhaon flooded the small Russian comics market with translated versions of, among others, *Spiderman, X-Men, Fantastic Four, Justice League, Avengers, Ultimate X-Men,* and *Gen*[13].

28. Among the most noteworthy monographs: Richard Reynolds's *Superheroes: A Mod-ern Mythology* (1992); Peter Coogan's *Superhero: The Secret Origin of a Genre* (2006); Charles Hatfield's *Hand of Fire: The Comics Art of Jack Kirby* (2012); Scott Bukatman's *Hellboy's World: Comics and Monsters on the Margins* (2016); Carolyn Cocca's *Superwomen: Gender, Power, and Representation*; and Ramzi Fawaz's *The New Mutants: Superheroes and the Radical Imagination of American Comics* (2016). Superheroes also made major inroads into video games, televi-sion, and film. We may remember the late twentieth and early twenty-first century, in fact, as the Age of the Multimedia Superhero, when—thanks partly to advances in special effects technology—the genre earned widespread familiarity, acclaim, and major box office clout.

29. As noted by Scott Bukatman: "Superhero comics present body narratives, bodily fan-tasies, that incorporate (incarnate) aggrandizement and anxiety, mastery, and trauma. . . . The superhero body is everything—a *corporeal,* rather than a *cognitive,* mapping of the subject into a cultural system" (*Matters*: 49). For my discussion of superheroes and embodiment, see Alaniz, *Death.*

sion of a jettisoned "ordinary" alter ego, itself bears much of the superbody's "power"—which attests to its fetishistic essence (*Super*: 32).

The costume serves as the sine-qua-non marker of the genre, which in turn gives the superbody permission to perform its amazing, hyperreal feats. Chief among its traditional features: strength, control, unboundedness—an utter denial of disability.

Finally, the superhero functions as a *visual* signifier, a literal mask or persona to put on and wear, effecting an ontological shift (Clark Kent "becomes" Superman). To the extent that the superhero signifier also expresses a particularly nationalistic message, the assumption of such an identity intimately relates the new persona to US values, however discredited. To sum up: A globally recognized (often reviled) shorthand for can-do US optimism and physical perfectibility, the superhero provides an alluring, coherent, but problematic body narrative of transformation into the amazing, the superhuman; a new, powerful identity or super-persona; and a potent hypermasculinity.

At first, the Russian reaction to such loaded imagery was almost immediate dismissal to the realm of the absurd and silly. (As noted, home-grown versions of nationalist-tinged hypermasculinity such as the *Brother* films had arrayed their heroes in more down-to-earth garb, not capes and primary-color underwear. This makes them no less fanciful.) First and foremost, superheroes struck post-Soviet Russians as patently alien and false.[30]

Various Russian artists set out from this assumption to lampoon the superhero and its ideological message—in the process embracing its peculiar brand of male-driven lunacy. A 2003 story by KOM veteran Alim Velitov,[31] "Batman," parodies the superhero's cult of youth. Batman, now aged, with a long beard, turns to a goateed, no-longer teenage Robin in the Batcave. "Don't go anywhere," says Robin, lounging on a couch with some snacks, in front of a television. "Let's see what's on the tube." "No, Robin," replies the older man. "We can't leave the city unpatrolled." Batman calmly proceeds alone, on foot, through a Gotham beset by muggers accosting women, suicides tossing

---

30. Komiksist Alex Khatchett said in 2005: "When Americans see Superman flying through the air, they think, 'Oh, freedom, truth, justice, the American way. When we see him flying through the air, we think, 'That looks stupid' or 'How come he's horizontal?' or 'Down with American imperialism!' or whatever. For them superheroes have 50+ years of baggage that they just don't have for us" (Alaniz, *Komiks*: 116). Russian acquaintances often told me things like, "Men in tights—that's not our kind of thing [*ne po-nashensky*]," though this was belied first in the late 1990s by innumerable Russian online sites in which one could read and download new superhero comics in translation almost as soon as their release in the States, and later by the rise of domestic superhero comics publishers, first and foremost Bubble.

31. Velitov began his career in the late Perestroika era with the first Russian comics studio, KOM. He later belonged to Khikhus's Moscow-based studio People of the Dead Fish (LMR).

themselves from buildings, and other evidence of urban decay. The elderly hero strides along, paying it all no mind. Nearby, the supervillain Penguin tries to break into a bank with some explosives, but only succeeds in blowing himself up. "The Penguin's up to his old tricks again," Batman muses, moving on. Finally, Batman walks up to a cashier's station and receives his pension. He then says, "Okay, Joker, enough hiding. Come on out." Batman's old nemesis, himself aged and using a cane (though still grinning maniacally) appears, and the two walk away arm in arm. "Let's go," says Batman. "I've got money for whiskey" (10).

Another Velitov story, "Game Over" (Kerdyk, 2003), shows superheroes in an even more cynical light, and counters their nationalist, specifically US, image with a native sensibility of its own (see figure 6.2). Spider-Man appears in Superman's[32] high-rise kitchen window, declaring, "Superman! Hurry, a giant Cheburashka's attacking the city!" Superman, a surly look on his face, is busy at the stove, and replies, "Damn. My eggs burned. You again, huh, Spider?" With less than heated enthusiasm, Superman flies out the window, mumbling, "Oh, well. Let's go!," Spider-Man swinging on his web close behind. Sure enough, a giant Cheburashka (the Soviet-era children's book and film character) is knocking down skyscrapers, declaiming that he will liberate the people from "the superheroes and their aggression" and replace them with "genuine, spiritual animated films about the hedgehog in the fog and Gena the crocodile."[33] Spider-Man pulls out the titanic creature's stop, and Cheburashka shoots off into the sky, rapidly deflating. But the superheroes' victory is short-lived; an enormous Gena the crocodile (in his trademark hat and coat) sneaks up behind them and chomps them into oblivion.

In each of these depictions, superheroes seem ineffective at best, uncaring at worst. In any case, they are harmless; their utter unreality dooms them to the inverse of agency (Gena the crocodile can always reinflate Cheburashka; Batman and the Joker are just two more old men getting drunk). Their hyper-masculinist project collapses with only the slightest push, while Velitov's "cartoony" style emphasizes their visual absurdity.

Other artists, however, adopt the superhero and its y-chromosome silliness in more adaptive ways. In Khikhus's story, "Little Red Riding Hood: A Christmas Tale," the eponymous blonde heroine discovers that impersonating her

---

32. Note that Velitov, like many Russian superhero parodists, ignores the issue of corporate universes; DC and Marvel characters freely mingle.

33. This was, incidentally, not the first attempt to marry superheroes and Cheburashka. The journal *Mukha* published a parody of the *Teenage Mutant Ninja Turtles* called "Cheburashka Ninja" written by Vitaly Mukhametzyanov and Oskar Serov, with art by Dmitry Fedotov (*Mukha*, no. 13 [1993]: 19–33).

FIGURE 6.2. "Game Over" by Alim Velitov (2003)

babushka (grandmother) is not the wolf of legend, but Batman. After dispatching some hunters with karate chops (which draw blood and break bones), the good-natured Batman is shocked to hear Little Red Riding Hood thinks he plans to eat her: "You dunce [*dvoechnitsa*]! I'm failing you in English and Biology! Bats don't eat little girls!" The two reconcile and eventually become a flying, crime-fighting duo. A caption reads: "Batman took Little Red Riding Hood to the city, got her registered, and they took to defending Gotham together. Merry Christmas!" ("Krasnaia": 43).

Where Velitov presents superheroes as ridiculous, if jaded, male cretins in costume, Khikhus's Batman appears as some sort of sensitive-to-a-fault New Age man: friendly but effective in a fight, quick to take offense when his good motives are questioned, always ready to forgive and move on. In replacing the original fairy tale's wolf (with its dark, violent, sexual overtones), the superhero defuses its threat ("Bats don't eat little girls!"), turns the helpless lass into a fully empowered superheroine in her own right, and provides fraternal care and affection. Once more, though, an expressionistic art style renders the action into a silly fantasy hard to take seriously.

But no komiksist mastered the plot devices, clunky dialogue, and juvenile fun of the superhero like Alexei Lipatov, whose 2000 story "Stalin vs. Hitler" represents a particular peak in the genre's appropriation for a specifically Russian audience: It conflates the male-driven kulachniy boi with sci-fi weaponry and nukes; superhero–supervillain epic battle with the Great Patriotic War; and snatches of historical speeches with the generic "super-rant" (delivered through hilarious German and Georgian accents and speech impediments).

The story recounts a mythical final showdown between the cloaked, magic-empowered Führer in his mountain fortress (decorated with Celtic and other occult runes) and a similarly caped, baton-wielding Stalin. The two spout lines that resonate with both the Bronze Age superhero fan as well as the reader versed in the Soviet version of World War II history: In a thick Georgian accent, Stalin thunders, "I offered you friendship, but you chose to start a war. Now I've come to destroy you"—to which Hitler replies, "Caucasian untermensch! I am now at the peak of my powers! . . . In my hands I wield all the power of the German nation! This power will wipe you from the face of the earth! Ha ha ha ha ha ha . . . !" Between cackles, Hitler fires beams of pure energy at his foe, from his bare hands ("Stalin": 135–136).

But, reeling in his moment of crisis, Stalin thinks back to his training years before at Razliv (the settlement north of St. Petersburg where Lenin hid in a hayloft, composing treatises, in 1917). His Master, speaking with a lisp (Lenin had trouble pronouncing r's), advises him, "Ouw powew lies in the laws of histowical inevitability!" Posed like the many statues in his honor, his hand upraised,[34] Lenin passes on the power to his protégé, who strikes back at Hitler with enormous force, exclaiming in his thick accent, "My marshal's baton is the incarnation of the unyielding will to victory of the multi-ethnic Soviet peoples!" (136–137).

The tale continues in this vein, with numerous references to Soviet-era speeches, slogans, and the historical record (such as Hitler's rumored flight to Argentina at the end of the war, the "Wheel of History," the V-3 and V-4 German rocket programs, the scarred Waffen-SS colonel Otto Skorzeny, and

---

34. On the standardization of Lenin's pose in representations of the Soviet era, see Bonnell, *Iconography*: 150–151.

much else). It also touches on the superhero convention of the alter ego (e.g., Clark Kent/Superman) through the fact that Stalin and Hitler invented their names: To the Führer's desperate offer of a peace settlement, the "Leader of Peoples" responds, "Schicklgruber and Dzhugashvili might have arrived at some agreement, but for Stalin and Hitler reconciliation is impossible!" (137).[35]

Lipatov ends the story with Hitler mistakenly believing he has arrived in Valhalla after his death, only to have Stalin inform him, "There is no Valhalla. Any seminarian will tell you that" (a sly allusion to Stalin's prerevolutionary past as a seminarian in Georgia). Hitler is simply cast into Hell; the word "KANETS" ("*konets*," or "the end," in a faux Georgian accent)[36] closes the tale (145).

"Stalin vs. Hitler" brings together a conceptualist strategy of pastiche with a US underground comix sensibility of anarchic play for a withering critique of the hypermasculinist superhero (whose body comes to stand in for the nation). At the same time, it fulfills to a T the genre's celebration of fantasist absurdity, ratcheting up its excesses at the same time it belittles them. Where the Versace-wearing troglodytes of *Novy Komiks* and Velitov's insouciant superhero simulacra ultimately refer first and foremost to themselves and their time (the late 1990s and early 2000s), Lipatov's obsessively intertextual work calls for a handle on both the specifically Soviet minutiae of the past, as well as the inescapably US idiom of the conventions it deploys to make meaning. Like Khikhus's fairy tale–derived "Little Red Riding Hood," "Stalin vs. Hitler" instantiates a hybridized poetics that meets the superhero "halfway"— a "respectful" mockery.

Some of those same mixed feelings vis-à-vis superheroes (and the mass culture foreignness they embody) seem especially evident in the work of KOM veteran Askold Akishin, an avowed devotee of Western genre material since the Soviet era (when it was officially discouraged, even condemned). His 2006 comics essay "R. I. P." opens with a panel showing a memorial statue to the deceased Captain America,[37] and the narration:

---

35. Lipatov seems to have lifted many of the illustrations from Marvel Comics of the mid-1980s. The work of the artists Sal Buscema, Ron Frenz, and P. Craig Russell seems to have been especially plundered (the final image of Hitler in Hell, for example, is copied verbatim from Russell's work on the 1982 graphic novel *Elric of Melnibone: The Dreaming City*)."Lenin" looks suspiciously like the bald, bearded superhero the Druid, who was a member of the Marvel Comics super-team the Avengers in the 1980s. All this attests to how carefully Lipatov absorbed the style of the so-called Bronze Age of the superhero genre in crafting his allusion-driven work. As with the Soviet-era trivia, the superhero too has a history, which the artist obsessively mined for his hybrid conceptualist opus.

36. The word, spelled as pronounced, also reflects the influence of Preved, the internet-based, youth-driven style of alternative Russian orthography.

37. A quotation of the cover of *Captain America* vol. 1, #113 (May 1969), art by Jim Steranko.

When I was a pioneer,[38] I really loved comics. Especially American ones.

The years passed. Once, looking over some old magazines, I stumbled upon a terrible picture.

Captain America. He had died in 1968!

He had lived only 27 years?! (21)

The narrator goes on to detail, in sarcastically mordant tones, the deaths of various heroes over the years: Thor, Green Lantern, Green Arrow, the Fantastic Four, the Hulk ("He died on an alien planet, far from his homeland": 22),[39] and others, all drawing on actual stories from different series. Like Lipatov, Akishin pays homage through visual quotes, in this case to the art of Jack Kirby, Herb Trimpe, and so on, while retaining his own recognizable style. Oddly, in the work's most sardonic panel, he shows a man crying bitter tears over a statue of Popeye, with the caption: "The sailorman Popeye died of old age!" (23). Akishin sneeringly promotes an equivalence between the more "realistically" drawn superhero and the "manly" cartoon Popeye. The hyperbole attains its climax in the conclusion, showing a tombstone with a characteristic *S* and another panel of a Metropolis in ruins:

In January, 1993, Superman died. Later on, of course, they resurrected him. But this wasn't the same Superman![40]

America, too, was destroyed. Everybody died!

What then was the point in living? (23)

Akishin enacts a "love-hate" posture with the superhero that reflects its journey in Russia from derogated bourgeois pulp in the Soviet era to market usurper in the new free economy. The narrator laments the passing of these figures—nostalgic and exotic at once—and in doing so "calls the bluff" of the genre's typical approach to death. He feigns the naïve belief of a reader who has not internalized the resurrection ethos of superheroes (what the blogger Ozymandias calls "the revolving door of death") and accepts their demise as real—willfully misreading them precisely the way a culture cut off from the genre's conventions for over fifty years would. At the same time, Akishin gives

---

38. The Pioneers were a Soviet youth group, roughly equivalent to US Boy Scouts.

39. Among other swipes, Akishin quotes a panel from page 3 of *The Incredible Hulk* vol. 1, #112 (February 1969), with art by Herb Trimpe and Dan Adkins, in which the jade giant is zapped (though not killed) and the "pietà" cover of *The Mighty Thor* vol. 1, #127 (April 1966, art by Jack Kirby).

40. A reference to the 1992–1993 "Death of Superman" storyline.

vent to a death wish[41] culminating in a postapocalyptic Metropolis. An "inva-sive species," superheroes have no natural habitat in Russia, "R. I. P." declares, but neither can they be ignored, given their enormous if problematic role in world comics culture.[42] Could the genre ever be incorporated into the komiks firmament in some way that will seem organic and palatable to Russian tastes? That was the question.

In the early 1990s, the artist and comics collector Ilya Kitup had expressed his own problematic relationship with American superheroes in his fanzine *Propeller* by rewriting them: He whited out the word balloons in an issue of *Superman* and inserted his own absurdist dialogue. In a similar vein, the komiksist Alexander Remizov seemed content to poke fun at the conventions of superheroes, such as the silliness and inconvenience of the X-men's cos-tumes, in various short works of the 2000s published on his blog.

Conversely, in 2008, Red Shark press advertised a new venture to publish a first-ever line of Russian superheroes, including Captain Russia, The Wolf, and Night Guard, to capitalize on the release of the video game *Chaos City* (*Gorod khaosa*).[43] Their unpromisingly overmuscled figures and opportunistic publication seemed to underscore comics scholar Waldomiro C. S. Vergueiro's 2000 observation:

> Outside the United States, superheroes seem to be created much more as a marketing strategy to gain domestic markets than as a viable indigenized alternative. Unfortunately, the experience so far has demonstrated that such characters have very few possibilities of changing the environment in which they are produced. Unless other factors strongly intervene, they have not the slightest chance of winning the battle against North American superheroes. ("Brazilian": 176)

The Tema komiksmen Vladimir Sakov told me in 1996 he does not believe the Russian literary tradition of "the little man and the state" allows for such bizarre and "facile" expressions of masculinity as Superman: "Our comics pro-ceed from the idea of the anti-hero. . . . He is a regular person, he doesn't have to stand out with the size of his muscles, etc., that is, his outward appear-

---

41. See Freud, "Thoughts": 298–299.

42. The situation is somewhat analogous to that of two Cuban comics creators of the 1960s, Virgilio and Marcos Behemaras, who expressed their affection for American superhero com-ics through anti-US, *Mad*-style satires of the genre in their series *Supertiñosa*. See Merino, *El Cómic*: 178–192.

43. It remains unclear to me whether the series ever actually launched.

FIGURE 6.3. Klash contemplates a decrepit city of vice and misery—and does nothing about it in "Inspector Klash" by Alexei Nikanorov (mid-1990s)

ance. . . . He is one of us, he is close to us [*on nam blizok*]" (Sakov interview, 1996).

Sakov's nativist rejection of the superhero makes Alexei Nikanorov's "Inspector Klash," a series of short stories from the mid-1990s, especially attractive as a Russian alternative to the genre's usual macho posturings. Klash, a disheveled, ordinary muzhik given to philosophizing, wanders through a horrible post-Soviet Russia of rampant crime, dilapidated infrastructure, and urban misery—in short, bespredel. He muses that someone should do something about all this chaos, that he himself should give up his vices and assume the mantle of hero—but by the end of these vignettes he has either dropped the idea and returned to his usual vodka-soaked pleasures in strip bars or else found that whatever action he did take was ineffective, misguided, or made things worse (see figure 6.3).

It's not that Klash is weak—he can handle a gun and once he decides on a course of action he will carry it through—but a hyperawareness of his ultimate inadequacy before the enormity of society's problems as often as not enervates his will. (Not for him the can-do attitude and big-picture denialism of the

US superhero.) While not as coarse or misogynistic as *Novy Komiks, Klash* makes a similar point about the futility of old-style heroism in the new Russia, effecting in essence a humorous parable. Klash is, in his own street-level way, a complex image of masculinity: equal parts Hamlet, Yojimbo, and Oblomov.

Russian treatments of superheroes and their discontents, such as those of Akishin, Velitov, and Nikanorov, as well as the works of Volegov and *Novy Komiks,* reflect the great shift in dominant fictions that beset the familiar models of masculinity in the Yeltsin and early Putin eras. These komiks' responses to the new reality run the gamut from reactionary backlash to primary-color parody. Much as they abused it, these artists acknowledged that the entry of this novel genre into the culturescape brought with it new ways of "being a man." The question is, given the altered circumstances, what both Russian men and the superhero genre would do next with those novel possibilities.

Recalling Erofeyev, komiks may indeed serve as "the mirror to man's collapse, the cheery pictures that accompany our own decomposition," but even if their *subjects* are unidimensional, this does not mean *they* need be. The denigration of the traditional male model is a given, these works seem to say; where can we go from here?

The Superhero Explosion

The answer was not long in coming.

With the run-up to Putin's 2012 return to the presidency (amid the largest antigovernment protests of the post-Soviet era), Putinism *toute courte* began to assert itself. This fact is inseparable from the sort of cultural expressions that arose at precisely this time, especially those of Bubble—the first successful mainstream superhero comics publisher.[44] In particular, I want to return to my focus on the superhero body. Helena Goscilo has persuasively argued that the representation of male bodies in the cinema of this period pointed to one ultimate referent:

> As under Stalin, so during Putin's reign, the leader's body is supreme and must be impervious to the slings and arrows from which the average man suffers, for in addition to its individual status, it is a symbolic "kremlin"— the royal body described by Ernst Kantorowicz, inseparable from the body politic. In post-Soviet Russia that mythologised body, impregnable and

---

44. Recall too that the venture's main investor, Aram Gabrelyanov, was a major ally of Putin.

spectacular but absent from the screen, can belong only to Vladimir Putin. ("Body": 105)

And much as in Lilya Kaganovsky's discussion of the male subject's bodily suffering and dismemberment in service to Stalin in Soviet literature (see *How*, especially chapter 2), Bubble's *Major Grom* enacts an oddly masochistic drama in which the genre conventions of bruises, scars, contusions, bandages, hospital stays, and lost consciousness serve as markers of the hero's devotion to preserving order (read: state power). For all that, the series, launched along with the rest of the original Bubble superhero line in 2012, presents a remarkably mixed and disorienting picture of contemporary Russia, neither fawning nor wholly damning—in essence an exploration of the male hero's role vis-à-vis a corrupt state.[45]

"Plague Doctor," the series' first arc, written by Bubble founder Artyom Gabrelyanov and Yevgeny Fedotov, with art mostly by Konstantin Tarasov, does not flinch from portraying the country's hopeless rot (spoiled rich kids who elude justice, businessmen above the law), as well as the many class and social divisions fueling the rage of the young (mass protests occur with some regularity, and even cops debate whether revolution might help matters or make them worse). Igor Grom, a tough-guy police detective whose surname means "thunder," whose headgear and jacket evoke the look of a 1920s communist, and who sports "lightning" eyebrows lifted from Frank Hampson's Dan Dare, squares off against a serial killer inspired by medieval iconography named the Plague Doctor. Though that setup forms just the tip of a very large iceberg that comes to take on national, even global, significance.

In issue #9 (June 2013), a naked Grom must navigate the Garden of Sinners, a perverse amusement park and escape rooms complex, in order to access the antidote to poison that will kill him in ten minutes. The park, in addition to deadly traps, poses riddles and puzzles based on medieval notions of sin, such as greed, cruelty, and stupidity. But before anything else, it seems calculated to physically and mentally torture Grom with pecking crows, explosions, near-drowning, hallucinations, and the Plague Doctor's incessant taunts via loudspeaker. Grom's muscled physique is rendered both impressively rugged and perilously vulnerable: the tormented hero in defense of a transcendent state.

---

45. In this the series recalls the mystery novels of Boris Akunin, especially *The State Counsellor* (2000). As the hero Erast Fandorin glumly states, "Russia's eternal misfortune. Everything in it is topsy-turvy. Good is defended by fools and scoundrels, evil is served by martyrs and heroes" (188).

Major Grom's predominant message on masculinity—not unlike that of another Bubble series, *Demonslayer* (see chapter 4)—comes down to an old-fashioned, heteronormative, patriarchal portrait of a strong, virile man in charge;[46] Grom's reporter girlfriend Yulia even keeps calling him "my super-hero" (see, for example, Gabrelianov, Fedotov, and Tarasov, *Mayor Grom* #5: n.p.). But Gabrelyanov and Fedotov include some fascinating cross-currents to that vision. Grom's younger partner, Dima Dubin, poses a twenty-first-century "metrosexual" alternative: He knows all about social media and the internet (Grom hates it, preferring "real life"); he has a softer, more diplomatic approach to investigation (Grom beats information out of suspects); and, most compellingly, he is willing to call out the country's problems, even partly sympathizing with antigovernment protesters (which leads to one of them stabbing him). Yet Dubin can still punch out a muscle-bound opponent in a fight club bout (Gabrelianov, Fedotov, and Tarasov, *Mayor Grom* #2: n.p.).

But no figure poses a greater challenge to traditional male power than the Plague Doctor, eventually revealed to be internet titan Sergei Razumovsky, founder of the social media network Vmeste (Together). The effete Razumovsky,[47] whose name derives from *razum* ("mind" or "reason"), forms a powerful counter to the manly, action-driven Grom—in ways typical to the genre.[48] In other ways, though, Razumovsky embodies some potent contemporary Russian contradictions: He wears a plague doctor mask and dispatches victims according to their "sins," using medieval imagery to clothe what looks like a modern vendetta against crime;[49] his millions-strong online following spills onto the streets in angry antigovernment protests, lending him far more

46. As Gabrelyanov told me: "We made Major Grom into someone honest, ordinary and good, to show that people like that exist. There's a lot of them. It's just that people write more about the bad ones, the killers, because that sells better" (Gabrelianov interview, 2013). He referred to the lyrics of the song about he character written by GGC featuring Krasivy: "Strong, smart, a police badge—that's Major Grom" (silen, umen, politseisky zheton—eto Maior Grom). See lyrics here: https://pesni.guru/text/ggc-ft-красивый-майор-гром.

47. Razumovsky seems tailor-made to set off readers' gaydar. A genius devotee of art and culture, he often appears androgynous, clad in swirling back feathers, recalling shojo manga series like Ikeda Riyoko's *Rose of Versailles* (1972). In a scene reminiscent of the interaction between the queer villain Silva and James Bond in *Skyfall* (directed by Sam Mendes, 2012), Razumovsky compliments the naked Grom's buff physique: "My god, you have a magnificent body!" In separate panels for each, he even caresses Grom's "powerful neck," "steel legs," and so on (Gabrelianov, Fedotov, and Tarasov, *Mayor Grom* #8: n.p.).

48. Ever since Superman's first nemesis, the Ultra-humanite, a cerebral villain in a wheelchair introduced in 1939.

49. The Plague Doctor's methods recall other Putin-era blends of medievalism and contemporaneity, from Vladimir Sorokin's novel *Day of the Oprichnik* (2006) to Daria Desombre's *The Sin Collector* (Russian original *The Spectre of Heavenly Jerusalem* [*Prizrak nebesnogo Ierusalima*], 2014), a sort of Dan Brownesque murder mystery in which the history- and occult-obsessed villain similarly dispatches victims through ancient means.

populist credibility and power than a gun or a good right hook; most crucially, Razumovsky makes a rather decent case that he's not a villain at all, but a principled patriot intent on dismantling a deeply corrupt system—by first taking it over legally, through winning an election (of course, his manipulation of public sentiment, he reckons, will help him assume the presidency). His followers dub him "The Citizen," a force for progressive good. "The people will help me!" he tells Grom in a dream. "I am merely the match, with which everything has begun! The fire will do the rest" (Gabrelianov, Fedotov, and Tarasov, *Mayor Grom* #7: n.p.) (see figure 6.4).

The narcissistic Razumovsky, then, is an Adrian Veidt–like figure determined to take onto himself the "necessary" sacrifice of lives so as to effect change.[50] In short, a revolutionary—at a time when such sentiments have little purchase in mainstream Russia (widespread discontent notwithstanding). More to the point, they can lead to real grief, even death. When Grom points this out to him, Razumovsky answers: "I am prepared to risk my life for the sake of a better future . . . are you?" (Gabrelianov, Fedotov, and Tarasov, *Mayor Grom* #7: n.p.).

Major Grom's themes and imagery, such as legions in plague doctor masks battling riot police, draws from Alan Moore and David Lloyd's *V for Vendetta* (1989)—and especially its 2005 film adaptation—for a pointedly political portrait of 2010s Russia. Even after the Plague Doctor is defeated and order restored, the nation's inequality and lawlessness linger, like a bad taste in the mouth. The hero's victory is hollow. (Gabrelyanov and his collaborators would continue to explore such troubling subject matter in subsequent arcs.)

Yet as Bubble was putting forth a familiar image of hardy, physically dominant men as the genre's coin of the realm (while subtly critiquing that model), others at about the same time followed the explicitly parodic line from the 1990s. None succeeded more prominently than Sergei Kalenik, a mid-twenties PR freelancer who uploaded his *A Man Like Any Other* (*Chelovek kak vse*)[51] to its own site, Superputin.ru, in summer, 2011. Building on previous satires like *Gryzlovman* (2009),[52] Kalenik created an absurdist, gag- and reference-filled

---

50. Razumovsky recalls the political radicals from Dostoevsky's *Demons*, who discuss "lopping off a hundred million heads" (405) in order to save the world, as well as *Watchmen*'s Veidt, who defends his plan to create utopia by way of mass murder: "*Someone* had to take the weight of that awful, necessary crime" (Moore and Gibbons: 409).

51. Kalenin wrote the script, with art supplied by Katya Zashtopik (aka Dopingirl) and daskunst (aka Otto Schmidt).

52. In 2009, an anonymous group named Unknown Team uploaded *Gryzlovman* (*Chelovek-Gryzlov*), a satire based on Boris Gryzlov, white-haired speaker of the State Duma and leading figure of the United Russia party. In cape and spandex, he saves the city from an exploding gas pipeline.

FIGURE 6.4. Igor Grom debates revolution with Razumovsky/
the Plague Doctor in *Major Grom* #7 (2013)

action adventure mixing politics, superheroics, and the Keanu Reeves vehicle *Speed* (directed by Jan de Bont, 1994).

In the story "Part One: The Phantom Menace," Putin appears in the white *gi* (a sort of kimono) he uses for judo, to do battle with an al-Qaeda cell, drive a bus with a bomb planted on it, and fend off zombies protesting inequality in Russia.[53] "No need to rock the boat!" he answers, throwing a zombie to the mat. His sidekicks are Nanoman, aka then-president Dmitry Medvedev, a gnome tech nerd who transforms into a bear (playing off his name, derived from *medved'* or "bear") and Sechin, aka Igor Sechin (head of the state's *siloviki* faction), who remains invisible the entire time and shoots zombies in the head. When Putin asks him, "How's reality coming along?" he answers, "In the proper direction"—a funny if chilling reference to the manipulation of reality that has become a common staple of governance in twenty-first-century Russia (Kalenik, "Chelovek"). Within a week, the Superputin site racked up over 5 million views (InoTV, "Vladimir"). Kalenik and his collaborators released subsequent episodes later in the decade.

Other notable 2010s superhero parodies included Roman Gorbachev and Dmitry Ivanov's *The Keepers* (*Blyustiteli*),[54] uploaded to his VKontakte and other sites in 2013. These were heroes in a banal, deflating key, including the Incredible Alk (from the Russian word for "alcoholic"); Captain Mail (Kapitan Pochta); Robopope; Tsenzura (censorship), a woman who appeared naked except for black bars over the naughty parts; Savingsman (Sberman); Supercop (Superment); and Normalman (Normalny). A number of the characters' names were elaborate puns, like Roskomnakha (blending Roskomnadzor, the state media regulator, and *rosomakha* or "wolverine").

The cover of a 2011 KOM studio reunion book spoofed superheroes, with Askold Akishin in the guise of the Hulk, Misha Zaslavsky as the Punisher, Alexei Kapninsky as the mighty Thor, Igor Kolgarov as Spider-Man, and so on. Literary references abounded in several superhero parody works. Ilya Obukhov's freewheeling 2013 interpretation of Vladimir Mayakovsky's poem "A Cloud in Trousers" (1915), part of the St. Petersburg Mayakovsky Museum's commemoration of the Silver Age and early-Soviet era poet's 120th birthday,[55] reads like a weird/funny fever dream. Any superhero fan worth their salt will

---

53. The zombies wear blue buckets on their heads, in reference to the "Blue Bucket Brigades" protesting the blue flashing sirens (*migalki*) (mis)used by government officials on Moscow's often jammed streets. "Down with privileges on the roads!" they yell. "Only ambulances and fire trucks!" They also demand, "Give us back NTV!," an allusion to oligarch Vladimir Gusinsky's independent television station taken over by the state's proxies in 2001 (Kalenik, "Chelovek").

54. One might also translate *blyustiteli* as "guardians" or "custodians."

55. Obukhov contributed this work to the museum's Mayakovsky Manifesto project.

recognize the allusion in Obukhov's cover: He models it on that of *Amazing Fantasy* #15 (the first appearance of Spider-Man, from 1962; art by Jack Kirby and Steve Ditko). Add to the list perennial superhero send-ups like KOM veteran Alim Velitov's *Supervalenok* (*valenok* refers to a type of felt boot), in stories dating back to the early 2000s.

As discussed earlier, other authors mined the history of the genre for inspiration, in works like Filipp Sosedov and Roman Onishchcenko's *Pantheon: Cult of Duplicity* (2012–2016); Alexei Volkov, Kirill Kutuzov, et al.'s *Dr. Lucid* stories (2014); Volkov and Alexei Gorbut's *Conquerors of the Impossible* (2017); Volkov, Kutuzov, and Gorbut's series *Thief of Shadows* (2019); and Volkov, Gorbut, and Madibek Musabekov's *Mir* (2020).[56] At the movies, meanwhile, audiences stayed away in droves from the execrable *Guardians*, the first Russian superhero feature film (directed by Sarik Andreasyan, 2017; see Alaniz, "Sarik").

One superhero work of the third post-Soviet decade stood out as the most truly innovative: Georgy "Gosha" Elaev's *Tyuman* (2016), a psychedelic, X-rated parable of alienation and modern-day energy extraction in the provinces. The hero derives his mystical powers from narcotic oil flowing through his veins and his name from Tyumen, a major fossil fuels industry hub in Siberia (where Elaev lived), while the series' demented gonzo vision takes in a resurrected Rasputin (minus his penis) and extraterrestrial invasion, among much else. *Tyuman* channels the satirical spirit of US underground comix classics like Manuel "Spain" Rodriguez's *Trashman* and Gilbert Shelton's *Wonder Wart-Hog* for a tragicomic meditation on power in Putin's Russia.

In the collection-cum-graphic novel *Eternity Smells Of Oil*[57] (2018), Elaev combines elements from Viktor Pelevin's mind-bending 1996 novel *Chapaev and Emptiness*[58] with anti-consumption tirades, oddly contemplative pornographic scenes, an exploration of childhood bullying, and a redemptive devotion to the US superhero the Phantom (based on Elaev's own upbringing, as he told me)[59] for a tale about what I can only describe as existentialist identity theft. In one scene, the evil "City Manager" reveals that he has stolen the hero's image in order to sell Tyuman-related knickknacks and merch, like masks, plush toys, action figures, comics, even a dildo. "Now you are simply

---

56. We may translate *Mir* as "peace" or "world." Bubble's translation retains *Mir*.

57. The title comes from Siberian punk legend Yegor Letov's song "The Russian Experimental Field," included in the 1989 Civil Defense album of the same name.

58. *Chapaev i pustota*, translated in the US as *Buddha's Little Finger* and in the UK as *The Clay Machine Gun*.

59. Elaev interview, 2019.

FIGURE 6.5. "You have been simply monetized!
Ha-ha-ha!" cackles the "City Manager," wearing a
Tyuman mask, in *Tyuman: Eternity Smells of Oil* (2018)

a product, a brand, an ad slogan for the consumerist masses!" cackles the villain. "You have been simply monetized! *Ha-ha-ha!*" ("Vechnost'": n.p.) (see
figure 6.5).

Not since Roman Safarov's *Man-Mold*[60] has the Russian superhero trod
in such deliriously coarse territory; not since Nikanorov's Klash stories has
the figure ventured into such philosophical, even metaphysical, terrain in its
(self) examination of masculine and genre paradoxes. For Tyuman is both
demigod-like—capable of creating mass oil spills and opening dimensional/
time rifts—yet oddly helpless before vast ideological and sociocultural forces
(like neoliberalism) that remake the world before his eyes. Above all *Tyuman*
is a baroque and dizzying meditation on the dehumanizing symbolic and literal capital of oil in contemporary Russia. (Of course, it goes without saying—but it always needs saying—that Russia's fossil fuel extraction policies are
environmentally ruinous, especially to those who live in the regions involved.)

60. See Alaniz, *Komiks*: 135.

By decade's end, Russians had a variety of superheroes to choose from in print, at the movies, on the internet—even in real life. In the lead-up to the 2019 Moscow City Council elections, Kalenik scored another satirical coup with *Who Will Save the Universe? Sharapova: People's Deputy* (2019), on the colorful Moscow City Duma deputy Olga Sharapova, which appeared digitally and as a booklet.[61] Dmitry Diachenko's *SuperBobrovs* comedy film series[62] dealt with an ordinary family blessed with superpowers. A popular 2019 online animated cartoon by Vyacheslav Kotov pitted US superheroes against Russian *bogatyry* (folktale knights), and even allowed the viewer to choose who would win; by August 2020, it had garnered 5 million views.[63] And in 2016 the "Khimki Batman" prowled the streets on the outskirts of Moscow dressed as his namesake, nabbing drug dealers; police later arrested him.[64]

In their 2020 book *Superheroes and Masculinity: Unmasking the Gender Performance of Heroism,* Sean Parson and J. L. Schatz write: "Investigating how superheroes operate is imperative for understanding how the contemporary imperial form of hegemony both develops and sustains itself in spite of the violence that it creates in the name of peace" ("Introduction": 2–3). In the case of Russia, domestic superheroes—like so much else—ultimately pointed back to the leader of the nation, who by the end of the decade had secured power through at least 2036 (barring the kryptonite of true democracy, that is). 'Til then, a real man is in charge. "Putin's masculinity," writes Helena Goscilo, "is grounded in the body and what that body can withstand—a material guarantor that, as Putin learned, reassures the public" ("Putin's": 184). A fawning 2017 exhibit at Moscow's Artplay Design Center, "Putin Is a Superhero," literalized the metaphor (*The Moscow Times,* "Putin").[65]

Yet as we have seen, the lineage of superhero comics in Russia is replete with parodic puncturings of traditional masculinity no less than of the very idea of heroism itself. For every "Putin Is a Superhero," there are several *A Man Like Any Other.* Laughter, as Bakhtin reminds, is its own superpower.

During a 2019 radio roundtable on superheroes, moderator Galina Larionova opined, "Superheroes conquer us not with their superpowers, but with the

---

61. The artist was unnamed. Kalenik posted the piece via the blogging platform Tilda (http://supersharapova.tilda.ws/) on September 7, 2019. It also appeared on other sites.

62. Two films were released: *The SuperBobrovs* (*Superbobrovy,* also known as *Super Family,* directed by Dmitry Dyachenko, 2016) and *The SuperBobrovs: National Avengers* (*Superbobrovy: narodnye mstiteli,* aka *Super Bobrovy: Better Than Avengers,* directed by Dyachenko, 2018).

63. Watch it here: https://www.youtube.com/watch?v=SlLjIxl1Mi8.

64. See Afonskiy, "V Podmoskov'e."

65. The exhibit's organizers declared that the show "depicts the current president as a modern superhero . . . whose many talents and skills can fittingly be characterized as 'supertalents' and 'superpowers'" (*The Moscow Times,* "Putin").

choice about how to use them. They lift our spirits and show how the world is changing" (Larionova, "Poteriat'sia"). I submit that superhero comics serve as just such a barometer for the changing latitudes accorded male identity and its discontents in post-Soviet Russia,[66] and how these might differ from those of the West. Alexander Kunin made a related point in 2014: "We must have our own path, we must touch upon our own history. We don't need Superman, we need a hero with our own face" (Panfilov, "My").

---

66. And female identity as well, though superheroines appear more rarely in Russian comics. One example: the short-lived *Moshka* (*The Gnat*, from Tien Press, 2016), by writer Anton Karzov and several artists. See also my discussion of Bubble's *Red Fury* in chapter 7.

CHAPTER 7

Elephants and DJs

Komiks *and Disability*

A scene late in *Corrections Class* (*Klass korrektsii*, directed by Ivan Tverdo-vsky, 2015), a hard-hitting film about disability in Russia, shows a mother, Svetlana Viktorovna (Natalya Pavlenkova), struggling to push her paraplegic teen daughter Lena (Maria Poyezhayeva) in her wheelchair up a two-track cement ramp outside the local high school. But the ramp, which we had seen in the process of construction earlier in the movie, has a fatal flaw: a gap of several inches between it and the sidewalk—too wide for a wheelchair to overcome. Worse than useless, the ramp is a spit in the face; a bureaucratic nod to inclusivity with no actual follow-through. It drives Svetlana Viktorovna, who has more than enough troubles in her life, to hiss with rage: "Thank you very much, my dears. Great job."[1]

Equal parts maudlin melodrama, documentary exposé, and black farce, the scene is not exactly fiction (though the film is). It had a real-life basis.

In the fall of 2012, a popular series of memes emerged on the Runet (Russian internet): pictures of the many inaccessible spaces for wheelchair users in Russian cities, turned into absurdist set decoration by ramps built impossibly steep; ramps with trees and other objects blocking the way; broken ramps with wide cracks; and ramps leading to/from nowhere (e.g., into walls). "The

---

1. See Alaniz, "Corrections" for a detailed discussion of disability in post-Soviet Russian cinema.

inaccessible-ramps meme gained popularity not as [a] representation of the problem of disability inclusion in Russia," wrote anthropologist Cassandra Hartblay, "but as a joke about the country's infrastructure, ironic evidence of dysfunction in Russian daily life" ("Good": 3).[2] She goes on to call the ramps "an overdetermined symbol, or a red herring for access" in postsocialism (4).

As the makers of *Corrections Class* knew, disability could also serve as an arresting subject for drama. In 2017, the mainstream comics publisher Bubble also foregrounded this facet of human experience as never before in its "Second Breath" initiative, when it revamped and relaunched many of its series (see chapter 4). The title *Red Fury*, fronted by sexy super-spy Nika Chaikina, was replaced with *Allies* (*Soyuzniki*), an ensemble series that featured Chaikina and her team of operatives. That wasn't the only change.

As readers learned early in "Before the Dawn," the first story arc, their beloved heroine had undergone a harrowing ordeal. She awakes, after horrible dreams, in a hospital, surrounded by doctors. The events at the end of the *Red Fury* series (a battle involving zombies) have resulted in unthinkable trauma: Chaikina has lost both legs above the knee. Unable to accept the new reality, the recent amputee lashes out, screams in horror, tries to wish it away in a storm of emotions that lasts the entire first issue of *Allies*.[3]

Much of the critical and fan reaction to this turn of events focused, curiously enough, on two things: Chaikina's "helplessness" and her drastic loss of sex appeal. Reviewer Alexander Talashin, for example, wrote: "The girl tries to convince herself that it's just a bad dream. But the doctors convince her of the opposite: the once beautiful thief and secret agent Red Fury is now a helpless invalid" ("Komiks"). A reviewer at Wicomix warned that the stark revelation of Chaikina "turned into a gray, ailing shadow of herself" will "cast the unprepared reader into a state of shock" ("Retsentsii").

Indeed, our heroine's portrayal in *Allies* differs markedly from what we saw in the previous series. There, Chaikina often appeared in skintight catsuits or revealing outfits, her bosom and posterior quite available to the gaze. The cover of #11 (August 2013)[4] showed her in a skimpy bikini made of jungle foliage, her hand coyly up to her mouth, while the cover to #18 (March 2014)

---

2. International athletes who came to Sochi for the 2014 Paralympics reported similar disappointing encounters with Russian infrastructure, despite the unprecedented coverage and popularity there of the games themselves (see F. Bernstein, "Ramp"). Times had changed. The Soviets refused to take part in the first Paralympics in 1980, on the grounds that, as one representative put it, "There are no invalids in the USSR!" (Phillips, "There").

3. For discussion of similar trauma scenes in US Silver and Bronze Age comics, including in *Fantastic Four* and *Tales of the New Teen Titans*, see Alaniz, *Death*: chapter 4.

4. By Mike Krome and Sabine Rich.

as well as to the third trade paperback collection (2015)[5] somehow lets the gazer look through the fabric of her pants, at a thong cleaving her buttocks.[6] A variant cover to #28 (January 2015) by Konstantin Tarasov features her in the infamous brokeback pose.[7] And the covers did not lie; more of the same awaited the reader in the stories. In short, cheesecake galore.

But now, in her hospital gown, she looks thin and wan (not voluptuous as before), with two chief expressions: wide-eyed bewilderment and profound gloom. (Later, as she tries to escape what she realizes is a fake hospital, grim determination takes over.) A "tragic" alternate cover to *Allies* #1 shows Chaikina downcast in her wheelchair, recalling her former partners and adventures, imagery of which dominates the space above her. The cover communicates that Chaikina's life as a hero and as a woman is effectively over.[8]

She herself seems to believe that. When a doctor tries to console her by saying, "You're not dead," she replies with: "I don't even know if that's a plus . . ." He holds out the possibility of prosthetics: "We can help you to get back up on your feet. Literally. If you'll let us . . ." She answers, looking away, "What if I don't want to get back up?" (Devova and Erofeeva, *Soiuzniki*: n.p.).

A dichotomous two-page sequence in *Allies* #1 achingly visualizes Chaikina's new sense of vulnerability and life as an amputee (see figure 7.1). In verso, a series of seven thin tiers depict her drab routine in the hospital bed: physical therapy, exams, bathing, feeding "day after day." Facing in recto, in sharp contrast, we see a splash page of Nika in her bed, reaching up and linking hands with her ghostly idealized self (with legs), who dangles down from a wire, the hospital's ceiling transformed into a wavy, fiery-red circus tent. She is escaping into her past, notes the former Red Fury in a textbox, "where I can pretend that I'm still capable of doing something . . ." But a song whose lyrics accompany the imagery casts a dark shadow on Nika's fantasies. "Easy Street," by the Collapsable Hearts Club, had not long before appeared in season 7, episode 3 (2016) of *The Walking Dead*—in scenes of torture; in other words, Nika has quite a ways to go to abandon her lost identity as an able-bodied person and accept who she is now, with all her gifts. (That journey begins soon enough as she utilizes her battle skills to aid in her own rescue.)

---

5. By Konstantin Tarasov.

6. *Red Fury* was originally drawn by Oleg Okunev, who according to publisher Artyom Gabrelyanov based her look on "the redheaded girl with large breasts" (Christina Hendricks) in the US TV series *Firefly* (2002–2003) (Cherniavskiy, "Artem").

7. On the "brokeback pose" representation of women in superhero comics, see Cocca, *Superwomen*: 12.

8. The supposed incommensurability of disability with superheroic adventure is reductively summed up in Talashin's remark: "It's hard, after 50 issues of whirlwind action, to see Chaikina in a hospital bed" ("Komiks").

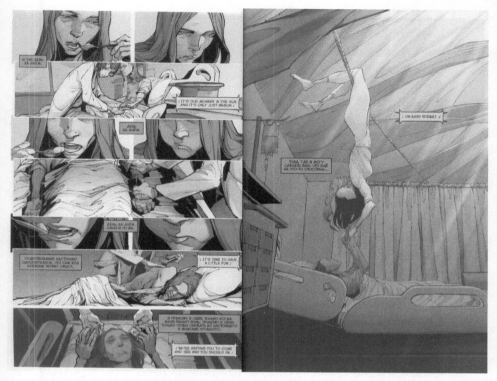

FIGURE 7.1. Nika Chaikina/Red Fury convalescing from her leg amputations, from *Allies* #1 (2017). Written by Natalya Devova, with art by Alina Erofeyeva.

For all its ableist presumptions about the value (or lack of it) that accrues to particular types of bodies (especially young female bodies), the opening chapters of "Before the Dawn" represent a fascinating turn in Russian mainstream comics' portrayal of disability—all the more remarkable for taking place in the action-adventure genre, still more so for its maiming of a (let's face it) soft-porny heroine.[9] The Wicomix reviewer repeatedly used the word *realistic* in their assessment, as in "a realistically portrayed . . . swamp of hopelessness and despair." For all the angst, or indeed because of it, the reviewer sees in Chaikina's misfortune a step forward for the character and the genre, well worth

> the pain, tears, panic and hysteria of a much-loved heroine, who from a sex symbol, a clone of Lara Croft and an intrepid spy, has suddenly transformed

9. Nika Chaikina's physical transformation likely had something to do with the new, all-female creative team: writer Natalya Devova, artist Alina Erofeyeva, and colorist Viktoria Vinogradova.

into a living and fragile person. . . . Nika's fans are probably not too happy
to see her like that, but this condition, without a doubt, provides the comic
with drama—real, hard-earned, not false at all. ("Retsentsii")[10]

It would not be the first time mainstream comics readers have linked disability with greater "realism," a hallmark of the US superhero genre since the
1960s.[11] But *Allies'* "progress" in this regard followed similar breakthroughs
in the alternative sphere and other sectors of the industry; the same year as
"Before the Dawn," *I Am an Elephant!*, the first graphic novel devoted to the
disabled experience, written by a wheelchair user, saw release.

With twenty-first-century Russian readers' increasing acceptance of comics—for decades derogated as a "foreign," half-literate medium—the amount
of graphic narrative work by marginalized groups grew as well, in particular
since Putin's 2012 return to the presidency. The accessibility, visceral impact,
and easy dissemination of comics (especially through the internet) made them
an attractive vehicle for voices and imagery otherwise occluded in contemporary life. This chapter discusses graphic narrative by and about the disabled—a
population itself long ignored in mainstream Russia.

I will offer a brief overview of the situation for people with disabilities in
Russia after the collapse of communism, and present some case studies of the
disabled experience in post-Soviet society as described in words and pictures
by nondisabled and disabled comics artists. How do these artists represent
the disabled body as a site of contention and human dignity? How do their
visions coincide with and complicate the rhetoric of disability rights movements in Russia? How do they reinforce or resist the medical model of disability, a lightning rod for disability rights movements in the West? How do the
visual–verbal strategies of comic art uniquely communicate the experiences of
lives too often lived in the shadows, lives of frequent hospitalizations, chronic
illnesses, bodily pain, and social exclusion?

In what follows I am guided by the key insights of disability studies scholar
Rosemarie Garland-Thomson:

> Representation structures rather than reflects reality. The way we imagine
> disability through images and narratives determines the shape of the mate-

---

10. Bubble editor Roman Kotkov called "Before the Dawn" "a complex story about a person who had everything, and suddenly loses it all (including her legs) and tries to find herself
in a world of mutants and superpowers . . . one of the most emotional and powerful comic
books we've ever done" (Parker, "Russia").

11. On the use of disability for dramatic purposes and "heightened realism" in Silver and
Bronze Age superhero comics, see Alaniz, *Death*: chapter 2 and passim.

rial world, the distribution of resources, our relationships with one another, and our sense of ourselves.

The aim of much disability studies is to reimagine disability, to reveal how the storied quality of disability invents and reinvents the world we share. Disability studies challenges our collective representation of disability, exposing it as an exclusionary and oppressive system rather than the natural and appropriate order of things. ("Disability": 523)

The representational stakes for the disabled, even in a long-ignored medium like graphic narrative, seem particularly high in Russia, given this social group's near-total abnegation during and after communism, and its only very recent rise to public awareness.

The Representation of Disability in the Post-Soviet Era

As noted, with the breakup of the USSR in 1991 Russia returned—ready or not—to full-blown capitalism. Hyperinflation, the collapse of social services, poverty, and a host of other social ills made life exceedingly difficult for the disabled, some of whom were reduced to begging in the streets (Norton, "Slow"). While living in Moscow in the early 1990s, I found it not at all unusual to see people with deformities of various sorts pleading for alms in metro stations and on the streets. Many Russians, accustomed to a reality "scrubbed" clean of such sights in the Soviet era, reacted with shock.[12]

In the first post-Soviet decade, the disabled were just another group ill-served by both the state and the faltering new economy—a group that gained (for many Russians) a startling new visibility. A variation on an oft-heard anecdote from my Russian acquaintances went much like this: "When I first went to the West, I thought how terrible it was that so many people with disabilities were on the streets, how sad that was. But then I realized that we in Russia must have just as many if not more, only we have them hidden away. They can't go out because of the terrible conditions," and so on.

If disabled people in Russia had remained mostly invisible, this had nothing to do with their choice, but instead was due to the lack of an infrastruc-

---

12. The rise in coverage of the disabled during Perestroika had highlighted the long-standing mistreatment and social exclusion of a population literally hidden from view by the Soviets. Sarah Phillips writes: "The high rates of institutionalization, the relative lack of education and employment opportunities, and the low economic status of most persons with disabilities—problems that only came to light after Gorbachev's policies of *Glasnost* (openness) and *Perestroika* (restructuring)—speak volumes about the [Soviet] state's inability or unwillingness to ensure equal rights to people with disabilities" ("There").

ture to accommodate them, whether at home (e.g., five-story walk-ups with no elevators—or if they had them, broken or too narrow to accommodate a wheelchair) or in public (treacherously potholed, cobblestoned, and curbed sidewalks, no ramps). Now, in the new capitalistic world, they were too often seen as drains on society's dwindling resources, despite the novel lip service to "humanitarian values." Writing in the journal *Stolitsa*, Ksenia Klimova described the disabled's plight in her short semi-biographical piece "Steps" (1994):

> Everybody has apparently noticed that people with disabilities exist, but they don't acknowledge their right to a sense of their own dignity and their own life, the right to have a job, friends, happiness, and to acquire all of this all you have to overcome . . . that's right, is a flight of three steps at the entrance.
>
> You won't hear the word "cripple" behind your back very often any more. But the bureaucrats often use the phrase "what for?" What do people with disabilities want clubs, sports, competitions, and exhibitions for? It all requires resources and effort. Why not wait until the country gets a bit richer? (143)

Of course, in the 1990s, few Russians were getting richer—quite the opposite.

On the other hand, new possibilities were opening up for people with disabilities, despite the recurring economic crises. Wheelchair-using athletes in integrated city marathons, like Moscow's, were now a common sight. In St. Petersburg, Yury Kuznetsov founded the activist group We Are Together (My-vmeste) in 1991. Building on the work of Soviet activists like Lev Indolev, such organizations proceeded from a civil rights model, demanding equal education, jobs, and access rather than mere benefits from a paternalistic government. But internalized attitudes proved hard to overcome for many. As sociologist Elena Iarskaya-Smirnova wrote: "The ideology of the disabled's dependence on the state and society is so deeply rooted in mass consciousness, that the legal frameworks [*modusy*] in regard to the disabled raise doubts for no one" (*Odezhda*: 171).[13]

With Putin's consolidation of power in the 2000s, the disabled steadily gained more prominence in the culture. Academics and disability rights activists pressed for more inclusion, including Irina Yasina, former director of the Open Russia foundation and a wheelchair user. In public appearances as well her memoir *History of an Illness: In Search of Happiness* (2011), she explicitly

---

13. Iarskaya-Smirnova here is writing not exclusively about Russia.

tied disability to other human rights struggles in Russia. The cover to a 2004 textbook, *Access to Higher Education for People with Disabilities: Problems and Perspectives,* edited by D. V. Zaitseva, set forth the ideal: a photograph of two smiling young women in wheelchairs, presumably students on their way to class.[14] No "ramps to nowhere" in sight.

In the Medvedev (2008–2012) and later Putin administrations (2012–?), infrastructure improvements, such as the wiring of disabled people's homes for greater internet access, and legal reforms gave some grounds for hope.[15] Russia signed on to the United Nations Convention on the Rights of People with Disabilities in 2006; parliament ratified it in 2012. On July 10, 2011, the Russian government dedicated a memorial to the disabled veterans once housed on Valaam Island.[16] Patriarch Kirill, leader of the Russian Orthodox Church, took part in the ceremony.

Still, despite real gains in the spheres of politics and access, Russia's disabled community remained largely excluded from mainstream society. Particularly in the realm of representation, the picture remains very mixed. Not enough has changed since disability scholars Pavel Romanov and Iarskaya-Smirnova argued in 2006:

> Fairly often the mass media sees as its mission to arouse the public's sense of pity and compassion for the disabled, and to take to task the activities of the state. Emphasized are all sorts of problems caused by the inability to hold a job; the struggles with work that people with disabilities have to go through; while more positive experiences receive less attention: disabled people's achievements at work, their successes in life. The accent is placed on how "courageous" the person is in the overcoming of his infirmity, or else what a trauma for the family a "defective" child represents. People of all walks of life, solely due to their physical handicaps, are uniformly represented as pathetic, unfortunate creatures. Relatively rarely are the disabled

---

14. The picture adheres to Garland-Thomson's "realistic" model of disability representation in photography (see "Seeing": 363–371).

15. See Human Rights Watch, *Abandoned* and *Barriers* for useful summaries of government policy regarding the disabled through the mid-2010s.

16. Stalin, partly from fear of an uprising by disabled World War II veterans, as well as his desire "to silenc[e] or den[y] any negative aspects" of the war, ordered many of them permanently exiled to such far-flung places as the far-North Valaam Archipelago (Phillips, "There"). The graphic artist Gennady Dobrov (1937–2011) produced a series of portraits of the disabled residents of Valaam and other such centers from 1974 to 1980. The series, titled "Signatures of the War" ("Avtografy voiny"), strikingly reflects both the dignity and living conditions of the veterans, which the Soviet government kept hidden from the outside world.

presented as professionals participating in socially significant events, in the making of decisions. (*Politika*: 217)

Three incidents in the 2010s, two involving major celebrities (who take up a large portion of the media landscape) emblematized the contemporary situation. In 2015, in Nizhny Novgorod, supermodel Natalya Vodyanova's sister, who has autism and cerebral palsy, and her nanny were asked to leave a café, in violation of the law on the "social protection of disabled people." The media uproar led to the café's investigation and closing (Ponosov, "V Nizhnem").[17] In a September 2016 press conference, pop singer Sati Kazanova declared that her charity Culture and Life does not deal with "sick, squinty-eyed, broken-backed children—forgive me, Lord" (bol'nymi, kosymi, krivymi, prosti Bozhe, det'mi). The predictable blowback led Kazanova to issue an online apology (*TBK*, "Sati"). Finally, in summer 2019, in Samara, disabled performance artist Arseny "the Pest?" (Arseniy "Vreditel' li?") sat in his wheelchair on a small platform attached to the exterior of a five-story building, level with the fourth floor. Steps and a double-track ramp led off to the abyss. Seven years after the "ramp to nowhere" viral memes, the artist said he pulled the stunt to draw attention to the persistent problem of inadequate infrastructure for disabled people (*Lenta*, "Khudozhnik"). Notably, apart from celebrities, most of these incidents involved "defenseless" children—still the primary mode through which Russian media infantilize and marginalize the disabled.

Perhaps no literary figure better represented the turbulent crosswinds of disability representation in early twenty-first-century Russia than Rubén González-Gallego, author of *White on Black* (2002), a controversial novel/memoir devoted to the injustices of the Russo-Soviet institutionalization of the disabled. The text had been painstakingly tapped out by a person with severely limited use of his fingers. Abandoned by his Spanish mother at birth due to his cerebral palsy (doctors had lied to her, saying the baby had died), González-Gallego was raised in a Soviet orphanage (*internat*), a "Gulag archipelago"–like existence[18] that he chronicles with penetrating frankness and a fierce rejection of pity:

---

17. The report I am citing, from the newspaper *Rossiyskaia Gazeta*, used the phrase "suffering from cerebral palsy and autism" (Ponosov, "V Nizhnem"), which most disability rights activists consider ableist terminology.

18. In 2014, Human Rights Watch released a report, *Abandoned by the State*, which paints a damning picture of the Russian government's neglect of children with disabilities in state orphanages. Conditions had changed much too little since the time of González-Gallego's Soviet upbringing.

I am a hero. It's easy to be a hero. If you don't have hands or feet, you're either a hero or dead. If you don't have parents, rely on your hands and feet. And be a hero. If you don't have hands or feet, and in addition you've contrived to come into this world an orphan—that's it. You're doomed to be a hero to the end of your days. Or else kick the bucket. I'm a hero. I have no other choice. (1)

Despite its problematic "overcoming" narrative of disability depiction, whereby the onus of survival and thriving lies on the shoulders of the individual (not society), González-Gallego's angry broadside received the 2003 Russian Booker Prize. The book paved the way for more sensitive depictions, such as Alexander Snegirov's novel *Petroleum Venus* (*Neftyanaya Venera*, 2008), about raising a child with Down syndrome, and Mariam Petrosyan's remarkably successful novel *The House Where . . .* (*Dom, v kotorom . . .*, 2009), itself set in an internat—albeit one infused with a high degree of mysticism and allegory. An expanded 2016 edition of the novel included fan art by readers.

In post-Soviet cinema, the popular image of the disabled tended also to emphasize pathos and sentiment, though more complex portraits have steadily increased in number. A 1998 comedy/thriller, *Land of the Deaf* (*Strana glukhikh,* directed by Valery Todorovsky), capitalized on the public's lurid interest in a "Deaf mafia." The period film *Of Freaks and Men* (*Pro urodov i lyudei,* directed by Alexei Balabanov, 1998) harkened back to the grotesque bodies of the freak-show era through its objectification of helpless conjoined twins and a blind woman. Later works such as Tverdovsky's *Corrections Class* pushed back hard against such "weak" depictions, though they overcompensate by showing disabled people doing horrible things, in this case thieving and committing a brutal gang rape. Myroslav Slaboshpytskiy's *The Tribe* (*Plemya*), a 2014 Ukrainian film on deaf criminals told entirely in sign language, also belongs in this category.[19]

The bland neoliberal tolerance for the disabled in twenty-first-century Russia is perhaps best represented by the romantic comedy *Love with Limits* (*Lyubov s ogranicheniami,* directed by Dmitry Tryunin, 2017), about a man who pretends to need a wheelchair in order to take advantage of state work programs benefiting the "disadvantaged"—a sort of disability-drag version of the 1986 film *Soul Man* (directed by Steve Miner); a closer cousin is the Johnny Knoxville comedy about faking one's way through the Special Olympics, *The Ringer* (directed by Barry W. Blaustein, 2005).[20] Meanwhile, series like *Love for*

19. On cinematic representations of disability in Russia, see Alaniz, "Cinema" and "People."
20. Vladimir Rudak's *Pineapple* (Ananas, 2016) follows a similar plotline. Rudak, a wheelchair user, wrote the graphic novel *I Am an Elephant!,* discussed further on.

Love (directed by Sergei Ashkenazi, 2013), about star-crossed paramours (one of them in a wheelchair), defined the limits of the acceptable on television. It will likely not surprise the reader that in these mainstream depictions, almost all of the disabled roles are played by able-bodied actors.

Disability manifested more rarely in popular music, and tended toward the metaphorical, as in the 2005 song and album *Disabled People* (*Lyudi-invalidy*) by the faux-lesbian girl duet t.A. T.u. A popular 2011 song and video, *"Our Nuthouse Is Voting for Putin"* ("Nash durdom golosuyet za Putina") by Rabfak, circulated online in the run-up to the 2012 presidential election. The video featured dehumanizing footage of homeless and mentally ill people.[21]

In 2013, the Russian Ministry of Health numbered citizens with disabilities at 13 million, or about 9 percent of the population (Human Rights Watch, *Barriers*: 15). This includes about 500,000 children. Russia remains officially committed to reforms that will achieve a more equal society for disabled people. But as noted, many problems remain. For one thing, the 2012 Dima Yakovlev law, which bans US families from adopting Russian children, remains in force. The effect of the law has been to leave tens of thousands of adoptable disabled children to languish in state orphanages.[22] Offering grounds for hope: a new generation of disabled activists (many of them artists), including Arseny "The Pest?," Alyona Levina, and Asya Cherepkova.

Disability in Russian Comics after Communism

In the era that saw the rise of a post-Soviet disability consciousness in Russia, comics artists were drinking from the same fountain, so to speak, as everyone else. The following highly selective survey provides only some of the highlights, but it also traces a similar change in attitudes over time.

Igor Kozhevnikov's one-page children's story "Mishka" (*Veles* #7, 1995) typifies the link between disability and villainy/malevolence. In it we see Mishka, a cute bear who always wants to help but ends up making things worse, running into an unnamed wolf on crutches, with his leg in a cast. "Poor wolf," says Mishka. "It's so hard for him to walk." The childlike bear approaches the angry-looking predator and says, in all friendliness, "Wolf, I know how to help you! You should tie springs to your crutches!" The wolf, bearing his fangs

---

21. See it if you must here: https://www.youtube.com/watch?v=0nARQdxIYMc. And read F. Bernstein, "Ramp" for a critique.

22. Enacted in retaliation for the US's Magnitsky Act, which addresses Russian corruption, the law was named after a child adopted by US parents who died from neglect in 2008 (see Zelenova, "Invisible").

in a smile, replies, "Good boy, Mishka." A thought balloon, however, betrays his real feelings: "Now I'll be able to catch up with all the rabbits!" Once the crutches have been outfitted with large metal springs, Mishka waves a flag with the word "Start" on it, as at a foot race. The wolf thinks, "Oh, boy, I'm really gonna fly!" The penultimate panel shows Mishka reeling from a nearby impact, denoted by the sound effect "Bang!" In the final panel, the wolf—now with both legs and an arm in casts, and using a wheelchair—chases after the bear-child in a rage, swinging his crutch like a weapon.

We see a more ameliorative late 1990s and early 2000s example of disability representation in *Magnificent Adventures* (*Velikolepnye Priklyucheniya*), an optimistic-to-a-fault youth-oriented series launched by psychologist Dmitry Smirnov, with art by Andrei Ross. Among a group of wholesome, healthy, and active young people, we find Webik, a "cool" bespectacled computer geek and wheelchair user, who gets around town in a snazzy, Ferrari-like car. In all things Webik maintains a positive outlook, telling a sensitive friend upset by bullies, "Just react to everything with a sense of humor, poet! Imagine that a frog is croaking at you from a swamp. Are you going to get offended at it?" (Smirnov and Ross, "Kanikuly": 9). One gets the sense that it will take more than just a cheery attitude to resolve the problems that beset Russia's disabled population, but Smirnov's turn-of-the-twenty-first-century series stands out for its radical portrait of a paraplegic young man as happy and thriving.

KOM veteran Igor Kolgarev's one-pager "He Is with Us" ("On ryadom," 2005) returns us to an older—even ancient—style of disability portrayal. A devout Baptist Christian, Kolgarev presents a simple story that retains a traditional view of the disabled as beings worthy of love-pity, blessed by God: A boy in a wheelchair with his mother (who looks glum) happens upon a Bible on the street, just as a rainstorm begins; he picks it up, and in a flash of "power-line" brilliance, miraculously stands up, saying, "Jesus!" (n.p.). In Kolgarev's comics vision, disability is a problem healed through steadfast faith—and that's about it. Conspicuously missing: historical context and socioeconomic justice, that is, the responsibility of a modern state (rather than a divine power) to guarantee equal treatment to all citizens, regardless of religion or ability.

My next selection has its origins on the opposite side of the political spectrum from Kolgarev, though it too conscripts the disabled body into a higher—in this case nationalist—project. *Story of a Real Man* (*Povest' o nastoyashchem cheloveke*, 2006) by Yevgeny Gusev tells the famous real-life story of Alexei Maresyev, a WWII fighter pilot shot down by the Germans in 1941. Maresyev refused to stay grounded, despite losing both legs. With the aid of physical therapy and prosthetics, he flew again to carry on the fight. In this adaptation of a 1948 socialist realist film,[23] produced by a foundation headed by Maresyev's son, we see very little of the emotional turmoil that seized the similarly injured Nika Chaikina in *Allies*; Maresyev is all grit and gumption. A shining example of the "New Soviet Man," whose heroic feats prove his superiority to capitalist models of masculinity, our hero insists, "I will fly!" as he sweats through therapy in a one-page montage sequence. "Absolutely I will!" he declares, tossing his crutches away in the final panel, recalling a Charles Atlas ad. After only eighteen months, Maresyev proves his manly mettle by not only returning to air combat, but by dancing a traditional Russian folk dance on his new wooden legs (Gusev, *Povest'*: n.p.). *Story of a Real Man* portrays Maresyev's struggle as one of heroic, masculine overcoming and patriotic fervor.

The rise of a viable comics industry in Russia, more or less congruent with Putin's third term, saw an influx of disability-related works in translation, including David B.'s *Epileptic* (2011) and María and Miguel Gallardo's *María and Me* (2014) from Boomkniga, and Charles Burns's *Black Hole* (Comics Factory, 2017), as well as the Marvel series *Daredevil*, about a blind superhero. The graphic narrative of Salekhard native Yulia Nikitina (aka Ner-Tamin) stood out in this era, especially her series of fantasy graphic novels, *A Sorcerer's Travels* (*Puteshestvie charodeya*, 2013). The protagonist, Lit, initially has a body impaired by magic, figured by his deformed legs, which end in pointed tips. The visual metaphor marks his social isolation, a device that falls squarely in David Mitchell and Sharon Snyder's category of disability as narrative prosthesis.[24]

Nikitina would dispense with such devices in her allegorical memoir *The Book of the Body* (2014), a wordless narrative that embraces and transcends mortal flesh through a complex scheme of myth and symbol. As she told me: "Very likely the whole of *The Book of the Body* is about how the mortal body lives, suffers, receives pleasure, goes through changes. About how a person senses this body like an extension of the self, like something separate, or like precisely who she is at a particular moment in time" (Nikitina email interview, 2016).[25] Another autobiographical work, *Schism* (*Razdelenie*, 2015), most

---

23. *Story of a Real Man* (directed by Alexander Stolper, 1948) was based on Boris Polevoi's popular 1946 account by the same name. A DVD of the film was bundled with the graphic novel adaptation.

24. On the narrative prosthesis in comics, see Alaniz, *Death*: 34 and chapter 6.

25. Nikitina went into more specifics on January 2014, on her Live Journal page, where she uploaded the piece: "Embodiment [*telesnost'*] is a painful subject for me, and for a long time I more or less preferred to live as if my body did not exist. But my body took measures to prove the opposite, and it managed to attract some attention to itself. *The Book of the Body* was necessary for me in order to come to grips with the link between consciousness [*soznanie*] and

explicitly and lyrically renders the ill, disabled, *and* beautiful body, meriting comparisons to Al Davison's *The Spiral Cage* (1988/2003).

From its opening confession—"I could never boast of having great health. / Most northern children can't"—*Schism* (aka *Disassociation*) puts forth an intensely personal and intimate meditation on a vexed body/mind dichotomy exacerbated by illness. In white letters against a mostly black background, Nikitina writes:

> Over the course of my life I've gotten really sick a lot, and picked up the habit of disassociating—splitting myself into pieces.
>
> I needed to do this in order to deal with the pain, and with the shame I felt from not being able to properly control my own body. ("Razdelenie": n.p.)

The artist literalizes that split, depicting her body broken up by mirrors, panel framing, the page compositions themselves. (The piece's title could also be translated as "disintegration.") A splash page shows the narrator in profile, staring sullenly down, at an absurdly empty space below her chest. "Sometimes I think it's better not to have a body at all" declares a block of text written on her upper torso.[26]

Schism stages a war between flesh and spirit familiar from generations of Russian religious thought,[27] though here utilizing the cartoonist's visual–verbal toolkit to make her physical suffering vivid in ways inaccessible to language alone.[28] Moreover, Nikitina's stubbornly material avatar for her pain—a wolf-like shadow-dog—has personality and life, no less so than David B.'s dragon

---

form, in which the body is situated. . . . *The Book of the Body* is my attempt to conceptualize the connection between culture and nature, the means through which the corporeal and the mental are unified in one being. In so much as I was born a woman, this is for the most part a book about the female body." The Live Journal account has since been deleted.

26. Nikitina's imagery recalls the absurdist poet Daniil Kharms's progressively disappearing "redheaded man" in his "Blue Notebook #10" (ca. 1937), which some have read as a coded depiction of the Stalinist purges: "There was a redheaded man who had no eyes or ears. He didn't have hair either, so he was called a redhead arbitrarily. / He couldn't talk because he had no mouth. He didn't have a nose either. / He didn't even have arms or legs. He had no stomach, he had no back, no spine, and he didn't have any insides at all. There was nothing! So we don't even know who we're talking about. / We'd better not talk about him any more" (*Today*: 45).

27. See, for example, Irene Masing-Delic's discussion of the nineteenth-century philosopher Nikolai Fyodorov's highly influential "Common Task" ("obshchee delo"), a cosmic program for spiritual transcendence over mere matter (*Abolishing*: chapter 4).

28. As Elaine Scarry has argued, the "objectlessness" of pain (i.e., its lack of a referent) resists representation by discourse and other means. On the other hand, in language that seems pertinent to Nikitina's work, she writes, "The only state that is as anomalous as pain is the imagination" (*Body*: 162). On comics' representation of psycho-physiological states such as illness and trauma, see Chute, *Graphic*: 2–7 and El Refaie, *Autobiographical*: 60–65.

to represent the "curse" of his brother's disease in *Epileptic* (2000) or Katie Green's "scribble-scrawl" to symbolize anorexia in *Lighter Than My Shadow* (2016). One moment it menacingly bares its sharp fangs, the next it peacefully lies on the narrator's stomach, immobilizing her in bed. "You've got to be kidding me," she grouses.

The next panel shows her facing the reader, calmly holding the dark-gray animal in her arms like a pet. "And it's big," she says. "This is the fruit of the schism between mind and body." As the creature grows and grows, it comes to blot out all of reality; white text once more against solid black declares: "When that happens, I usually end up in the hospital." For the next two pages, we see the bifurcated narrator-self on her hospital bed ("I"), floating on a vast ocean of inky black ("I's" pain—which also constitutes "I"). The imperative and the struggle to accept the pain as part of herself, rather than an alien imposition, consume her. A medicine bottle contains the words: "It's not my fault, after all. My body hurts." Outside the bottle, in white against black, the additional text: "It is my fault. I couldn't cope with it."

The narrator comes to an uneasy resolution: "I have good days and I have bad days." On this page she is split yet again, in two separate panels with facing profiles: One of them shows her with her eyes closed and monstrous bat-like shapes swirling around her; in the other she resembles a sphinx, eyes open, stars shining in the sky. Nikitina represents her divided self as Sirin and Alkonost, magical bird-women of Slavic mythology. In a later page she appears at an art gallery, hanging up pictures. The text declares, "Poor health doesn't mean I can't have work and goals." Crucially, Nikitina insists on personal health as a social concern, a shared interdependence. The narrator speaks with another woman; they discuss their dietary needs and phobias. "You don't have to give a reason, but don't stay quiet," the text says. "Don't just put up with it." The author here exhibits the other-orientation of what literary scholar Arthur Frank calls the "dyadic body," one

> immersed in a suffering that is both wholly individual—my pain is mine alone—but also shared: the ill person sees others around her, before and after her, who have gone through the same illness and suffered their own wholly particular pains. She sees others who are pained by her pain. Storytelling is one medium through which the dyadic body both offers its own pain and receives the reassurance that others recognize what afflicts it. Thus storytelling is a privileged medium of the dyadic body. (*Wounded*: 36)

In its conclusion, too, *Schism* powerfully rebukes subject–object distinctions, blurring the lines between health/illness, body/society, and joy/despair, in favor of a radical holism. Another page of white lettering on black pronounces: "Diseases don't make you better or worse. They don't give you any special rights. But they must be acknowledged, so you can live happily. / Dissociation does not help." The final two pages lend visual form to that argument. Nikitina displays her physique split into different framed portraits: an ear, an arm, a headless body, and so on—mirroring the "dismemberment" page layouts from before. Comics, like all media, chops women up into bite-size pieces, the page suggests. But a caption avers: "I am not a collection of diseases, I am not the parts of my body." The "transformative" concluding page shows her nude, all in one piece, with the picture frames behind her, empty. She holds the largest frame, the one that contained the headless body on the page before. The transition creates the effect that the woman has stepped out of the frame at the same time as she has gathered all her parts together. "I'm whole," she declares, looking straight at the reader.

Nikitina's *Schism* affirms that what needs "overcoming" is not disability, illness, or even pain—they are all manifestations of the organic self—but the restrictive, reductive frameworks in which bodies (in particular women's bodies) are often cast. Disablement stems from (internalized) social division, which sees only parts and not wholeness. *E pluribus unum*. In elaborating that thesis, the introspective author exploits an array of graphic narrative techniques that in their complexity and expression yield nothing to other media; the comics-skeptical Russian reader might even have to concede that other media would have trouble conveying the message so clearly and so movingly. For as comics scholar Bart Beaty notes, "The ability to move between representational and subjective modes . . . distinguishes the comics form from the traditions of portrait painting and situates the play of reality and subjectivity as central to the autobiography project" (*Unpopular*: 164).

Nikitina's startling work indeed belongs to a tradition of autobiographical graphic narrative that, in the words of Hillary Chute, "takes up the question of ethics in relation to notions of self-constitution in the face of trauma" (*Disaster*: 4). It exhibits what literary scholar G. Thomas Couser calls the "postcolonial impulse" of disability memoir to "define oneself in resistance to the dehumanizing categories of the medical and health-service institutions" (*Signifying*: 46)[29]—a characteristic of much Graphic Medicine as well.

Yana Smetanina's *The Residents of Psychiatric Hospital No. 5 in Kot'kovo* (2013), a series of nonfiction graphic works, shares that will to expose the hid-

---

29. Couser elaborates further: "Autobiography . . . can be an especially powerful medium in which disabled people can demonstrate that they *have* lives, in defiance of others' commonsense perceptions of them. Indeed, disability autobiography may be regarded and taught as a postcolonial, even an anticolonial, phenomenon, a form of autoethnography" ("Disability": 605).

den corners of suffering in which too many disabled people still languish. Displayed at the second Feminist Pencil exhibit in Moscow in fall 2013[30] (under the auspices of the Second International Media Strike Festival of Activist Art), the simple black and white portraits with accompanying biographical text show women shivering, mumbling, staring vacantly into space. In one, a middle-aged patient, "Tan'ka from Khimki, 53," haughtily looks on, a cigarette dangling from her mouth. The text explains, in part: "When she swears her speech becomes articulate. Such gestures, as if she'd been in prison for 70 years. / But she has a Moscow State University education. She was brutally raped for the first time at 7. Repeatedly as an adult." As Smetanina explained in her artist statement, "Almost all of these women were rape victims and precisely because of that they'd either lost their minds or depleted their strength and will to live" (quoted in Lomasko, "Viktoriia").

Wrenching and provocative, these drawings contrast sharply with the long tradition of dehumanizing the disabled in portraiture. For example, Dziga Vertov's early Soviet depiction of patients at a mental institution, in his series of documentary film shorts *Kino-Glaz* (1924), represented them mostly for purposes of mockery. Smetanina's portraits seek to connect the reader with the lived reality of her traumatized subjects, and by extension with the reality of the abuse of countless women in Russia.

Two 2010s works in particular centered a sustained engagement with themes of disability justice, in ways we can truly call unprecedented in Russian comics. In the next sections, we turn to them.

"No One Cares about People Like Me"

The Izhevsk artist Tatyana Faskhutdinova's collaborative twenty-one-page biography "Unknown Stories From the Life of Lyonya Rodin," part of the first Feminist Pencil exhibit in 2012,[31] presents itself as accessible to younger readers through its youthful idiom and subject matter—but most of all, through its unflinching directness. The titular Rodin, a twenty-four-year-old friend of Faskhutdinova's, is a man who uses a wheelchair—in a city designed with something other than him in mind. But Rodin, in his first-person narrative, must deal with more than the familiar ramps to nowhere, broken lifts, inaccessible trams, hard-to-navigate sidewalks, and the threat of homelessness. The

---

30. Curated by art historian Nadezhda Plungian and graphic reporter and comics artist Viktoria Lomasko.

31. Curated by Lomasko.

prejudice, ignorance, and gawking stares of ordinary citizens take if anything a greater toll on his psyche. Faskhutdinova's artist statement read, in part:

> Lyonya Rodin is my friend. He's disabled from birth. . . . I wanted to tell not so much about the absurd situations that drive you mad, that happen to him over and over again, because of people's indifference, because of society's ill-preparedness and unwillingness to take the disabled into account, as much as about his ability to have a social life, to dream, to make plans and carry them out, his passion for work, about the complete absence of anger over his fate, about his inner calm and pride, despite the severity and even cruelty of his circumstances. (Lomasko, "Viktoriia")

One of those "absurd situations" involves a hysterical landlady who stares aghast at Rodin in his wheelchair when he comes to inquire about a rental. "How much are you renting out the apartment for?" he asks. "Aaa! He can even talk, too!" she yells, hands to her face. "People often take me for an extra-terrestrial," Rodin wryly comments in the accompanying text. On the next page, the young man confronts the depressingly common impediment of inaccessible public transport. At the entrance to a tram car—one without a ramp or lift—Rodin can only sit in his chair. The tram driver scolds him through the window: "Hurry up and get on!" The text concludes: "In our town, no one cares about people like me. Here we don't have the right conditions for disabled people to get around" (n.p.).

Rodin's daily experiences confirm Hartblay's ethnographic observations that "a few exceptions aside, the infrastructure of outdoor public spaces does not meet the minimum standards of accessible design according to Russian law and international standards" ("Good": 6).[32] In language that sounds provocative given our present study, she elsewhere notes, "Russian infrastructure is caught in an overdetermined *caricature* as a bastion of 'bad' design, or bad implementation of 'good' design. This *caricature* is tied up in thick historical processes that link good design to governance, democracy, economic development, and modernity" ("Good": 3; my emphasis). (If so, we might say that the status of "Unknown Stories from the Life of Lyonya Rodin" as a comics work helps to convey all the better the sadistically *cartoonish* nature of disabled people's daily existence in Russia.)

But Faskhutdinova and Rodin's story does not dwell on such frustrations, which they portray with more than a tinge of black humor. Lyonya maintains

---

32. For more on the infelicities of Russian infrastructure vis-à-vis the disabled, see also Human Rights Watch, *Barriers*: 18.

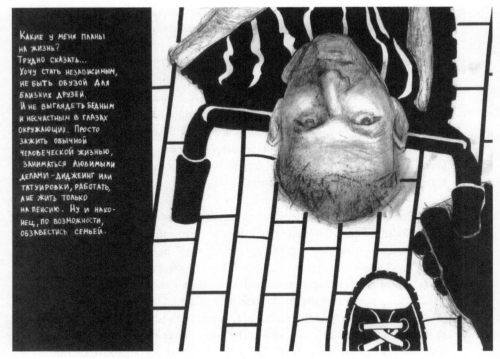

FIGURE 7.2. The conclusion to "Unknown Stories from the Life of Lyonya Rodin" by Tatyana Faskhutdinova and Leonid Rodin (2012)

a vibrant social circle as a DJ and a tattoo artist. He even engages in that classic young person's pursuit: annoying the neighbors with loud music. Rodin further shatters stereotypes about the "fragility" of disabled people with reckless and rowdy behavior. "My favorite extreme sport is going down the stairs," he explains. "Tons of adrenaline. I still don't know how I didn't bust my head." The accompanying drawing shows Rodin in his chair at the top of a creaky-looking set of stairs, about to launch himself. Here and throughout the piece, Faskhutdinova presents her subject's life in a series of expressionist drawings (ink for physical environment and bodies, soft pencil for faces and heads) that blend photorealism with the handmade aesthetic of woodcuts, creating an effect both intimate and disorienting.

The final panel depicts Rodin close on, in an upside-down portrait (see figure 7.2). We look down on him, from the point of view of someone pushing his wheelchair from behind, a hand on the grip and a sneaker visible. Rodin looks directly at the presumed able-bodied reader as he delivers his contemplative monologue:

What plans do I have for my life? Hard to say . . . I want to become independent, not be a burden to my close friends. And not look poor and unfortunate to those around me. I just want to start living a normal person's life, do the things I like: DJ-ing, or tattooing, work instead of living on a pension. And, well, finally, ideally, start a family.

That last remark especially would shock and scandalize large segments of contemporary Russian society, which continues to routinely infantilize the disabled (as the media portrayals of the Vodyanova and Kazanova scandals suggest). That people in wheelchairs would have sex lives, much less procreate, for many remains a taboo notion. Rodin's penetrating gaze, straight on, thus reads as an indictment of how modern Russia forecloses the human potential of its millions of disabled citizens.

As a "postcolonial" testimony (in Couser's terms), "Unknown Stories from the Life of Lyonya Rodin" limns an affirming, emancipatory image of its subject—a real-life version of Webik, minus the fancy car—without shying from a critique of ableist social conditions endemic to Russian culture. Rodin's personal is the political every disabled person must navigate as part of their daily routine. Faskhutdinova celebrates an unusual life—but also points fingers where they need to be pointed.

I Am an Elephant!

To a considerable extent, the foregoing serves as prologue to the first Russian graphic novel devoted to a disability theme, Vladimir Rudak and Lena Uzhinova's *I Am an Elephant!* (Boomkniga, 2017). Wheelchair user Rudak, a noted filmmaker, musician, playwright, and author from Petrozavodsk,[33] collaborated with Uzhinova, longtime comics artist and animator, based on their shared interest in narratives about disabled people.[34] The result, based on one

---

33. Rudak told me his band Kto Kak Mozhet ("Everyone for Himself," more or less) recorded its first album in 1997, though it took years of overcoming barriers (personal, physical, and cultural) before they performed live. He has published a novel, *Eternal Sugar* (*Vechniy Sakhar,* 2010) and a collection of short stories, *The Sole Arrow* (*Edinstvennaia Strela,* 2014), among other work. On his remarkable 2006 film *Tough Guys Don't Dance* (*Krutie ne tantsuyut*), a noir rap opera set in a world where almost everyone uses a wheelchair, see Alaniz, "Cinema." In full disclosure, I helped organize the Pacific Northwest premiere of Rudak's 2016 film *Pineapple* at the University of Washington. That same year he also worked with Cassandra Hartblay at the University of California at San Diego on a play devoted to the lives of disabled people in Petrozavodsk.

34. In 2015, Uzhinova published her minicomix *Miracle,* made up of one-page stories dealing with people who are either born with disabilities or who acquire them as a result of trauma,

of Rudak's unproduced semi-autobiographical plays, sets forth a meandering, often surreal series of first-person monologues detailing the journey of the paraplegic Anton, a young man paralyzed in an accident.

Anton's struggles to understand and accept his new identity, his family's search for various mystical cures, his depression and frustrations with the women he still longs for, his entertaining aperçus on life with a disability in contemporary Russia, and his interactions with other patients at his rehabilitation center comprise much of the content.[35] That description, however, elides a lot of what makes Rudak and Uzhinova's work remarkable as graphic narrative. For one thing, from the first panel the reader is made aware that she is watching a performance: Anton appears on stage, curtains parted, with the first row of the audience visible from behind as our protagonist addresses them (and us) (5). The self-consciously "theatrical" framing recalls both the pre-Soviet tradition of the lubok (see Alaniz, *Komiks*: 19–20, 84–85) and the rambling poetics of a long stand-up comedy show.

Most audaciously of all, for most of the novel our stand-up comic Anton materializes onstage in the doubled guise of (1) a full-grown elephant, loquacious and often obnoxious, and (2) a lifeless rag doll that the elephant manipulates with his trunk. The effect of all these devices feels like Nikitina's *Schism* (with its copious visual symbols of the war between spirit and flesh) crossed with a Penn and Teller routine.

For the most part, *I Am an Elephant!*'s reviewers took such cartoony hijinks in stride, possibly because Uzhinova's "cutesy" high-contrast black and white art—all curves, stage lighting, big eyes, and grand pachyderm emotions—looks well-suited for children. As a writer for *Regnum* noted, "[Rudak] presents himself to a drawn audience and to us the readers as an Elephant, kind and attentive, happy and sad, but in the main alive and very, very nimble" ("Slon"). Indeed, the elephant-Anton never seems to stand still: whether arguing over the phone with a food delivery service, dancing like a vaudevillian (with hat and cane), traversing a body of water on an ice floe, and so on. (A cliché of Marvel Bronze Age comics—"How can something so big move so fast?"—definitely applies to him.)

---

who nevertheless live full lives. As Uzhinova told me, "We need to talk about these things, because they happen, and nobody knows why. They're miracles." Uzhinova is also known as the award-winning animator of *Zhikharka* (2006). I discuss Uzhinova's graphic memoir *My Sex* in the conclusion to this study.

35. In some of its heteronormative male set pieces, *I Am an Elephant!* recalls dramatic films about paralyzed men, such as *The Waterdance* (directed by Neal Jimenez and Michael Steinberg, 1992) and *Born on the Fourth of July* (directed by Oliver Stone, 1989).

More commonly, though, reviewers responded to the novel's highly unusual tone: "not solemn/tragic, or heroic/heavy, as is the custom with conversations about disability, but lively, light, fusing together the comical and the sad into one whole" (Volkova, "Komiks"). Despite what the *Regnum* reviewer calls its irreverence and "ironic fashion" ("Slon"), *I Am an Elephant!* registered first and foremost as a socially activist work drawing attention to a marginalized community in a new way—through the "fun" medium of comics.

One reviewer responded in more personal terms. Maxim Trudov, writing for the online site *Comics Trade,* sneeringly derided the political correctness often invoked in discussions of historically oppressed groups:

> We can't say anything bad about the disabled, even if you're a famous journalist from Channel One. You can't doubt the talent of the disabled, and only heartless people can refuse to let them participate in music competitions. You can't laugh at disabled people if you yourself are not disabled—as the main character constantly reminds us. ("Nechestniy")

Those readers not driven away by such discourse soon come to see Trudov as a more complex figure—given that in the course of his review he comes out as a paraplegic wheelchair user himself, someone positioned to understand Rudak's perspective better than most. "Absolutely, we need to talk about the disabled in Russia—and preferably not in a romcom with a banal title," he insists, referencing the 2017 film *Love without Limits.* He concludes, "If you're looking for something in the style of *Epileptic* or *Persepolis,* only shorter and of domestic manufacture, don't miss the graphic novel *I Am an Elephant!* ("Nechestniy").

That endorsement by a disabled comics reader of Rudak and Uzhinova's work, placing it in the front ranks of global comics culture, was echoed by the attention it attracted in the mainstream press, unusual for a graphic novel. The good coverage led Boomkniga to offer a larger than normal print run (*Takie dela,* "V Sankt-Peterburge"). Still more rarely for Russian comics, the book was included in the 2017 White Ravens catalog, the Munich International Youth Library's list of works with special significance for young readers.

Not unlike Nikitina (who uses a lot less humor), *Elephant*'s authors initially delineate the disabled psyche's agon as a sharp dichotomy between mind and matter, often literally rendered in black and white hues. On a page divided equally between upper and lower halves, the elephant-Anton pushes the doll in a wheelchair forward to the reader (see figure 7.3). "A lot of time will pass before we once more become a unified whole," he says in the top panel, "and for now I cannot accept this motionless creature into my family." He continues

FIGURE 7.3. Elephant-Anton introduces his
body, signified by a passive rag doll

in the lower frame: "Let me introduce you. This is me. More accurately, this is my body." Everything about this page is designed to contrast the two panels: In the upper, we see the elephant's expressive face unimpeded as he speaks, while the doll with its empty "X" eyes—cartoon shorthand conventionally meaning "dead"—is cut off at the chest; in the lower, we have a full-body view of the doll, but can no longer see the elephant's face, only his trunk. Uzhinova's solid black background makes the white figures stand out, creating another strong contrast (26).

The dual-identity trope has a long tradition in comics (most famously in the superhero genre), but it has a disproportionate presence in graphic narrative about disability in which the subject strives to come to terms with a recalcitrant physiology. For example, the Canadian cartoonist Georgia Webber in her memoir *Dumb: Living without a Voice* (2018) resorts to a "doubled" avatar (one of them represented in red) to visually portray the experience of painfully losing the ability to speak. Such narratives, *I Am an Elephant!* more than most, tend to flirt with the notion of the stubbornly "flawed" body as subordinate to a transcendent soul, where the "true" I resides—a juxtaposition that risks rendering the disabled experience as a fundamentally split identity, a sort of severe body dysmorphia—before reconstituting body and mind into an integral identity by work's end.

The mind/body hierarchy stands out in moments when elephant-Anton crudely tosses about doll-Anton with his trunk, holding it upside down and sticking it with catheters in a hospital bed (52), propping it up next to another doll in women's clothing (55), placing it on a child's duck ride toy (80), and dancing with it in a symbol of reintegration (102 and the cover), to name but a few instances. And of course, the elephant gets all the lines. It's as if Rudak and Uzhinova agree with Herr Settembrini in Thomas Mann's *The Magic Mountain* (1927), when he tells Hans Castorp and his cousin: "A human being who is first of all an invalid is *all* body; therein lies his inhumanity and his debasement. In most cases he is little better than a carcass" (100).

In this sense, we might think of the elephant as a quasi-superheroic figure whose dynamic and wide-ranging (read: "fun") antics are enhanced by the supremely passive inertness of the "alter ego" doll. In other words, our "nimble" pachyderm hero functions as a walking, talking *disavowal* of the vulnerable, disabled body. The elephant himself speaks of it in something like these terms, when he tells the doll: "Remember, they only think you're a hero because you haven't swallowed a mess of pills out of despair. An elephant has thick skin. This is symbolic. A crippled person needs to have a thick mental skin" (93).

As Rudak told an interviewer:

Lena made the book's protagonist an elephant, but this is of course an allegory. The elephant is a recurring image in my work. Every person has an injury of some sort, especially those who have met with a disability. The first years go just towards accepting yourself, and during this time you can't escape from the division of the world into an inner part, that's stayed the same as before, and an external part, with a bunch of limitations. So that you won't lose your self-control and not get overly affected by the carelessly spoken words of others, you need a thick mental skin—your own kind of elephant costume, to protect you from post-traumatic stress. (*Takie dela*, "V Sankt-Peterburge")[36]

I would add that the elephant "costume"—conceived by Uzhinova after reading Rudak's script—not only literalizes the metaphor of "thick skin"; it also compels the reader to acknowledge disabling environments and inaccessible venues. After all, how easy would it be for a full-sized elephant to go through a human-sized door? As I've argued previously, the unconventional "super body" (a category in which our elephant falls) prompts a rethinking of normal public spaces and their presumptions about which bodies inhabit them.[37]

In any case, if Anton-elephant is a kind of superhero, and Anton-doll his alter ego, we soon see a four-panel "origin story" set at the hospital on the day of his accident. In a scene familiar from many Graphic Medicine narratives, a doctor coldly explains the hopelessness of the case to Anton's mother. The doll lies on a bed, as if thrown there. Textboxes read:

The doctor showed my mother the pictures, which she didn't understand at all.

He held up the negative before him at arm's length, accompanying it with commentary adapted for people without medical training. She nodded, holding back tears, digesting with difficulty everything that was going on.

Fracture of the spine.

I thought this wasn't any more serious than a fracture of a hand or a foot. It would heal. (27)

That first reaction—flat-out denial of the new disabled identity—resonates too with the memoir literature of those with mobility impairments brought on by accidents or illness later in life. Simi Linton, for example, writes:

I have become a disabled woman over time. I certainly would have rejected such a title in the beginning. It could precipitate my death. Consign me to an itty-bitty life. . . .

---

36. On the elephant avatar, Rudak elaborated to me, "The hard skin represents psychological defense, the fact that I have to be thick-skinned. Because certain phrases might hurt me, like 'Hey, look at that disabled guy.' I must not react, I must not let that into myself" (Rudak interview, 2017).

37. On the incompatibility of the "monstrous" superhero body with its urban surroundings, see Alaniz, *Death*: 89–91.

For me and other disabled people, the process of claiming disability as an identity and the disabled community as our own is complex. I crept toward it, then skittered away. I remained for a long time an eavesdropper, a peeper. (*My Body*: 107–108)

Terror over an "itty-bitty life" with no horizons as a result of disablement consumes most people in these circumstances. It is a stage one needs to traverse to adjust to the new reality, to the long period of rehabilitation, and everyone does it at their pace.[38] As Rudak told me:

People think that if they find themselves in such a situation, their lives have ended. That their active life will be over. There's no help, no rehab centers. That's what they think, that they won't have anything to do with other people ever again. They'll just rot at home, not going out. All society knows that. Me too. I came from that. . . .

The first time you see the hospital, you hate it. It's all so gloomy. But you get to like it, get used to it. You start joking around, you make friends. You come to realize that this is possible, like other things. Like your disability, it becomes a part of your life. (Rudak interview, 2017)

We see a negative example in the case of another patient whose story Anton recounts, a paralyzed man so convinced he would walk again that he even named a date on the calendar when it would happen: "He yelled out to the whole hospital courtyard that he would give away his wheelchair to whoever wanted it" (16). The date passed with no change in his condition.

Rudak and Uzhinova balance the black absurdism of such scenes with savage attacks on the able-bodied world's hypocrisies and presumptions about disabled people. They cast a particularly jaundiced eye on self-serving media stereotypes of the sort Iarskaya-Smirnova documented, dismantling the tropes of disability-themed movies such as *The Sea Inside* (*El Mar Adentro*, directed by Alejandro Amenábar, Spain, 2004):

The director will show the true power of the spirit trapped in an unmoving body.

So that the story will move the viewer, we need a particular set of devices: a mournful voiceover, sad music (preferably piano) and, of course, the object itself.

---

38. On disability brought on by accident as a life "not worth living," see Shapiro, *No Pity*: 260.

> Let's say a man in a wheelchair. His legs must be covered by a checkered
> lap blanket.
>
> After all, everybody believes that a paralyzed man's legs get cold. Not his
> soul, though. Or his heart. (33)

Other vignettes recall Faskhutdinova and Rodin's descriptions of the dread
and contempt inspired by disabled people simply being out and about in public. In a two-page sequence, elephant-Anton takes his dressed-up doll-self for
a stroll in a park on a sunny day. "They say that positive thoughts[39] make a
person's life more balanced," remarks the elephant, "so he should look only at
pleasant things, which will provoke no perturbations in the enlightened soul."
On the next page, a couple sit on a bench, their heads grotesquely turned away
180 degrees, to the sunset. "Some are afraid to look in my direction, lest they
draw misfortune to themselves," we are told. The couple then turns around to
see them, with a sour look on their faces: "All of a sudden our eyes will meet,
and my sickness will make the leap on over to them." The elephant concludes:
"Many people say, 'Oh, we're all vulnerable,' but they themselves don't really
believe that. They think they're the chosen ones, that they're special." In the
background, a man talking to a woman is about to unknowingly step in an
open manhole (108–109).

But the authors save their most virulent critiques for the popular notion
of the disabled's brave face before unimaginable misfortune—what Western
disability rights activists call "inspiration porn." As Anton-elephant explains:

> A millionaire wants to be loved for something other than his money, and a
> disabled person wants to be loved for something other than fake heroism
> made up by someone else.
>
> It's really dangerous if people start accusing you of heroism. Then they
> can treat you however they want.
>
> You'll put up with anything. After all, you're a hero. (52)

Quite a pointed rebuke to the "overcoming" narrative of González-
Gallego's *White on Black,* for whom the phrase "I am a hero" serves as a kind
of credo.

One last attribute of the elephant-Anton persona—another historically
associated with superheroism—bears mention: its unexamined portrait of
masculinity. As Iarskaya-Smirnova has argued, the intersectional psychody-

---

39. The elephant's decidedly post-Soviet phrase *pozitivnye mysli,* a calque from the English
"positive thoughts," implies a critique of neoliberalist can-do attitudes. I thank Miroljub Ruzić
for this insight.

namics of the disabled Russian male can lead to identity crises over not "measuring up" to a "real man" ideal:

> The social definition of masculinity showers praise on strength and invincibility, an idealized physique and youth, while perceiving bodily functions in and of themselves as something self-evident. A disabled person finds it difficult to fulfill the norms and values corresponding with this definition, due to physical and social taboos which govern access to education, employment and institutions of power. A man resisting the stigma of disability can still achieve the expected status which will be associated with empowered social roles and gain recognition in the public sphere, but all the same his masculine identity will deviate from the stereotypical. The construction of manliness [*muzhestvennost'*] in the context of disability goes beyond medical frameworks and recognizes social restrictions as a basis for the difference experienced in daily life as a consequence of marginalization and social exclusion. The gender identity of the disabled in Russia, on the one hand, in large measure takes on the form of those restrictive social institutions in which men and women find themselves—but on the other hand, through personal emancipation and collective participation, there takes place a transformation of society's negative view of disability. (*Odezhda*: 173)

While Rudak and Uzhinova's graphic novel indeed contributes to a rethinking of Russian society's "negative view of disability" (as indicated by its reviews and press coverage), it does almost nothing to encourage a reassessment of hegemonic models of Russian masculinity. In this respect, *I Am an Elephant!* is not much of an improvement over Maresyev's testosterone-driven portrait in *Story of a Real Man*. (Come to think of it, Lyonya Rodin's macho "extreme sports" posturing might fall into this trap, too.) The problem, as I've written previously in regard to film representations of disabled masculinity, is that the onus of "proving" one's male bona fides despite physical impairment too often means ignoring a lot of baggage, that is, leaving unquestioned the problematic fundaments of what, after all, being "a real man" has often meant.[40] Masculinity too easily blurs into toxic masculinity. This in mind, I find it hard not to see the elephant/doll split in gendered terms: abusive, logocentric "masculine" elephant victimizing passive, "feminized" silent doll.[41]

---

40. See my comments on *Murderball* (directed by Dana Shapiro and Henry Alex Rubin, 2007) in Alaniz, "Cinema."

41. Paul McIlvenny's description of Al Davison's self-representation in his graphic memoir *The Spiral Cage*, on living with spina bifida, seems all too relevant to *I Am an Elephant!*: "In citing himself in relation to his impairment and normative notions of the masculine body,

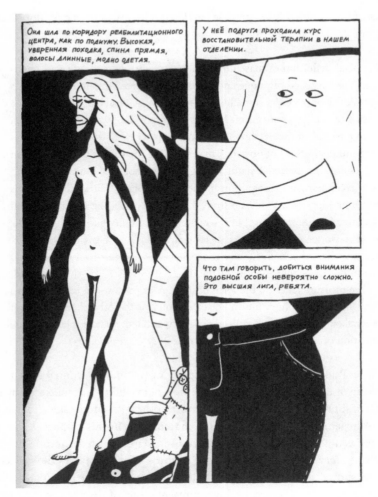

FIGURE 7.4. Faina makes her entrance

Perhaps the novel's greatest pitfall in this regard is its sexism. Faina, a young woman with whom Anton grows infatuated (she sometimes comes to the rehab center; they also talk regularly on the phone), comes off as a man's egregious caricature of femininity: talkative, unstable, and self-obsessed. One reviewer described her as a "spectacular hysteric" who "carries on a non-stop

---

Davison often resists the cultural inscription of his body as the masculine 'feminine.' He refuses to be still, to be inactive, to lack mobility, to be confined by so-called aids to mobility, and so he may be accused too easily of conforming to hegemonic norms of masculine conduct" ("Disabled": 119).

stream of utter nonsense" (Bondareva, "Kogda"). In her physical character-istics, Faina resembles something a couple of notches above a sex doll, with swollen lips and long eyelashes. When she first appears, a dramatic spotlight shining down on her, the textbox excitedly reads: "She walked along the cor-ridor of the rehabilitation center, like on a catwalk. Tall, with a confident gait, her back straight, hair long, dressed to the nines" (see figure 7.4). Despite the description of her wearing clothes, Faina looks like a naked Barbie doll in her separate vertical panel, which reaches from top to bottom of the page. Another panel shows a close-up of her hip and thigh in skin-tight jeans, as the elephant further remarks that she belongs to an out-of-reach "higher league." This page as a whole enacts a disconcerting objectification: The elephant's trunk extends from its own right-hand panel across the gutter into Faina's panel, swaying, seeming to block the doll from accessing her body. The elephant's tusks, as well as the doll's stubby limbs, all look suggestively erect. (The doll, it must be said, never looks more active and "aroused" than here [39].)

This brief excursus into *I Am an Elephant!*—a groundbreaking work that merits much more thorough investigation than I've given it here—opens up what I hope is a productive line of questioning into its virtues and shortfalls as a graphic narrative depiction of disability in Russia.

IN THEIR COMICS, the Bubble studio, Tatyana Faskhutdinova, Lyonya Rodin, Yulia Nikitina, Vladimir Rudak, Lena Uzhinova, and other artists represent-ing the contemporary Russian experience of disability prominently show the distance covered by both graphic narrative and people with disabilities in the post-Soviet era. Younger komiksisty in part inspired by their work, such as Anna Baturina, Vitaly Lazarenko, and Andrei Chapygin,[42] continue that mis-sion, while acknowledging how far the disabled in Russia still have to go.

A scene late in *I Am an Elephant!* encapsulates that dual sense of hope and open-endedness. We see Anton, no longer bifurcated into elephant and doll, his identity fully integrated now as simply a human being in a wheelchair. He explains to the reader that, while his mother is still pursuing mystical cures for his paraplegia, this time in far-off Buryatia, he himself "[doesn't] want to go anywhere." The next panel, taking up the bottom half of the page, shows Anton sitting in his chair, looking out a window. The window itself is mostly a blank white slate, standing out against the solid black wall, a sort of negative image of Malevich's *Black Square*. That emptiness represents potential, end-

---

42. They published stories on the blind (Baturina) and a man in a coma (Lazarenko and Chapygin) in the Space Cow Comix anthology *Black Milk*.

less vistas—a canvas upon which to write one's destiny. The flame motif on the wheel of Anton's chair (similar to a design on Rudak's own chair) hints at movement, daring, adventure—at some point (129).

But for now, Anton is content to sit and contemplate whatever he gazes at outside his room. We don't see his face, so that Uzhinova could in fact be representing not the narrator but all disabled men (people?), including the young man from earlier who refused to admit he had permanently lost the use of his legs. We can read the image as an all-encompassing vision of disability liberation and empowerment. Ditto Anton's narration: "I understood that I'm healthy. Even in my dreams I don't walk anymore . . ." (129).

For me, the scene brings to mind two remarks, both by Russian disabled men.

The first comes from Rudak, who in our interview told me about his first independent metro ride with other wheelchair users, fellow patients at his Moscow rehabilitation center, in the mid-1990s. They went to Sparrow Hills, a nice place to get an overlook of the city. After the long rehab following his accident, it felt like a liberation. The awe still in his voice, Rudak said that on that day, "it was like curtains had parted on a window, and I could make out the sea beyond it" (Rudak interview, 2017).

The second remark comes from the St. Petersburg disability rights activist Yury Kuznetsov, who in 2000 told a reporter: "Having now lived independently a long time, with no one watching over me, I can say that there's nothing harder than to be free. Freedom is responsibility for every act that you yourself carry out. And you yourself answer for their consequences" (My, "Chetyre": 33).

CONCLUSION

The Nonfiction Turn

Let us sum up: Upon their rocky origins in the tumultuous 1990s, post-Soviet Russian comics contended with a shattered economy, domination of the market by foreign brands, and deep public disdain for the form as inherently frivolous and subliterate. Despite some remarkable masterpieces, much of the material produced in the Yeltsin era—in such genres as science fiction, adventure, and humor—proved of such shoddy quality as to confirm Russian preconceptions of comics as trash. In any case, too few people bought it to sustain an industry. That began to change with the rise of internet culture in the mid-to-late 1990s, bringing with it new avenues for community-building and dissemination of works, as well as the first major comics festivals, KomMissia and Boomfest. These put *komiks* on the Russian cultural map as never before,[1] preparing the soil for the important breakthroughs of the late 2000s and early 2010s: the manga boom, translations of US and Western classics (like *Maus*), the launch of Bubble. Readers started paying attention.

---

1. As Alexander Kunin told an interviewer in 2014: "Comics in Russia were in a marginal position for a long time. Before we couldn't break through anywhere with them, everything was done on pure enthusiasm. Khikhus proved that comics are an art form. In the first years of [the KomMissia festival's] existence, it was precisely on this that they laid the stress" (Panfilov, "My").

No less a cultural barometer than the hallowed literary and arts journal *Oktyabr*[2] declared in 2014:

> The main breakthrough is happening just now—the formation of a large readership interested in the development of Russian comics.
>
> In point of fact, it is time to moderate our imperial snobbism. So what if we were raised on Chekhov, Gogol and Dostoevsky (and by the way, there also exist comics about the latter), this doesn't at all mean that we need to reject a less traditional art. Modern comics, after all, were long ago put on equal footing with literature and film in Europe, America and Japan. In this light, it wouldn't hurt Russian writers to experiment a bit and master another mode of expression, while it wouldn't hurt Russian readers to finally put Proust, Dostoevsky, Hérge and *Persepolis* on one shelf. (Bondareva, "Komiks")

That cheery picture of Russian and French *belles lettres* making shelf space for comics (as was actually happening in bookshops) would strike some literary purists as heretical ("*Persepolis*?!"), while it made others feel liberated, modern, connected at last to a vibrant global culture. By mid-decade that Western-style acceptance of graphic narrative as a legitimate art form—however begrudging in some quarters—was already bearing fruit with the rise of a new comics genre, one directly tied to the fraught question of contemporary Russians' grappling with history and, well, *reality*.

The Smithereens of Meaning

In the words of Seth Graham, "The Yeltsin and Putin eras were both characterized by attempts to locate, gather, and find new uses for the smithereens into which virtually all categories of meaning had been smashed during the collapse of the Second World" ("Two"). In these attempts, the country's long and anguished history was press-ganged, especially by Putin, to serve the current grand narrative vision of a great Russian state.

We see a dramatic and disturbing recent example in the "Russia—My History" project, a network of state-sponsored multimedia theme parks that present an "official" version of the past, from the foundational Kievan Rus period to the post-Soviet era. With parks in over twenty Russian cities, the project

---

2. *Oktyabr'* (*October*) was founded in 1924 by the Moscow Association of Proletarian Writers (MAPP). In the post-Soviet era it had a liberal slant.

grew quickly from its immediate origins in the November 2013 exhibition "The Romanovs," at the Manezh in Moscow.

The version of history on view in these venues—whether the 1917 revolutions, World War II, the Stalin or other eras—betrays the deep involvement of the Russian Orthodox Church. (In fact, one of its primary organizers and conceptualists is Metropolitan Tikhon, a church bishop, writer, and rumored personal confessor to Putin.) As a result, and as discussed by sociologist Ekaterina Klimenko, the experience of visiting these exhibitions resembles a single-track train journey—with little opportunity to deviate from a set route:

> Composed of halls, which, much like in a palace *enfilade*, flow from one into another, [they create] a space-time of Russian history: advancing along the corridor-shaped space of [the] park exhibitions, a visitor travels through time, from ancient Rus' to contemporary Russia. Importantly, visitors' progress through the exhibitions of the historical parks is heavily predetermined by the latter's spatial constitution. Having little freedom in choosing either which of the exhibition halls to view and which to miss out, or in what sequence to observe the halls of any of the four exhibitions, a visitor, thus, follows the path set out by the historical parks' creators. As she does so, the history of the Russian state and that of the Orthodox Church unfold before her eyes: the two are represented in the parks as indissolubly intertwined. ("Building": 5)

This attempt to meld secular and religious understandings of Russian history—sort of a live version of *Russian Ark*, Alexander Sokurov's 2002 single-take journey through a ghost-filled Hermitage Museum—predictably leads to some rather severe contradictions, says Klimenko: "In the historical parks, the Russian Revolutions are cursed, while the USSR, the state that emerged in their aftermath, is glorified" ("Building," 6).[3] Such oddities became a staple of the Putin era's "history wars" between the state and academics (as brought up in my discussion of the 2019 "Medinsky vs. comics" case), a disturbing trend on the road to full-blown autocracy—a road Russia has traveled before. The "Russia—My History" project would seem a validation of two writers' *aperçus*, one Russian ("Nothing in the world ever ends"),[4] one not ("The past is never dead. It's not even past").[5] Thus, to have purchase on some sort of viable,

---

3. A global TV audience saw a similarly strange mash-up of history and wishful thinking during the 2014 Sochi Olympics opening ceremony.

4. Dostoevsky, *Demons*: 292. The line is echoed in, of all places, Alan Moore and Dave Gibbons's superhero series *Watchmen*: "*Nothing* ends, Adrian. Nothing *ever* ends" (409).

5. Faulkner, *Requiem*: 73.

egalitarian future, the country has more need now than ever of alternative voices, voices spanning the society, voices in schools and halls of power, in the streets and performance stages and museums, voices on the written page, online and off.

In this book I have cast a wide net, to give the reader as varied and rich a portrait as possible of the contemporary Russian comics scene, because diversity is strength. That sentiment prompts me, in the closing pages that follow, to posit *komiks* too as one of those vital alternate voices speaking truths to power today. For, parallel with Putin's increasingly vise-like grip on the nation, there arose something else: a new industry and culture devoted to graphic narrative as a profitable business and bona fide art form. Better to say *rose from the ashes,* especially the ashes of the 1990s' failures in this direction, but fed too by that era's crucial breakthroughs. More than that: I call this book *Resurrection: Comics in Post-Soviet Russia* because what we see today is in many ways old vodka in shiny new bottles. I need not reargue the case from my first book; it is in any case no longer controversial to claim that throughout its history (including the Soviet era), Russia created and consumed graphic narrative in many different forms.

Let us now turn to one of the most recent and groundbreaking of those shiny new bottles—indeed a promising vehicle for said alternative voices— what I call Russian comics' Nonfiction Turn. In this movement, the subject's engagement with history and identity—whether personal, national, or both— powerfully asserts itself, first and foremost to "find new uses for the smithereens" of post-Soviet meaning.

The Nonfiction Turn

Partly as a reaction to Putinism, especially of the third-term strain, a wave of "serious"[6] nonfiction graphic narrative got underway by 2013. It would crest

---

6. "Serious" in more ways than one. In a case of what we might call accidental nonfiction comics, a 2015 Sergei Elkin cartoon shows two police officers, an official in a black suit, a woman with a briefcase (perhaps representing child protective services), and a dog at the door of an apartment. One of the officers bangs on the door, yelling, "Sidorov family, open up! The authorities got word that you haven't turned on your TV in a long time!" A 2019 news report detailed the trials of a real-life Sidorov in Samara province, a father of three boys whose neighbors denounced him to the authorities because Sidorov did not own a television. The neighbors felt Sidorov's sons were being deprived of popular culture, like the classic Soviet children's series *Cheburashka.* Also, one of the sons had taken up crocheting, which the neighbors considered a "non-traditional orientation" for a boy. The report noted the similarities to Elkin's four-year-old cartoon (Koroleva, "V samarskoi").

later in the decade, as Putin remained entrenched, authoritarianism grew, and political options narrowed. These works, by veterans and newcomers, in many cases represented a leap forward in length, sophistication, and maturity for Russian comics, just as they were finally attaining the critical and popular respect long afforded comic art in other countries.

Nina Mickwitz, in her *Documentary Comics: Truth-Telling in a Skeptical Age,* persuasively argues for folding comics autobiography, journalism, travelogues, memoir, biography, and related nonfiction works of the last fifty years into an overarching conceptual framework, namely "a mode of address through which audiences and readers are invited to accept that the persons, events, and encounters signified are actual rather than imagined" (7). She elaborates: "At stake, overall, is the undertaking of narrating and visually representing events, persons, and experiences of the actual and sociohistorical world, within the affordances and limitations of given forms and media" (159), in this case graphic narrative.[7] These are comics, as Joseph Witek expostulated as far back as the 1980s, which through various means advance a "claim of truth" (*Comic Books*: 11).

Not that any such claims need be honored. In fact, as discussed by such scholars as Charles Hatfield, Bart Beaty, Michael Chaney, Hillary Chute, Benjamin Woo, and others, "fact-based" comics of whatever sort, through their very status *as* comics, trouble the notion of a "direct" and "straightforward" depiction of some stable "real." Jared Gardner stated the case better than most:

> The comics form necessarily and inevitably calls attention through its formal properties to its limitations as juridical evidence—to the compressions and gaps of its narrative (represented graphically by the gutterspace between the panels) and to the iconic distillations of its art. The kinds of truth claims that are fought over in the courts of law and public opinion with text-based autobiography are never exactly at issue in graphic autobiography. The losses and glosses of memory and subjectivity are foregrounded in graphic memoir in a way they never can be in traditional autobiography. (Gardner, "Autobiography's": 6)

Note, as Gardner and others contend, that comics' foregrounding of these "losses and glosses of memory and subjectivity" paradoxically redound to the enhanced sophistication of the reading experience and readerly engagement with the real-life subjects depicted; graphic narrative's very artificiality as a visual–verbal medium, its patent constructedness, vouchsafes a form of truth-

---

7. In her book, Mickwitz applies concepts from documentary cinema, among other fields.

telling. In other words, nonfiction comics may be as "truthy" (in the Colbertian sense) as they are "true," but by making their fakeness more explicit than other media (you kinda can't miss it), they offer a form of reassurance, of transparent "honesty." We arrive at a highly subjective and skewed view of the world inflected through a unique artistic consciousness(es)—and all the more "reliable" for that. (It is folly, by the way, to try to avoid scare quotes when dealing with these matters.)[8]

Such an understanding obtains whenever comics grapples with the "real" (those scare quotes again), as it does in autographics, which "generally invite us to theorize subjectivity, genre and the reader's engagement with the autobiographical in new terms," going so far as to "undermin[e] the authority and integrity of autobiography's traditional humanist subject: the autonomous individual and universalizing life story that became definitive for life writing in the West" (Whitlock, "Autographics": 232–233). Relatedly, I wish to emphasize how nonfiction graphic narrative often blurs genres and approaches in its aesthetic tussles with the recalcitrant "facts of the matter." As Kent Worcester expounds about comics journalism: "Significant contributions to the genre have a pronounced autobiographical component, and political concerns are rarely if ever far from the surface, even when they are refracted through the lens of individual experience" (Worcester, "Journalistic": 143).[9]

Lastly, we should take one more thing into account. Despite the slipperiness of any notion of truth, the gravitational pull of Philip Lejeune's "autobiographical contract" (however discredited) will tend to hold sway. Even the most gap-filled and self-sabotaging nonfiction work will still convey some sense of artistic unity and (it bears repeating) truthiness—its aura of the real, so to speak. As Elisabeth El Refaie puts it, "The powerful cultural conventions governing the construction and interpretation of works labeled as autobiographical will nevertheless lead many authors to aspire to—and their readers to expect—some kind of a special relationship between a narrative and the life it purports to represent." This "special relationship" she calls "performed authenticity" (137).[10]

---

8. Hillary Chute argues: "An awareness of the limits of representation . . . is integrated into comics through its framed, self-conscious, bimodal form; yet it is precisely in its insistent, affective, urgent visualizing of historical circumstance that comics aspires to ethical engagement" ("Comics": 457). See also Charles Hatfield's discussion of autobio comics avatars in *Alternative*: chapter 4.

9. See also Benjamin Woo's excellent discussion of comics journalism, Joe Sacco, and Walter Benjamin's "storyteller" in "Reconsidering."

10. I'm reminded of nothing so much as the old George Burns quip: "Sincerity—if you can fake that, you've got it made." (The sentiment apparently dates back at least as far as the French writer Jean Giraudoux.) Less cynically, we may point to Lynda Barry's useful neologism,

In any case, said features of nonfiction comics—its truth-telling claims, artfully presented—played an indispensable role in graphic narrative's late-twentieth-century mainstream acceptance as a medium capable of tackling "weighty" subjects. To take nothing away from the important breakthroughs of Chris Ware's made-up *Jimmy Corrigan, the Smartest Kid on Earth* (2000) or Alan Moore and Dave Gibbons's *Watchmen* (1986), it is nonfiction that has received the lion's share of readerly and critical attention and accolades, and proved the most influential—especially outside the world of fan-driven genre series.[11] I speak of course of such canonical and lauded works as those by Justin Green (especially his galvanizing 1972 *Binky Brown Meets the Holy Virgin Mary*), Art Spiegelman, Robert Crumb, Keiji Nakazawa, Aline Kominsky-Crumb, Jack Jackson, Harvey Pekar, Phoebe Gloeckner, Lynda Barry, Marjanne Satrapi, David B., Dominique Goblet, Fabrice Neaud, Joe Sacco, Alison Bechdel, Ariel Schrag, and innumerable others.[12] To be taken seriously, the market decided, you gotta get real.

It makes perfect sense, then, that in its long quest for cultural relevance, Russia's prodigal medium of comics would sooner or later turn to nonfiction as an authorizing mode, a way of reassuring the reader, "our voice speaks truths too."[13] As catalogued in my previous book, post-Soviet comics artists had a long tradition of reality-based and reality-adjacent image-texts to draw from: hagiographic and historical icons; the *lubok* (woodblock prints); propaganda posters; *diafilmy* (film strips); and cartoons, among other materials.[14]

"Reality," one could argue, mattered now more than ever in post-Soviet Russia, under Putinism's relentless assaults on it and creation of weaponized alternatives to it in ways that strongly recall the Soviet experiment (as reported in Peter Pomerantsev's *Nothing Is True and Everything Is Possible: The Surreal*

"autobiofictionalography." See also Kate Polak's arguments on "historio-metagraphics" shaping graphic narratives' reality effect (*Ethics*: 28). For her part, comics artist Ariel Schrag calls her autobiographical work an exercise in *"visualizing memory"* (quoted in Whitlock, "Autographics": 234).

11. On the influence, prestige, and value (i.e., symbolic capital) of comics, see Beaty and Woo's *Greatest Comic Book*.

12. On nonfiction and history comics of an earlier era, see Witek, *Comic Books*: chapter 1.

13. We may make an instructive comparison with the Czech comics boom of 2003 and after, which leveraged that country's literary tradition and history to "sell" graphic narrative as worthy fare to readers. See Alaniz, "History."

14. A short list would include Eufrosinia Kersnovskaya's (1908–1994) verbal–visual memoir of her ten-year ordeal in the Norilsk labor camp. Excerpts circulated in samizdat in the 1980s and appeared in 1990 in *Ogonyok* and *Znamia*, and were published as a whole in 2000 and 2001 as *How Much Is a Human Being Worth?* (*Skol'ko stoit chelovek?*). See also the work of Danzig Baldaev (1925–2005), the son of an "enemy of the people," who worked as a Soviet prison official. His sadistic secret drawings of prison life, published in 2009, paint a surreal and disturbing picture.

Heart of the New Russia, among other sources).[15] Artists' responses ranged from author Lyudmilla Ulitskaya's unflinching historical novels to Svetlana Alexievich's people's testimonials, from director Andrei Zvyagintsev's exploration of neoliberal Russia's moral failings to documentarians like Sergei Loznitsa and Marina Razbezhkina's "hunt for reality,"[16] to the street art of Pavel P183.

By the second decade of the twenty-first century, the social and market conditions in Russia had emerged for nonfiction comics to join the conversation.[17] Some even demanded that it do so. In 2017, comics scholar Alexei Pavlovsky cast down the gauntlet:

> I have a rhetorical question for Russian comics authors: why up to now have you not written one graphic novel about the Leningrad siege? Why is there still no contemporary comics work about what happened in the gulag? If you lived in and grew up in the 1990s, why have only [Olga] Lavrenteva in *ShUV,* [Vitaly] Terletsky in *Products 24* and [Yulia] Nikitina in *Land of Midnight* written about it articulately? . . .
>
> [We need] to write at last about life in Russia, its history and fundamental problems . . .
>
> You want to be timely? Draw something about Crimea, about Syria or the Donbass, just don't do it crudely [*poshlo*]. (Bondareva, "Chto")

Post-Soviet Nonfiction Russian Comics

As it happened, within two years of Pavlovsky's utterance important comics works about both the WWII-era siege of Leningrad and the horrors of the concentration camps did appear (discussed below).[18] As in the West, though, there emerged no one overarching term under which one could subsume the

---

15. If not even earlier; see Mikhail Epstein's comments on early modern Potemkin villages and post-Soviet Russian attitudes to reality and the *"prezentatsiya"* ("Origins").

16. As Razbezhkina terms the practice. In 2011, she and Mikhail Ugarov founded the School of Documentary Film and Theater, which teaches minimally interventionist methods resembling those of the Direct Cinema movement. See Kostina, "Hunting."

17. The 2011 Boomkniga publication of David B.'s *Epileptic* in Russian translation has the distinction of being the first major nonfiction comics work to enter the Russian market. See my introduction for a discussion of the Russian translation of Spiegelman's *Maus* (2013) and its reception.

18. As for comics about Crimea, the Donbass, and other matters related to the ongoing Ukraine crisis, Ukrainian artists were handling that well. See Alaniz, "Igor." Western comics artists had preceded Russians in the representation of such material; these included Chantal Montelier's *Tchernobyl Mon Amour* (2006), Igort's *The Ukrainian and Russian Notebooks* (2016), and

different kinds of graphic narrative based on real-life subjects; "social activist comics" (*sotsial'ny komiks*) caught on perhaps better than most. Kunin dates the movement to 2010, when "a series of projects appears, whose authors consciously chose precisely this theme and made it one of their professional orientations" (Evtushenko, "Seks").[19]

KOM veteran Alexei Iorsh deserves special mention in this regard. His socially and historically engaged comics practice has comprised the history of skinheads (2011; see Alaniz, "Flashy"); a short graphic biography of the Jewish child violinist slain by the Nazis, Abram "Musya" Pinkenzon (2010); and an account of art activism in comics (2013).[20]

Before that, individual artists and works going back to the early 1990s had touched on nonfiction themes, though the state of the market and distribution system made any sustained movement impossible. Among these I would include Yury Kamenetsky, Ezhen Shchedrin, and Askold Akishin's *Georgy Zhukov* (1991, Progress) a graphic biography of the famous Red Army Marshal; the series *Red Blood* (1992–1995, Veles), based in part on the experiences of an Afghanistan War veteran (see Alaniz, "Fragging"); Lena Uzhinova's 1999 short autobiographical piece "Story about My Eye" (Pro glaz, see my *Komiks*: chapter 8); the hagiographic 2006 biography of Alexei Maresyev, *Story of a Real Man* (see chapter 7); and short pieces published in the KomMissia and Boomfest catalogs.

No figure broke more ground than Nikolai Maslov, with his unvarnished, autobiographical *Siberia* (2006), which deals with his late-Soviet clinical depression, army service, the suicide of a brother, and other somber topics. Tragically, Maslov's influence was muted by the fact that he could only publish his work abroad,[21] and by the resistance to his then-unconventional vision within the Russian comics community at the time (see Alaniz, *Komiks*: chapter 7). Even today many younger fans and comics artists have not heard of him, nor seem aware of the debt owed to the approach he pioneered in Russia (as discussed in chapter 4).

What a difference a few years makes. By 2019, Kunin could comfortably tell an interviewer:

> The main thing is factual material: family problems, the discrepancy between what we want and what we have, the social conflicts in society, political pres-

---

Joe Sacco's comics journalism pieces "What Refugees?" and "Chechen War, Chechen Women" (*Journalism*: 29–72).

19. KomMissia 2012 featured the exhibit "Comics about Life" (Ignatenko, "Khikhus").
20. Access the latter here: https://issuu.com/ekaterinanefedkina/docs/prrus.
21. For a discussion of Maslov's later work (published in France), see Alaniz, "Food."

sure on people, propaganda, material insecurity, the suppression of tragic episodes in our history . . . We have all of this in our lives. And that means that we'll find comics-makers who take it as their obligation to tell about these things, using their artistic toolkit. (Evtushenko, "Seks")

Kunin could in fact have made this declaration a decade earlier. The year 2011 proved pivotal for Russian nonfiction graphic narrative: The social tolerance project Respect launched, its aim to distribute comics booklets, many based on real subjects, to young people across the country, and Boomkniga released *Forbidden Art,* Anton Nikolaev and Viktoria Lomasko's graphic reportage of the trial of the decade (both discussed in Alaniz, "Flashy").

Over the course of the 2010s, Lomasko emerged as the most prominent proponent of serious, socially activist comics and reporting that combines text with illustration.[22] By the end of the decade she had become the most well-known, most-exhibited[23] Russian comics artist and muralist[24] abroad, with arts residencies and commissions in Germany, England, the US, and other countries. Lomasko's work appeared several times on the popular comics website *The Nib.*

In her 2017 collection, *Other Russias* (published first in English by N+1; still unpublished in Russia though available online), Lomasko combines text, illustration, comics, and book design for a multilayered portrait of a divided nation, especially of its marginalized groups. Based on reporting and interviews, chapters explore modern protest movements, like that of long-distance truckers, the LGBTQ+ community, the Pussy Riot trial, and the shameful reality of modern immigrant-slaves in Russia.

---

22. Though she often disavowed the title of komiksist, preferring to describe what she does as "graphic reportage." As Lomasko said in 2011:

> Today there's a new generation growing up that already understands the language of comics. But people my age and older don't understand that language very well. We find it easier to read a more traditional type of narration. All the more so when such serious topics come up. Many people just don't want to hear anything about comics. When I met with the committee at [human rights organization] Civil Assistance, the word "comics" popped out of my mouth—and immediately I ran up against some negative perceptions: "Do you know what we're doing here? And you come to us with comics!" But graphic reportage—it even sounds different. And all the same this isn't just a different term; it looks different too. When I showed them *Forbidden Art,* their attitude changed. (Bashkirtsova, "Zapretnoe")

The link to this interview, published by the journal *Big City Buzz* under the title "Forbidden Art," no longer functions. The reader may now find the interview, reposted by Misha Zaslavsky, at https://forum.comicsnews.org/forum-f4/topic2471-75.html#p31575.

23. See, for example, her 2015 Oxfam-sponsored show "HIV: The Unequal Ones" at the Borey Arts Center in St. Petersburg.

24. On Lomasko's murals, see Plungian, "Immersivnoe."

Lomasko creates powerful, clashing juxtapositions by pairing antithetical constituencies across the page folds. In "Angry," part 2 of the book, the left page consists of a splash of a 2012 anti-government march, with several protesters in Pussy Riot–style balaclavas, one hoisting a Pride flag. On the facing page, also taking up all the real estate, we see a portrait of incensed elderly women and skinheads holding Russian Orthodox banners (one gives a fascist salute), yelling, "Put Pussy Riot in the trash!" The two groups walk "towards" each other, the cleave of the pages forming the troubled "front line" (136–137). Absolute polarization; no room for compromise or middle ground.

This particular piece looks more polished, but other works Lomasko produced on location, often in the middle of the events depicted. Many bear the traces of their unconventional creation. This is especially true of works made during the massive anti-Putin marches and government crackdown on protesters of 2011 and 2012. As she explained,

> It's impossible to draw without emotion in such conditions, to think about the reporter's mission. I myself am a participant, I too yell out along with everyone. And you get lots of different sensations from participating: sometimes you just feel a rumbling, your hands tremble. For example, on May 6 [2012], when they were starting the crackdown, I was drawing, but I had such a nervous line that I wasn't even able to finish the drawing. (Gulin, "Grafika")[25]

A different chapter in *Other Russias*, "The Girls of Nizhny Novgorod," also features Lomasko's "drawn from life" technique—though in a completely different setting from the protests. Here, she portrays the daily lives of prostitutes, a population rendered largely invisible in mainstream Russia. As she notes in the book: "I was able to spend between five and fifteen minutes at each 'office'—a rented apartment where sexual services are provided—during breaks between clients. I had to draw the series very quickly, on the spot, without making corrections" (*Other*: 107). Executed with a felt-tip pen on location, the quick, minimalist portraits capture the profound cynicism, boredom, and banality of sex work. One woman, smoking a cigarette, says, "Many guys just come to talk. We need to raise the fee for chats. Our brains are worth more" (118–119) (see figure 8.1). Another smoker sneers, "Some clients ask us to piss on them, but I'd be happy to shit on them on behalf of all women" (116–117).

---

25. She described her method: "For me it's important to draw at the site of the events. From these drawings, made on-site, I put together the reportage. What matters is the rhythm, the tempo of a quick drawing, the point of contact of the pen against the page. Sometimes I draw to produce a better drawing. The composition gets better, but it's less lively" (Lomasko email interview, 2012).

FIGURE 8.1. "The Girls of Nizhny Novgorod," from
Other Russias by Victoria Lomasko (2017)

Her insistent foregrounding of the subjects' words themselves makes Lomasko the Svetlana Alexievich of Russian graphic narrative. Like the 2015 Nobel Laureate, she has made it her mission to give voice to the voiceless: the destitute, the precarious, the losers in Putin's Russia. Her portraits allow readers to regard these people as more than words on paper, but to *see* them— more than that, to see them as she does: with compassion, even with love.

Askold Akishin, KOM studio veteran and father of Russian horror comics, followed a more linear and conventional career path—or at least as linear and conventional as a comics career could be in late and post-Soviet Russia. He, too, jumped on the nonfiction bandwagon in 2013 with *My Comics-Biography* (*Moia komiks-biografiia,* Boomkniga), in which he weaves his own personal and artistic development with the troubled fate of comics in his country. The artist redraws photographs, his old strips, original documents, and memories to recreate (and subtly reshape) his own life as well as the heady early days of the art form, going back to the late 1980s. The result somewhat resembles Yoshihiro Tatsumi's 2008 autobiography *A Drifting Life*, though with a lot more formal experimentation and incorporation of primary material. True to his title, Akishin creates a hybrid biography/chronicle of the birth of the Russian comics industry.[26]

The book's opening exemplifies its approach. In a self-portrait that looks taken from a photograph of himself at the drawing board in present day, Akishin begins to reflect on his personal history. A page-turn shows us the artist again, only decades in the past, as a much younger man. Here, too, he's making comics. "My first comics-biography was drawn in 1989," a caption reads. The bottom half of this page is taken up by that very first attempt: a two-tier strip, *Autobiography*, which first appeared that year in *Vechernyaya Moskva*, the Moscow journal where KOM's first works were published during Perestroika (1–2). Here and throughout his opus, Akishin inhabits and honors his artistic past.

Other parts of the book deliver perhaps a different message—remaking rather than recounting history. For instance, in his telling of KOM's origins, Akishin uses a circa 1990 photograph of the studio's chief editor Sergei Kapranov holding what looks like a poster or mock-up of a proposed comic book cover (artist unknown) and two other men (one of them looks like fellow KOM artist Ilya Savchenkov) (see figure 8.2). In his drawn image, Akishin takes some significant liberties with the content of the photograph: He reverses it; eliminates background details; changes the mock-up that Kapranov holds into a smaller item, a copy of KOM's first independent comics publication, *Breakthrough* (Proryv, 1990)—which just so happens to have a cover by Akishin; and replaces the presumed Savchenkov with his own portrait (as his middle-aged self). Furthermore, the third man (who has his back to us, looking down) now seems to hold his hands together in an attitude of prayer toward the comic book; also, Kapranov now smiles at the comic, though in the photograph he has a much more calm expression as he looks at the poster/mock-up (79).

---

26. Akishin depicted a poignant moment from KOM's 1990 debut book presentation: The artist Yury Lobachev, who had emigrated from the USSR in the 1930s to become a master of Yugoslav graphic narrative, returned to see comics flower at last in his own country (82). On Lobachev, see Alaniz, *Komiks*: 82. Full disclosure: Akishin also managed to squeeze into *My Comics-Biography* a panel of yours truly analyzing one of his works (he quotes Alaniz, "Serious") (91).

FIGURE 8.2. Left: A photo of the KOM studio's Sergei Kapranov holding a poster in the late 1980s. Right: Akishin reworked this photo for *My Comics-Biography*.

In short, through such "archival" reenvisionings, Akishin inserts himself into the center of the story in ways not quite in keeping with the documented facts. (This is to take nothing away from him as a seminal figure in Russian comics, by far the best-known and most critically acclaimed KOM veteran in the post-Soviet era.) Through such loose historiographical methodology, *My Comics-Biography* offers an object lesson in the malleability of the past—no state or Russian Orthodox Church required.

Very different from both Lomasko and Akishin, Lena Uzhinova stands out as the post-Soviet komiksist who has worked the longest in nonfiction subjects, especially the graphic memoir—even as her style is far more "loose" and cartoony, and less tied to realism, than theirs. In fact, style/content tension fuels much of her work, creating moments when the reader laughs, cringes, and feels horrified all at the same time—as when the young heroine in "Story About My Eye" (1999) almost has the organ in question accidentally plucked out by her mother. The "based on a true story" aspect of the proceedings only heightens the almost illicit readerly pleasure paired with discomfort. "Auto-biography has always been and remains an important characteristic of Uzhinova's creative practice," writes Kunin. "Life itself, her personal struggles, her own experience are an unvarying foundation for her works" ("Lena").

In her controversial graphic memoir *My Sex* (2014), Uzhinova (writing as Alyona Kamyshevskaya) strips the veil off Soviet-era sexual mores, inadequate sex education, lack of women's hygiene products and contraceptives, banal promiscuity, and rape culture, all in the author's trademark tragicomic style. Like an earlier, late-Soviet generation of women prose writers,[27] Uzhi-

---

27. On the transgressions, travails, and triumphs of late and post-Soviet Russian women's writing, see Goscilo, "Perestroika."

nova dives headlong into taboo territory heretofore unseen in Russian graphic narrative.

For example, the coming-of-age story, following her from childhood to adulthood, devotes a scene to the author's first menstrual period. It happens while at a Young Pioneer summer camp, in a world without tampons. The camp's staff makes Alyona shower in her panties in front of the other girls—who waste no time in confirming their suspicions: They humiliate her by pulling down her underpants to check for blood (30). Months later, the monthly curse complicates Alyona's interactions with an old friend (a boy); she retreats to a bathroom stall to sew a patch of cloth onto her undergarments. A stylized textbox, like graffiti on the stall, reads: "Something new was beginning, but I wasn't prepared for it" (35).

Among *My Sex*'s most disturbing scenes is Alyona's childhood encounter with a pedophile. At the time, her family was living in Algeria (her father worked for the Soviet diplomatic corps). During a get-together at Alyona's family apartment, an acquaintance, Rashid, surreptitiously sticks his tongue first into his very young daughter's mouth (she treats it as a "fun" game), then into Alyona's mouth. The violations occur off-panel; Uzhinova communicates her heroine's disgust and outrage through facial expressions (23–24).

In three page-width panels, we see Alyona's response to Rashid's vile kiss (see figure 8.3). Besides her scowl, a thought balloon encloses a skull and crossbones (the skull has Rashid's nose). She walks back into the adults' room with a sour look; Rashid is already sitting at the table with the other grown-ups:

But I couldn't talk—that would mean swallowing spit. His spit.

I sat around for a while longer without swallowing the spit, but I understood that there would be no miracle—nothing would change on its own.

And quietly I went to the balcony and spit it all out. (25)

The final panel shows her angrily doing just that as a light rain falls, like a baptism into a new reality—or as she had put it earlier, into "the horrors of man's world" (21).[28] *My Sex* veers dizzyingly from such unsettling, Debbie Drechsler–type episodes to self-deprecating humor, as when "Adolescent Alyona" appears posed only in her panties as Leonardo Da Vinci's Vitruvian Man, with various outfits and accessories assembled below, paper doll–like. "And so I became an adolescent," declaims a textbox, "with zits, hair growth in my 'bikini zones,' with a chest you couldn't hide under any sweater, and a full-blown, 100% inferiority complex" (36). Other scenes combine comedy

---

28. These late-Soviet childhood scenes differ sharply from those of Varvara Pomidor's in "Pravda" (2012), an autobiographical short story that also deals with bodily functions (especially defecation), but remains staidly sex-free. For a discussion of this work, see Alaniz, "Staring."

FIGURE 8.3. *My Sex* by Alyona Kamyshevskaya

and misogynist abuse, as when she depicts in all its fumbling awkwardness a date rapist pressing down on Lena and groping her on a couch. "Can I move now?" she asks. "No, a little more," he answers. "How about now? Can I . . . ?" "Not yet . . ." (43).

Though evocative of established "confessional" works by Aline Kominsky-Crumb, Phoebe Gloeckner, and Julie Doucet, among others, *My Sex* was nothing short of revolutionary for Russian comics, which had no such decades-long history of feminist representation. Reading it feels almost like being made privy to a huge societal secret: women's casual, day-in/day-out objectification, even dehumanization, by men—from the perspective of the object. Yet Uzhinova does not wallow in self-pity or victimhood; there's a certain trite givenness to the book's catalog of ordeals, which makes it all the more powerful, funny, and enraging.

Uzhinova herself, during the promotion of *My Sex,* stoked that "elicit" mood. The work-in-progress was presented in a 2012 KomMissia exhibit (the viewer had to bend down to enter a small room, like a "teenager's retreat," to view the artwork), as well as during a performance piece by the artist, held on March 8, 2013 (International Women's Day), in Tula (Kunin, "Lena").

Of course, not everybody appreciated the book. "It was very negatively received by our shop's readership," said Ivan Chernyavsky, co-owner of Chuk and Geek. "[Customers said] it was drawn too primitively, and that the theme wasn't worth it [*nezasluzhena*]. . . ." (Cherniavskiy interview, 2017).[29] On the other hand, Uzhinova's memoir became the subject of at least one master's thesis,[30] a very rare distinction for a contemporary Russian comics work.

Over the course of the 2010s, Uzhinova turned increasingly to non-autobiographical subjects, such as *I Am an Elephant* (2017), written by Vladimir Rudak, the first Russian graphic novel about disability. This work, too, had a real-life basis: Rudak's own experience as a paraplegic due to an accident (see chapter 7).

Her major work-in-progress, *Echo of Sandormokh,* represents another step away from autographics toward a wider nonfiction scope, and to decidedly political—even anti-Putinist—subject matter. The book recounts the struggle of historian Yury Dmitriev of the civil rights organization Memorial, who in 1997 discovered a mass grave determined to contain the remains of over 6,000 victims of the 1930s Stalinist purges. The authorities dispute that account, saying at least some of those killed were victims of the Finnish army, and/or that they were military dead, not civilian political prisoners. Dmitriev was later tried by the state on pedophilia and other charges, which most consider fabricated—another front in the country's history wars (Higgins, "He").

Uzhinova and her late husband Alexei Kostin began the project in the mid-2010s. As she explained it:

---

29. Let *Spidermedia*'s Yury Kolomensky represent the negative critical view: "The comic amuses with its form. It's autobiographical, it discusses frankly with its reader things that are improper to discuss, it's even unique for our comics market. But that's it. It has no artistic value . . . I see nothing unique in the unending sexual liaisons, in the deflowering by a person of Caucasian appearance, in the several abortions, and, of course, in the 'acceptance of god.' Over the course of my not very long but very full life, I have met people like the main heroine. These were interesting people, but not so interesting that I wanted to learn all the dirty details of their lives" ("Obzor").

30. Paula Järvilehto's "*My Sex*: Gender, Sexuality and Religiosity in Alyona Kamyshevska-ya's Autobiographical Comics" (Faculty of Information Technologies and Communication Sciences, Tampere University, Finland, 2020). I had a small, unofficial advisory role in its writing.

I began my comic arts practice by drawing autobiographical and absurdist works. At a certain point, my personal struggles started to be overtaken by something bigger than just my "I." After the presidential elections of 2012 it became clear to me that our hopes for freedom, the Constitution and human rights had all been wiped the fuck out (I have no other way to put it) by state businessmen and the state's business interests. . . .

When Alexei heard that they had jailed Yury Dmitriev on made-up charges, he proposed that we make comics about him. I agreed—we could. This is now our cause. (Uzhinova, "Nakhodka")

Toward the end of the third post-Soviet decade, nonfiction comics—in particular those dealing with national and personal trauma—exploded. It was as if Pavlovsky's challenge had been heeded—in spades.

In 2018, the leading liberal newspaper *Novaya Gazeta* launched a new rubric, *The Kafka Codices* (*Kafka Kodeks*), which it explained would "tell stories about insane legal proceedings in Russia . . . in the form of comics!" The paper elaborated: "Absurd stories (from the legal point of view), to which a court or other 'law enforcement agency' in one way or another has put the period (or period with a comma), absolving us from the obligation to double-check the facts, in and of itself begs to be represented in the form of comics" (Nikitinskiy, "Chto"). *NG* also provided readers the opportunity to rate the absurdity of the cases on its website. *The Kafka Codices* highlighted work by leading and cutting-edge komiksisty. In "Hedgehog through the Looking Glass" ("Ezh v zazerkal'e"), KOM veteran Alexei Iorsh recounted the plight of the *Daily Journal* (*Ezh* for short),[31] whose website the state blocked for "tendentiousness" (i.e., bias) simply for reporting on the 2012 anti-Putin protests. An accompanying article by Galina Arapova (lawyer and director of the Mass Media Defense Center in Voronezh) expounded upon the relevant legal issues. Other pieces featured Georgy Elaev on censorship in the arts, Mariya Snetkova on an egregious case of mistaken identity, Andrei Bilzho on the legal status of street musicians, and Darya Petushok on abuses of the law in the farming sector.[32]

2019 saw the release of *You Who Survived* (*Vy-zhivshie*),[33] a collection of four stories based on interviews with survivors of Soviet-era repressions

---

31. *Ezhednevny Zhurnal* (*Daily Journal*) is often called *Ezh* for short, coincidentally the same spelling as for "hedgehog" in Russian. Iorsh is also referencing Yury Norstein's classic children's animated cartoon *Hedgehog in the Fog* (1975).

32. To access the stories, see Nikitinskiy, "Chto." *Novaya Gazeta* closed down the feature in 2019 and gathered the stories in a print collection.

33. A pun on *survivors* (*vyzhivshie*). A perhaps better translation: *You Are the Survivors.*

and the Gulag.[34] Released originally online, the stories were accompanied by hyperlinks to the interviews and other materials (Pal'veleva, "Nesmeshnye").[35] The project was sponsored by Moscow's Gulag History Museum, whose director Roman Romanov said, "Reading these comics, we will touch the history of people who lived through the 20th century."[36]

The theme of historical trauma has seen its fullest treatment in Olga Lavrenteva's monumental *Survilo* (Boomkniga, 2019), a graphic biography drawn from interviews with the author's grandmother, who survived the arrest and execution of her father in the 1930s on false spying charges; exile; and the Leningrad siege of World War II. Among the country's most highly regarded comics achievements of recent years, it deserves praise as the Russian *Maus* (see Alaniz, "*Survilo*"). Lavrenteva often bases her work on factual material, such as in her earlier *The Trial of the Twelve* (2015), comics journalism on the legal proceedings involving members of Another Russia (an anti-Putin group).

Originally from the northern city of Salekhard, Yulia Nikitina (aka Ner-Tamin) is another critically acclaimed artist who frequently turns to nonfiction (though in a more poetic key). In her graphic novel *Land of Midnight* (*Polunochnaya zemlya*) and graphic memoir/travel narrative *Storm Diary* (*Dnevnik shtormov*) (both Boomkniga, 2018 and 2019, respectively), Nikitina blends the personal with the national by deploying the text/image capacities of comics for an exploration of the Russian landscape, reflective of an inner journey to grapple with social anxiety and trauma (I discussed her earlier works *The Book of the Body* and *Schism* in the previous chapter).

Other entities of varying ideological stripes put comics to "social activist" and educational uses. In 2017 the Moscow mayor's office created a 100-page comics booklet, *On the Rules of Behavior for Migrants in the City of Moscow*, in which figures from folklore warn newcomers against "hasty familiarity," "excessive pushiness," and eating on the street (BBC, "Meriia").[37] A less controversial social activist art project, Living Language, launched in 2015. Headed by translator and KomMissia organizer Anna Voronkova and Finnish artist Sanna Hukkanen, the project used comics to help preserve endangered lan-

---

34. Writers and artists who worked on the collection, which has a yellow color scheme, included Timur Bulgakov, Konstantin Chirkov, Anastasia Danilova, and Sofiya Elovikova.

35. *You Who Survived* bears comparison to *We Are Still at War* (*Ještě Jsme ve Válce*), a much larger and better-funded Czech social activist project also focused on twentieth-century historical trauma. See Alaniz, "Shoah."

36. Romanov said this in a 2018 promotional clip for the project. View it here: https://www.youtube.com/watch?v=k7DMw5LFTTo.

37. Though it was produced by the social organization Support for Working Migrants, critics faulted the booklet for, among other things, an overly confrontational stance toward migrants and for not taking cultural differences sufficiently into account.

guages of the northwestern Russian borderlands with Finland. Through ongoing workshops and collaborations with the populations in this region, they published comics in various local Finno-Ugric languages, including Sami, Komi, Karelian, Khanty, and Mari (Shil'kovskaia, "As kagakod").[38] Finally, in 2019, the prolific Akishin along with writer Dennis Dvinsky released *Akhmatova: Six Stories* (Eksmo), an episodic graphic biography of the seminal Soviet-era poet Anna Akhmatova.

In 2018, Radio Svoboda organized a roundtable to discuss the exhibition "New Activism," then at Moscow's Sakharov Center. The exhibit featured documentary comic art devoted to NGOs affected by the state's 2012 "Foreign Agents" law, under which more than 165 such organizations were declared "foreign agents," subject to close monitoring and audits. (Domestic and international observers decried the law as chilling free speech, since many of these organizations were critical of government policies.)

The roundtable, "Comics at the Intersection of Social Activism and Art," brought together NGO representatives and comics artists to discuss what nonfiction and social activist graphic narrative could contribute to the struggle against the "foreign agents" law. A number of speakers ironically declared themselves proud "foreign agents." In the course of the exchange, KOM veteran and exhibit curator Alexei Iorsh opined:

> At one point popular music unexpectedly started talking about human problems, rather than just being something people could dance to. Just like that, I think, it's way past time for Russian comics as a democratic medium for self-expression to grow up a little. Inside our community we have a lot of discussions about what Russian comics is, how it should look, and we all have our say in this insular artistic discussion. But that's the least interesting for us, generally speaking. What really interests us is how we can be useful to society. Many of us have already outgrown comics' childhood; this art form itself, all over the world, has outgrown it. (Fanailova, "Komiks")

Comics that have "grown up a little," that are "useful to society," serves as well as any formulation for what their promoters say nonfiction comics are, what they do. It is a developmental, even teleological definition: a stage reached, a childhood "outgrown." It fits well into a narrative of progress, from "puerile" 1990s to fully fledged, present-day "adult" struggles and triumphs.

---

38. Another example: a successful crowdfunding campaign for comics intended to help children accommodate to life after they leave their orphanages. See here: https://boomstarter.ru/projects/380862/57383.

Of all people, it seems former minister of culture Vladimir Medinsky inadvertently played a role in this reassessment of graphic narrative. His widely publicized dismissal of comics as being for "morons" (*debily*) at the 2019 Moscow International Book Fair (see chapter 5) seems paradoxically to have spurred popular interest in the medium. "After this, older people started coming to our stands," noted Stepan Shmytinsky of Komfederatsiya Press. "They said, 'Well, if the minister said that this is some sort of disgusting literature, then that means we should buy it.' I don't know, maybe this kind of prohibition worked for books in the Soviet Union, but it's good. One way or another in Russia we are seeing more and more comics on serious themes—before it was only Boomkniga who put those out" (Kolokoltsev, "Vidish'").

In 2019, Olga Lavrenteva went even further in this vein:

> I think that social activist comics and comics based on real events or the author's personal experience are the only possible direction for the development of Russian comics, because imitation—for example of superheroes— only leads to a dead end. But to narrate what's going on here, what we are witnessing—as it happens, that's the much more interesting and forward-looking path for our readers, no less than for our creators. (Evtushenko, "Seks")

Perhaps. But, without diminishing the remarkable works being produced in this genre, there would seem to exist a very real ceiling to how "developed" it can get in current Russian market conditions. For one thing, Lomasko doubted that many artists would even venture into this type of comics practice for the simple reason that it doesn't pay. There are still not enough foundations or patrons ("foreign agents" or not) to fund it on any consistent basis (Evtushenko, "Seks").[39] Bubble may be a kind of "prostitution," as some komiksisty believe, but it does remunerate its artists—in both lucre and prestige.

Chernyavsky told me that nonfiction would remain a niche interest for another reason: It burns bridges, getting artists into trouble, not only with the state but with their social circles, too. I had asked him Pavlovsky's question: Why don't we see more comics about the recent wars in Chechnya or Eastern Ukraine? "You understand, you could offend someone, destroy relationships," he said. "This is probably the main reason why people who aren't directly experiencing a bombing or a war, don't venture [into truth-based comics

---

39. That need not prove much of an impediment; many Western minicomix and small press artists do what they do for something other than money. Tyumen's Space Cow Press functions with that ethic too, as discussed in chapter 4. They increasingly publish nonfiction, especially autobiographical works.

about such matters]" (Cherniavskiy interview, 2017). In short, let us never lose sight of the fact that, much as it saddens me to type this, Russia under Putin is not a free society. In such circumstances, truth-tellers one way or the other tend to come to grief; their sad example dissuades others.

Which only makes the 2010s achievement of Russian nonfiction comics all the more important and worthy of support.

The End: "A Well-Forgotten Old"

Russia closed out the third post-Soviet decade with no shortage of disheartening news: military entanglements in Eastern Ukraine and Syria; prolonged suffering brought on by post-Crimea annexation sanctions; increasing crackdowns on free speech and political dissidence; widespread inequality and corruption; death camps for LGBTQ+ people in Chechnya; the legal extension of Putin's rule to 2036, if not beyond. This was not quite the future envisioned or hoped for by many who had renounced communism and ushered Yeltsin to power more than a quarter century before.

In the words of one of Putin's biggest admirers, "It is what it is."

To wit: In 2017, twenty-two-year-old blogger Ruslan Sokolovsky was arrested for violating the law against "incitement of religious hatred" for playing *Pokémon Go* in an Orthodox church in Yekaterinburg. He had posted a Christianity-bashing video about the game online. Sokolovsky received a three-and-a-half-year suspended sentence (Shurmina, "Russian"). On the other hand, the February 2020 trial of members of The Network (Set'), an anti-fascist group in Penza, resulted in lengthy jail sentences. Accused of domestic terrorism, the defendants insisted they had been tortured for their "confessions" (Roth, "Russian"). In August 2020, yet another of Putin's major political opponents, Alexei Navalny, fell victim to an apparent assassination attempt by poisoning, in Tomsk (BBC, "Alexei"). In early 2021, upon his return from Germany (where he received life-saving treatment), he was arrested and, at the time of this writing, is serving time for "parole violations."

Despite the increasing success and profile of comics, a chasm remained between mainstream and geek culture. In April 2019, the comics shop Chuk and Geek complained that the cell phone service provider Beeline was blocking text messages pertaining to comics, apparently because the word *miks* was a popular slang term for illegal drugs. The issue was resolved (Mazanov, "Magazin"). More seriously, in July 2020, Julia Tsvetkova, a young activist from Komsomolsk-na-Amur in the Russian Far East, was charged under the country's "anti-gay propaganda" laws for her feminist drawings of female genitalia and happy LGBTQ+ families, posted online. Her case drew global headlines (Vasilyeva, "Russian"; Mikisha, "Delo").

Like the rest of the world, Russia confronted the coronavirus crisis starting in early 2020. Over that summer, the official number of dead topped 16,000. By April, cases had been detected in every region of the country. That same month, *Novaya Gazeta* published Askold Akishin's mash-up of history, Graphic Medicine, and satire, "The Crown of Russia's Epidemic," a playful phantasmagoria of anthropomorphized plagues befitting the king of Russian horror comics, which drew numerous links between pandemics past and present.

Part 2, "The Extraordinary Adventures of the Italians in Russia,"[40] had the monsters in the present day, plotting their revenge for the failures of the Venetian Bubonic Plague campaign 700 years before. They are now led by the coronavirus, who dresses like Napoleon and commands, "And now to Russia, *fratelli!*" (see figure 8.4). But they are largely foiled again by heroic health care workers and social distancing measures in Moscow. (The strip appeared well before the pandemic in Russia peaked, with disastrous results, later that year.)

The still-young Russian comics industry negotiated this new threat as best it could. Yakovlev told me in May that sales in comics shops had fallen, but that was partly offset by increased orders through Boomkniga's website and through bookstores. He lamented, though, that visits by foreign authors were being cancelled. Art Spiegelman was on the guest slate of a book festival in Petersburg that autumn; now it seemed the festival would not happen. "I've been inviting him since 2009," he sighed.[41]

Yakovlev wasn't the only one who noticed a sharp drop-off in purchasing. In April, the site Geek City surveyed several comics publishers on how the pandemic was affecting their business and the industry in general. Their answers varied little: The Covid-19 crisis accelerated a slowdown in the market that dated back to 2017, driven by oversaturation and the fall of the ruble;[42] projects were being scrapped or postponed until the fall or even the new year; publishers were holding off on purchasing new foreign licenses—which still

---

40. Part 2's title plays on that of a late-Soviet film, *The Unbelievable Adventures of Italians in Russia* (directed by Eldar Ryazanov and Franco Prosperi, 1974). Akishin's title for the work as a whole puns on another late-Soviet film, *The Crown of the Russian Empire, or Once Again the Elusive Avengers* (1971), directed by Edmond Keosayan.

41. Personal correspondence, 2020.

42. According to Yakovlev, the percentage of Boomkniga books sold in comics shops had been dropping long before the coronavirus hit, from 40 percent in 2017 to 28 percent in 2019. Meanwhile, sales in bookstores were increasing. To Yakovlev, this meant that comics shops were bleeding customers and not replacing them with new ones (Afonin, "Slovo"), though of course it also meant that comics shop patrons were not the alternative comics publisher Boomkniga's primary customer base. Other indicators, though, did confirm Yakovlev's general observation. In short, the market had become saturated.

FIGURE 8.4. "The Crown of Russia's Epidemic" (2020), comics
about the coronavirus pandemic by Askold Akishin

made up the lion's share of profits; most comics shops and smaller presses,
especially in the provinces, probably would not survive; many were turning
to selling the electronic versions of their products to weather the storm (Afonin, "Slovo").

Comic Con Saint Petersburg 2020 was cancelled. Comic Con in Moscow
2020 took place online. Festival and con cancellations hit publishers hard.
Even Bubble's always-upbeat Roman Kotkov admitted that.[43] He did otherwise put on a characteristically brave face: "In the near future we will have
new releases, because to not release them and just sit down by the sea to wait
out the weather—in our opinion, that would just make the situation worse
for everyone." He added that Bubble had wisely closed down their line of
singly (floppies) not long before the pandemic; these stories were now available exclusively in electronic format and via their mobile app—until the trade
paperback collections. They were also putting out variant covers exclusively
for comics shops, to encourage people to patronize them. A number of publishers predicted the pandemic would deal a death blow to *singly* in Russia.

---

43. The festival cancellations meant catastrophe for many shops and presses, Kotkov said,
because of the immediate boost to sales such events provide. Many had eked out a living from
event to event (Afonin, "Slovo"). Not in 2020—and beyond.

Some warned that as a result of the crisis, the industry as a whole could contract by up to 40 percent (Afonin, "Slovo").[44]

In June, after months of lockdown, *Geek City* published a glaring headline announcing that Russian comics publishers' output had contracted by 70 percent. (The actual story painted a more complex picture, but still a disastrous one.) Jellyfish Jam noted that over the last month it had received only about 10 percent of its normal payments. Many were counting on the upcoming Bubble film *Major Grom: Plague Doctor* to "save" Russian comics in 2021. Its success could open doors for more comics adaptations and throw a financial lifeline to the industry, some mused (Kolokoltsev, "Vidish'").[45]

On July 1, 2020, the nation voted on a series of constitutional amendments, the chief of which allowed Putin to "restart" the clock on his term limits, meaning he could stand again in consecutive presidential elections beginning in 2024. In effect, this meant Putin could now potentially remain in office until 2036, when he would be 84 years old. The amendments thus set Russia back on the path to the sort of gerontocratic rule it last saw in the late-Soviet era. It also meant the country would remain on the path of oligarchy and authoritarianism that it had tread since Putin assumed office.

Lomasko reflected on these themes, as well as the peculiar circumstances of the vote, in "How to Change Your Constitution in a Health Crisis," published by *The Nib* in August 2020. The graphic reporter explains how a masked Moscow mayor Sergei Sobyanin had maintained a strict quarantine, even scheduling alternating days when residents were permitted out for walks so as to minimize interactions. "But when Vladimir Putin scheduled the vote for amendments to the constitution, the mayor immediately cancelled the lockdown," she writes, showing Putin with a large crown on his head, declaring "July 1st"—the date of the vote. Meanwhile, she notes, "People are no longer worried and live their ordinary lives as if there was no pandemic." A panel depicts several citizens in a field, sunning themselves, having a picnic, playing

---

44. Alexander Zhikarentsev, from Azbuka Press, had the gloomiest assessment: "I have said this and I will repeat it: we never had a comics industry in Russia. We had enthusiasts who tried to publish comics. And there were a lot of good people who opened the shops of their dreams, trying to sell those things that they liked. Unfortunately, this did not have time to develop into something we could call an industry. For this you need time, which we did not have, and a stable economy, which we had even less" (Afonin, "Slovo").

45. The film premiered in April 2021, and performed below expectations at the box office. However, it was picked up by Netflix for a record sum and has been critically well-received. Its effect on the Russian comics industry was minimal.

ball, while above them floats an official chart of new Covid-19 cases, showing a downward trend ("How").[46]

This was a portrait of banality and cynicism in the time of plague, a topical account of a global crisis from a very Russian, even a very Moscow, point of view. In English, on one of the most popular platforms for contemporary graphic narrative. This was Russian comics out in the world.

In late summer, 2017, I was interviewing my old friend Alexander (Sasha) Kunin in a Moscow coffee house. He was telling me about Khikhus' complicated handoff of KomMissia to him and his team over the course of 2013, as well as the many plans they had then for the festival's expansion, new projects, ventures, and sponsorships. And it all would have worked out beautifully, he said. Then he leaned toward me with a rueful smile:

Esli by ne odin nyuants. My zhivyom v Rossii. Zdes' nikogda ne znaesh' shto budet zavtra.

[If only it weren't for one nuance. We live in Russia. Here you never know what's going to happen tomorrow]. (Kunin interview, 2017)

Sasha's assessment expressed the centuries-long uphill climb for comic art in Russia (and much else besides). But that makes only more remarkable and exciting the achievements of the post-Soviet era, and the last ten years in particular.

If in the 1990s, and even in the mid-2000s, one person could do a reasonable job of covering the scene, today that is impossible. The sudden growth has been explosive and thrilling. But as I have tried to show throughout my years as a professional scholar, comics in Russia didn't just come from nowhere—certainly not just from the West and Japan. We are dealing here with a rich visual–verbal form of long indigenous pedigree—notwithstanding the short cultural memories and prejudices of the present day.

In short, *komiks* are not foreign or exotic or novel. That they have seemed so for so long is quite simply a failure of historical engagement and—in a regrettably ableist phrase—a case of willful cultural blindness. To keep changing that flawed perception, the comics industry, the fan community, and Russian comics studies all have their roles to play. There remains much ongoing

---

46. Summer 2020 marked the passing of Olga Ryabova-Alexeyeva, who ran the French bookshop Pangloss in Moscow, starting in the 1990s. Back then, it was the one store in the city where you could find *bande dessinée* and other comics, and became a hub for the nascent scene. It was there that Nikolai Maslov took his first autobiographical work to show the shop's owner, Emmanuel Durand, in 1996.

work of excavation,[47] validation, redemption, revival, interpretation, critique, and yes, financial stabilization. But as someone who has followed them for decades, more than ever can I say that today it feels like Russians see graphic narrative as an old friend at last being welcomed home.

Over the course of writing this book, I stumbled on a quote that, more than anything, captures why I chose to put the word *resurrection* in the title of this tome. In 2013, *Art Guide* was interviewing Boomkniga's Dmitry Yakovlev along with artist Varvara Pomidor. Let their exchange stand as my coda:

> AG: Just a few years ago, any journalistic report about comics began with a phrase like, "Comics is an exotic phenomenon for Russia. We have no tradition of comics." However, since the mid-2000s the country has been seeing a comics boom. They're getting published, read, drawn. On the internet whole communities of fans translate and publish them. Why have comics suddenly become so close to the Russian heart?
>
> VP: Apparently because people always gravitate to what's new . . .
>
> DY: . . . Especially when this "new" is actually *a well-forgotten old.*[48]

47. For example, see this fascinating 2019 report on Soviet "art brut" comics: Vishnevets-kaia and Yashnov, "V poiskakh."

48. Matveeva, "Komiksy." In Russian, Yakovlev's phrasing is "*khorosho zabytoe staroe*" (my emphasis).

BIBLIOGRAPHY

Admin. "Ekskliuziv: Aleksandr Kunin—Galdyrdyms ili Zhurnalistika skrinshota." *Spidermedia* (August 11, 2015). http://spidermedia.ru/comics/kunin-galdyrdyms.

Administratsiia Zheleznodorozhnogo rayona goroda Ekaterinburga. "Igor' Ermakov: 'Glavnoe, rebiata, serdtsem ne staret'!'" http://xn--d1abacdeqluciba1a2o.xn--80acgfbsl1azdqr.xn--p1ai/novosti/85638#photo=300e817ff04df0514c69af2f27a798b8.

Adorno, Theodor, and Horkheimer, Max. "The Culture Industry: Enlightenment as Mass Deception." *The Cultural Studies Reader.* Ed. Simon During. Routledge, 1993: 29–43.

Afonin, Sergey. "Slovo izdatel'stvam. Kak Pandemiia otrazilsia na komiksakh v Rossii?" *Geek City* (April 16, 2020). http://geekcity.ru/slovo-izdatelstvam-kak-pandemiya-otrazilas-na-komiksax-v-rossii/.

Afonskiy, Artem. "V Podmoskov'e ob'iavilsia Betmen, kotoriy napadaet na narkopritony." *Moskovskiy Komsomolets* (June 28, 2016). https://www.mk.ru/mosobl/2016/06/28/v-podmoskove-obyavilsya-betmen-kotoryy-napadaet-na-narkopritony.html.

Agentstvo gorodskikh novostei Moskva. "V. Medinskiy vyskazalsia protiv prepodavaniia istorii v formate komiksov (utochnenie)." September 4, 2019. https://www.mskagency.ru/materialy/2924177.

Akeema. "Vasia—ne gey." *Izotekst* (2012/13): 116–176.

Akhmirova, Rimma. "Putin podarit 13 millionov sozdateliam russkikh komiksov." *Sobesednik* (December 11, 2015). https://sobesednik.ru/obshchestvo/20151211-putin-podarit-13-millionov-sozdatelyam-russkih-komiksov.

Akishin, Askol'd. "Korona rossiyskoy epidemii. Chast' 1: Smert' v Venetsii." *Novaia Gazeta* (April 19, 2020). https://novayagazeta.ru/articles/2020/04/19/84973-korona-rossiyskoy-epidemii.

———. "Korona rossiyskoy epidemii. Chast' 2: Neveroiatnye prikliucheniia italiantsev v Rossii." *Novaia Gazeta* (April 21, 2020). https://novayagazeta.ru/articles/2020/04/21/85012-korona-rossiyskoy-epidemii-2.

———. *Moia komiks-biografiia*. St. Petersburg: Boomkniga, 2013.

———. "R. I. P." *Al'manakh risovannykh istorii*, no. 4 (2006): 21–23.

Akunin, Boris. *The State Counsellor*. Trans. Andrew Bromfield. Weidenfeld & Nicholson, 2008.

Alaniz, José. "Cinema without Barriers." *KinoKultura*, no. 16 (April 2007). http://www.kinokultura.com/2007/16-alaniz.shtml.

———. "Corrections Class." *KinoKultura*, no. 47 (January 2015). http://www.kinokultura.com/2015/47r-klass-korrektsii.shtml.

———. "Czech Comics Anthropology: Life and Story in *O přibjehi: Keva*." *Comics Forum* (May 11, 2012). http://comicsforum.org/2012/05/11/czech-comics-anthropology-life-and-story-in-o-pribjehi-keva-by-jose-alaniz/.

———. *Death, Disability and the Superhero: The Silver Age and Beyond*. University Press of Mississippi, 2014.

———. "Death Porn: Modes of Mortality in Post-Soviet Russian Cinema." *Interpretation of Culture Codes: Madness and Death*. Ed. Vadim Mikhailin. Saratov State University Laboratory of Historical, Social and Cultural Anthropology, 2005: 185–211.

———. "'Flashy' Pictures: Social Activist Comics and Russian Youth." *Eastern European Youth Cultures in a Global Context*. Ed. Matthia Schwartz and Heike Winkel. Palgrave Macmillan UK, 2015: 316–334.

———. "Food in Post-Soviet Russian Comics." *The International Journal of Comic Art*. Vol. 18, No. 2 (Fall/Winter, 2016): 216–233.

———. "'Fragging' the Afghan War: *Red Blood*." Forthcoming.

———. "'Hippies' and Pacifism in Igor Kolgarev's Militariisk Comics." *International Journal of Comic Art*. Forthcoming.

———. "History in Czech Comics: Lucie Lomová's *Divoši*." *Ulbandus*, vol. 15 (2013): 81–105.

———. "Igor Baranko and National Precarity in Ukrainian Comics." *Comics of the New Europe: Reflections and Intersections*. Ed. Martha Kuhlman and José Alaniz. Leuven University Press, 2020: 215–237.

———. *Komiks: Comic Art in Russia*. University Press of Mississippi, 2010.

———. "'Nice, Instructive Stories Their Psychology Can Grasp': How to Read Post-Soviet Russian Children's Comics." *Russian Children's Literature and Culture*. Ed. Marina Balina and Larisa Rudova. Routledge, 2007: 193–214.

———. "Notes from the Inside." *International Journal of Comic Art*, vol. 10, no. 2 (Fall 2008): 849–861.

———. "Omega the Unknown on the Spectrum." *Uncanny Bodies: Disability and Superhero Comics*. Ed. Scott T. Smith and José Alaniz. Penn State University Press, 2019: 35–58.

———. "'People Endure': The Function of Autism in *Anton's Right Here* (2012)." *Cultures of Representation: Disability in World Cinema Contexts*. Ed. Benjamin Fraser. Wallflower Press, 2016: 110–125.

———. "Sarik Andreasian: *Guardians*." *KinoKultura*, no. 58 (October 2017). http://www.kinokultura.com/2017/58r-zashchitniki.shtml.

———. "'Serious' Comics Adaptations of the Classics in the Late Soviet Era: Askol'd Akishin's *A Chronicle of Military Actions*." *International Journal of Comic Art*, vol. 13, no. 1 (Spring 2011): 235–248.

———. "The Shoah, Czech Comics and Drda/Mazal's *The Enormous Disc of the Sun*." *Journal of Modern Jewish Studies*, vol. 17, no. 1 (2018): 64–78.

———. "Staring Back at History: Varvara Pomidor and Russian Comics." *Transnational Perspectives on Comic Art and Feminism in the Nordic Countries and the Baltic Sea Region.* Ed. Kristy Beers Fägersten et al. Stockholm: Södertörn University: 239–253.

———. "*Survilo* and Historical Trauma in Contemporary Russian Comics." *International Journal of Comic Art,* vol. 23, no. 1 (Spring 2021): 5–32.

———. "Vision and Blindness in Alexander Sokurov's *Father and Son.*" *Cinepaternity: Fathers and Sons in Soviet and Post-Soviet Film.* Ed. Helena Goscilo and Yana Hashamova. Indiana University Press, 2010: 282–309.

———. "'We Are Here': *Trans*Siberia* and Queer Comics in Russia." ImageTexT. Forthcoming.

Aleksandrov, Nikolay. "Vladimir Morozov: Komiksy daiut vozhmoshnost' razvivat' oba polushariia srazu, liudi odnovremenno vosprinimaiut kartinki i tekst." *OTR Online* (September 4, 2018). https://otr-online.ru/programmy/figura-rechi/vladimir-morozov-komiksy-dayut-vozmozhnost-razvivat-oba-polushariya-srazu-lyudi-odnovremenno-vosprinimayut-kartinki-i-tekst-eto-vazhneyshiy-klyuch-k-ponimaniyu-togo-chto-est-komiks-33374.html.

Aleksandrov, Yuriy. "Desiat' let sto let nazad." *Russkiy Komiks.* Ed. Yuriy Aleksandrov and Anatoliy Barzakh. NLO, 2010: 7–8.

Alexievich, Svetlana. *Voices from Chernobyl.* Trans. Keith Gessen. Dalkey Archive Press, 2005.

Alimguzina, Il'mira. "Kto i pochemu ubil transseksuala v Ufe?" *Ufa 1* (February 2, 2016). https://ufa1.ru/text/gorod/129315224408064.html.

Alius, German. *Trans*Siberia.* Facebook. May 1, 2017. https://www.facebook.com/transcomicssiberia/.

Alyokhina, Maria. "Pussy Riot: Maria Alyokhina's Closing Statement." *Critical Legal Thinking* (August 20, 2012). https://criticallegalthinking.com/2012/08/20/pussy-riot-maria-alyokhinas-closing-statement/.

Anikina, Alena. "Aleksey Venediktov: Obognavshiy 'Vremia' so skorost'iu ekha." *Novye Izvestiia* (June 25, 2004). http://onair.ru/main/themes/view/THID__264/.

Anokhin, Aleksandr. "#iachitaiukomiksy—komiks-soobshchestvo protiv ministra Medinskogo." *Geekster* (September 5, 2019). https://geekster.ru/columns/yachitayukomiksy-komiks-soobshhestvo-protiv-ministra-medinskogo/.

———. "'Panteon: Kul't Dvulichiia' i Fillip Sosedov: kamen' pretknoveniia." *Geekster* (November 17, 2016). https://geekster.ru/hot-news/philipp-sosedov-panteon-tpb/.

Antonova, Maria. "Putin's Great Patriotic Purge." *Foreign Policy* (May 8, 2015). https://foreignpolicy.com/2015/05/08/vladimir-putin-great-patriotic-purge-victory-day-nazi/.

Antoshchenko, Egor. "Ia—nastoiashchiy comic book nerd." *Colta.ru* (October 30, 2015). https://www.colta.ru/articles/swiss_made/9079-ya-nastoyaschiy-comic-book-nerd#ad-image-0.

Applebaum, Anne. *Gulag: A History.* Anchor Books, 2003.

Arkhangel'skaia, Elizaveta. "Million dlia maiora: mozhno li zarabotat' na rossiyskikh supergeroev." *RBC Journal,* no. 4 (April, 2017). https://www.rbc.ru/magazine/2017/04/58cfaec89a7947b5c9715c1f.

Azarova, Aytalina, et al. "The Effect of Rapid Privatisation on Mortality in Mono-Industrial Towns in Post-Soviet Russia: A Retrospective Cohort Study." *The Lancet Public Health,* no. 2 (May 2017): 231–238.

Babintseva, Nataliia. "Komiksy i kompleksy." *Moskovskie Novosti* (April 8, 2011). https://www.mn.ru/newspaper/freetime/68145.

Bakhtin, Mikhail. *Rabelais and His World.* Trans. Hélène Iswolsky. Indiana University Press, 1984.

Barber, Lionel, et al. "Vladimir Putin Says Liberalism Has 'Become Obsolete.'" *Financial Times* (June 28, 2019). https://amp.ft.com/content/670039ec-98f3-11e9-9573-ee5cbb98ed36.

Barkov, Denis. "Kak vygodno pokupat' komiksy v Rossii." *Kanobu* (April 5, 2017). https://kanobu.ru/articles/kak-vyigodno-pokupat-komiksyi-v-rossii-370201/.

Barry, Ellen. "From a Novelist, Shock Treatment for Mother Russia." *The New York Times* (April 29, 2011). https://www.nytimes.com/2011/04/30/books/the-russian-novelist-vladimir-sorokin.html.

Bashkirtsova, Marina. "Zapretnoe iskusstvo." *Big City Buzz* (November 2011). http://bigcitybuzz.ru/2011/11/zapretnoe-iskusstvo/ [link no longer functions].

Basora, Adrian A., and Fisher, Aleksandr. "Putin's 'Greater Novorossiya': The Dismemberment of Ukraine." Foreign Policy Research Institute (May 2, 2014). https://www.fpri.org/article/2014/05/putins-greater-novorossiya-the-dismemberment-of-ukraine/.

Bassin, Mark, and Kelly, Catriona, eds. *Soviet and Post-Soviet Identities.* Cambridge University Press, 2012.

Bassin, Mark, and Kotkina, Irina. "The *Etnogenez* Project: Ideology and Science Fiction in Putin's Russia." *Utopian Studies,* vol. 27, no. 1 (2016): 53–76.

Battersby, Christine. *The Sublime, Terror and Human Difference.* Routledge, 2007.

BBC. "Alexei Navalny: 'Poisoned' Russian Opposition Leader in a Coma." *BBC* (August 20, 2020). https://www.bbc.com/news/world-europe-53844958.

———. "Meriia Moskvy narisovala komiks s pravilami povedeniia." *BBC* (January 16, 2017).

Beaty, Bart. "Pickle, Poot and the Cerebus Effect." *The Comics Journal,* no. 207 (September 1998): 1–2.

———. *Unpopular Culture: Transforming the European Comic Book in the 1990s.* University of Toronto Press, 2007.

Beaty, Bart, and Woo, Benjamin. *The Greatest Comic Book of All Time.* Palgrave Macmillan, 2016.

Belton, Catherine. *Putin's People: How the KGB Took Back Russia and Then Took On the West.* Farrar, Straus and Giroux, 2020.

Bennetts, Marc. *I'm Going to Ruin Their Lives: Inside Putin's War on Russia's Opposition.* One World, 2016.

Berezina, Nastia. "Komiks *Maus* o kholokoste sniali s prodazhi v moskovskom Dome knigi." *RBC* (April 27, 2015). https://www.rbc.ru/politics/27/04/2015/553defab9a794776dba89555.

Bernstein, Anya. "*Caution, Religion!* Iconoclasm, Secularism, and Ways of Seeing in Post-Soviet Art Wars." *Public Culture,* vol. 26, no. 3 (2014): 419–448.

Bernstein, Frances. "The Ramp to Nowhere? Disability in Contemporary Russia." Jordan Russia Center (December 8, 2014). http://jordanrussiacenter.org/news/putin-good-invalids-disability-contemporary-russia/#.XtBKW2hKjb1/.

Beumers, Birgit. "Myth-Making and Myth-Taking: Lost Ideals and the War in Contemporary Russian Cinema." *Canadian Slavonic Papers,* vol. 42, no. 1–2 (2000): 171–189.

Bigg, Claire. "Russia's New Disability Rules Prompt Outrage as 500,000 Lose Benefits." *The Guardian* (March 18, 2016). https://www.theguardian.com/world/2016/mar/18/russia-disability-rules-outrage-lose-benefits.

Bird, Robert. *Andrei Tarkovsky: Elements of Cinema.* London: Reaktion, 2008.

Birger, Liza. "Kupit' i zasmotret'sia. Kak graficheskie romany spasaiut bumazhnuiu knigu." *Kommersant' Vlast',* no. 26 (July 6, 2015): 38. https://www.kommersant.ru/doc/2747830.

Biriukov, Sergey. "Na 'Krasnom Oktiabre' otkrylas' vystavka, feministkaia po forme i chelovecheskaia po soderzhanii." *Trud* (October 19, 2012). http://www.trud.ru/article/19-10-2012/1283723_na_krasnom_oktjabre_otkrylas_vystavka_feministskaja_po_forme_i_chelovecheskaja_po_soderzhaniju/print.

Blomfield, Adrian. "Sexual Harrassment Okay as It Ensures Humans Breed, Russian Judge Rules." *The London Telegraph* (July 30, 2008). http://www.telegraph.co.uk/news/worldnews/europe/russia/2470310/Sexual-harrassment-okay-as-it-ensures-humans-breed,-Russian-judge-rules.html.

Bondareva, Alena. "Chto takoe rossiyskiy komiks?" *Rara Avis* (September 26, 2017). https://rara-rara.ru/menu-texts/chto_takoe_rossijskij_komiks.

———. "Kogda ty slon, tebe ne obidno." *Rara Avis* (April 17, 2017). https://rara-rara.ru/menu-texts/kogda_ty_slon_tebe_ne_obidno.

———. "Komiks. Vtorzhenie." *Oktiabr'*, no. 3 (2014). https://magazines.gorky.media/october/2014/3/komiks-vtorzhenie.html.

Bone, Harry. "Putin Backs WW2 Myth in New Russian Film." *BBC News* (October 11, 2016). https://www.bbc.com/news/world-europe-37595972.

Bonnell, Victoria E. *Iconography of Power: Soviet Political Posters under Lenin and Stalin.* University of California Press, 1997.

Borenstein, Eliot. "A Coat of Not Many Colors: Vatnik (Russia's Alien Nations)." *All the Russias* (May 2, 2019). http://jordanrussiacenter.org/news/a-coat-of-not-many-colors-vatnik-russia-alien-nations/#.XQAi_ohKjbo.

———. *Men without Women: Masculinity & Revolution in Russian Fiction, 1917–1929.* Duke University Press, 2000.

———. *Overkill: Sex and Violence in Contemporary Russian Popular Culture.* Cornell University Press, 2008.

———. *Plots against Russia: Conspiracy and Fantasy after Socialism.* Cornell University Press, 2019.

Borisenkova, Anna. "Narrativniy povorot i ego problemy." *Novoe Literaturnoe Obozrenie*, no. 3 (2010). https://magazines.gorky.media/nlo/2010/3/narrativnyj-povorot-i-ego-problemy.html.

Borodo, Michał "Multimodality, Translation and Comics." *Perspectives*, vol. 23, no. 1 (2014): 1–20.

Borovskiy, Aleksandr. "Novye russkie rasskazchiki." *Novye Rasskazchiki v russkom iskusstve XX–XI vekov.* Ed. Evgeniia Serousova and Ol'ga Klokova. Russian Museum, 2014: 5–29.

Bovt, Georgy. "Playing on Old Myths." *Russia Profile*, vol. 3, no. 3 (March 2006): 36.

Boycko, Maxim, et al. *Privatizing Russia.* MIT Press, 1997.

Boym, Svetlana. *The Future of Nostalgia.* Basic Books, 2008.

Brienza, Casey. "'Manga Is Not Pizza': The Performance of Ethno-Racial Authenticity and the Politics of American Anime and Manga Fandom in Svetlana Chmakova's *Dramacon*." *Global Manga: "Japanese" Comics without Japan?* Routledge, 2015: 111–130.

Brown, Edward J. *Russian Literature since the Revolution.* Harvard University Press, 1982.

Bukatman, Scott. *Matters of Gravity: Special Effects and Supermen in the 20th Century.* Duke University Press, 2003.

Bureau of Democracy, Human Rights, and Labor. "2018 Report on International Religious Freedom: Russia." United States Department of State, 2018. https://www.state.gov/reports/2018-report-on-international-religious-freedom/russia/.

Burko, Pavel. Interview with author. Moscow, January 2002.

Bustanov, Alfrid K. *Soviet Orientalism and the Creation of Central Asian Nations*. Routledge, 2014.

Cassidy, Julie A., and Johnson, Emily D. "A Personality Cult for the Postmodern Age." *Putin as Celebrity and Cultural Icon*. Ed. Helena Goscilo. Routledge, 2013: 37–64.

Cherniavskiy, Ivan. "Artem Gabrelianov—o russkikh supergeroiakh, 'Panteone,' i nedostatkakh 'Khranitelei.'" *Spidermedia* (November 26, 2012). http://spidermedia.ru/blog/vch/artem-gabrelyanov-glavnyy-redaktor-izdatelstva-bubble-o-russkih-supergeroyah-panteone-i.

———. Interview with author. Moscow, July 2017.

Chernov, Sergei. "Viktoria Lomasko's Portraits of Life." *The St. Petersburg Times*, no. 1789 (48) (December 4, 2013). http://sptimes.ru/index.php?action_id=100&story_id=38652.

Chirikova, Evgeniya. "Russia Is a Land of Protests and Activism. Really." *The New York Times* (September 12, 2019). https://www.washingtonpost.com/opinions/2019/09/12/russia-is-land-protests-activism-really/.

Chukovskiy, Korney. "Rastlenie detskikh dush." *Literaturnaia Gazeta*, no. 76 (2459) (1948). http://www.chukfamily.ru/kornei/prosa/kritika/rastlenie-detskix-dush-2.

Chute, Hillary L. "Comics as Literature? Reading Graphic Narrative." *PMLA*, vol. 123, no. 2 (March 2008): 452–465.

———. *Disaster Drawn : Visual Witness, Comics, and Documentary Form*. Harvard University Press, 2016.

———. *Graphic Women: Life Narrative and Contemporary Comics*. Columbia University Press, 2010.

———. "'The Shadow of a Past Time': History and Graphic Representation in *Maus*." *A Comics Studies Reader*. Ed. Jeet Heer and Kent Worcester. University Press of Mississippi, 2009: 340–362.

———. *Why Comics?: From Underground to Everywhere*. Harper Collins, 2017.

Clements, Barbara Evans. "Introduction." *Russian Masculinities in History and Culture*. Ed. Barbara Evans Clements et al. Palgrave: 1–14.

Cocca, Carolyn. *Superwomen: Gender, Power, and Representation*. Bloomsbury, 2016.

Collins, Sean T. "Uno Moralez!" *The Comics Journal* (August 16, 2012). http://www.tcj.com/uno-moralez/.

Comichron. "June 2015 Comic Book Sales to Comics Shops." *Comichron: Comics History by the Numbers* (2018). https://www.comichron.com/monthlycomicssales/2015/2015-06.html.

Conquest, Robert. *The Harvest of Sorrow: Soviet Collectivization and the Terror-Famine*. Oxford University Press, 1986.

Couser, G. Thomas. "Disability, Life Narrative and Representation." *PMLA*, vol. 120, no. 2 (March 2005): 602–605.

———. *Signifying Bodies: Disability in Contemporary Life-Writing*. University of Michigan Press, 2009.

Crary, Jonathan. *Suspensions of Perception: Attention, Spectacle and Modern Culture*. MIT Press, 1999.

Cuttle, Jade. "Russian Comics Gets Sales Boost after Culture Minister Calls Them Pathetic." *The Guardian* (September 17, 2019). https://www.theguardian.com/books/2019/sep/17/russian-culture-minister-dismisses-comics-as-for-those-who-cant-read-well.

Daughtry, J. Martin. "Russia's New Anthem and the Negotiation of National Identity." *Ethnomusicology*, vol. 47, no. 1 (2003): 42–67.

Denson, Shane, et al. "Introducing *Transnational Perspectives on Graphic Narratives: Comics at the Crossroads.*" *Transnational Perspectives on Graphic Narratives: Comics at the Crossroads.* Ed. Shane Denson et al. Bloomsbury, 2013: 1–12.

Devova, Natal'ia, and Erofeeva, Alina. *Soiuzniki: Kniga 1- Pered rassvetom.* Bubble, 2018.

Ditrih. "Interv'iu s CCR 2017: Ivan Cherniavskiy." *Comics Boom!* (October 28, 2017). http://comicsboom.net/interview/4506-intervyu-s-ccr-2017-ivan-chernyavskiy.html.

———. "Interv'iu s CCR 2017: Mikhail Bogdanov." *Comics Boom!* (October 11, 2017).

Dmitrieva, Daria. "Going West or Going Back?: Searching for New Male Identity." *Baltic Worlds,* Special Section 1–2 (2015): 57–63.

———. *Vek supergeroev. Istoki, istoriia, ideologiia amerikanskogo komiksa.* Izoteka, 2015.

Doak, Connor, Platt, Kevin M. F., and Strukov, Vlad. "The Transnational Turn in Russian Studies." *Newsnet: News of the Association for Slavic, East European and Eurasian Studies* (March 2020): 2–7.

Dobrenko, Evgeny. "Utopias of Return: Notes on (Post-) Soviet Culture and Its Frustrated (Post-) Modernization." *East European Thought,* no. 63 (May 2011): 159–171.

Dobrynin, Sergey. "Evoliutsionisty i natsionalisty." *Radio Svoboda* (June 20, 2017). https://www.svoboda.org/a/28569172.html.

Dony, Christophe, and van Linthout, Caroline. "Comics, Trauma and Cultural Memory(ies) of 9/11." *The Rise and Reason of Comics and Graphic Literature: Critical Essays on the Form.* Ed. Joyce Goggin and Dan Hassler-Forest. McFarland & Co, 2010: 178–187.

Dostoevsky, Fyodor. *Demons.* Trans. Richard Pevear and Larissa Volokhonsky. Vintage, 1994.

Drury, Colin. "Olga Misik: Teenage Girl Reads Constitution in Front of Putin's Riot Police during Moscow Protests." *The Independent* (July 31, 2019). https://www.independent.co.uk/news/world/europe/olga-misik-russia-protests-constitution-moscow-riot-police-putin-a9029816.html.

Duncan, Matthew. "Graphic Novelty." *The St. Petersburg Times: All About Town* (February 11, 2005): i–ii.

EAN (Evropeysko-Aziatskie Novosti). "Komiksy—eto polnotsenniy vid sovremennogo iskusstva." *EAN.* Undated (ca. 2011). http://eanews.ru/interviews/item173583/.

The Economist. "A Krisha over Your Head" *The Economist* (August 26, 1999). https://www.economist.com/special/1999/08/26/a-krisha-over-your-head.

———. "Russia's Uneasy Handover." *The Economist,* vol. 386, no. 8569 (March 1, 2008): 13.

Elaev, Georgii "Gosha." Interview with author. Seattle, November 2019.

Elaev, Georgy. "Against All Odds, Siberia's Indie Comics Scene Soars." *Broken Pencil* (December 25, 2019). https://brokenpencil.com/news/against-all-odds-siberias-indie-comics-scene-soars/.

Elder, Miriam. "Vladimir Putin Mocks Moscow's 'Condom-Wearing' Protesters." *The Guardian* (December 15, 2011). https://www.theguardian.com/world/2011/dec/15/vladimir-putin-mocks-moscow-protesters.

El Refaie, Elisabeth. *Autobiographical Comics: Life Writing in Pictures.* University Press of Mississippi, 2012.

Epshteyn, Alek. D. *Iskusstvo na barrikadakh: "Pussy Riot," "Avtobusnaia vystavka" i protestniy art-aktivizm.* Viktor Bondarenko/Kolonna, 2012.

Epstein, Mikhail. "The Origins and Meaning of Russian Postmodernism." *Re-Entering the Sign: Articulating New Russian Culture.* Ed. Ellen Berry and Anesa Miller-Pogacar. University of Michigan Press, 1995: 25–47.

Erofeyev, Viktor. "Comics and the Comics Disease." Trans. José Alaniz. *International Journal of Comic Art*, vol. 7, no. 1 (Spring/Summer 2005): 22–38.

——. "Soviet Literature: In Memoriam." Trans. Andrew Meier. *Glas*, no. 1 (1991): 226–234.

Eroshok, Zoia. "Nam nado nayti foto. Vystavka odnogo eksponata." *Novaia Gazeta*, no. 124 (November 8, 2017). https://novayagazeta.ru/articles/2017/11/08/74483-nam-nado-nayti-foto-avtora.

Eurocature. "Denis Lopatin." *Eurocature* (2020). https://eurocature.org/denis-lopatin.

European Commission For Democracy Through Law (Venice Commission). "Federal Law on Combating Extremist Activity of the Russian Federation." *Legislation Online* (March 30, 2012). https://www.legislationline.org/download/id/3707/file/RF_law_combating_extremist_activity_2002_am2008_en.pdf.

Evdokimova, Maria. "The History of Russian Comics: An Interview with Misha Zaslavskiy." *Comics Forum* (December 9, 2015). https://comicsforum.org/2015/12/09/the-history-of-russian-comics-an-interview-with-misha-zaslavskiy-by-maria-evdokimova/.

——. "Introducing Russian Comic Artists." *Comics Forum* (December 30, 2015). https://comicsforum.org/2015/12/30/introducing-russian-comic-artists-by-maria-evdokimova/.

——. "What Comics Are Published and Read in Russia?" *Comics Forum* (December 17, 2015). https://comicsforum.org/2015/12/17/what-comics-are-published-and-read-in-russia-by-maria-evdokimova/.

Evtushenko, Aleksandra. "Seks, sud i preodolonie trevozhnosti: kak rossiyskiy sotsial'niy komiks pomogaet govorit' na slozhnye temy." *Takie Dela* (March 29, 2019). https://takiedela.ru/news/2019/03/29/socialnye-komiksy/.

Fanailova, Elena. "Komiks pro inostrannykh agentov." *Radio Svoboda* (January 14, 2018). https://www.svoboda.org/a/28953506.html.

Faskhutdinova, Tat'iana, and Rodin, Leonid. "Neizvestnye istorii iz zhizni Lioni Rodina." Dmitriy Yakovlev Live Journal Page (October 13, 2012). https://guprus.livejournal.com/223217.html.

Faulkner, William. *Requiem for a Nun*. Knopf Doubleday, 2011.

Finger, Bill, and Kane, Bob. "The Legend of the Batman—Who He Is and How He Came to Be!" *The Batman Chronicles Volume 1*. Ed. Dale Crain. DC, 2005: 138–139.

Fischer, Craig. "Fantastic Fascism? Jack Kirby, Nazi Aesthetics, and Klaus Theweleit's Male Fantasies." *International Journal of Comic Art*, vol. 5, no. 1 (Spring 2003): 334–354.

Fomenko, Andrey. "Risovannye istorii." *Art1* (September 16, 2013). https://art1.ru/2013/09/16/risovannye-istorii-23175.

Foucault, Michel. *The History of Sexuality: An Introduction. Volume I*. Vintage, 1978.

Frank, Arthur. *The Wounded Storyteller: Body, Illness and Ethics*. University of Chicago Press, 1995.

Frazier, Thomas Carey. "Russia's Little-Known Comic Book Scene Is Strange and Beautiful." *Vice* (December 9, 2016). https://www.vice.com/en_us/article/ywnabj/russias-little-known-comic-book-scene-is-strange-and-beautiful.

Freud, Sigmund. "Thoughts for the Times on War and Death." *Standard Edition of the Complete Psychological Works of Sigmund Freud*, vol. 14. Ed. James Strachey. Hogarth Press, 1957: 275–300.

Frimmel, Sandra. "Teatr na Taganke: reportazh odnogo protsessa." Afterword to Viktoria Lomasko and Anton Nikolaev, *Zapretnoe iskusstvo*. Boomkniga, 2011: n.p.

Gabrelianov, Artem. Interview with author. Moscow, September 2013.

Gabrelianov, Artem, Fedotov, Evgeniy, and Tarasov, Konstantin. *Mayor Grom.* "Chumnoy Doktor. Chast' 1," vol. 1, no. 1 (October 2012).

———. *Mayor Grom.* "Chumnoy Doktor. Chast' 2," vol. 1, no. 2 (November 2012).

———. *Mayor Grom.* "Chumnoy Doktor. Chast' 4," vol. 1, no. 5 (February 2013).

———. *Mayor Grom.* "Chumnoy Doktor. Chast' 6," vol. 1, no. 7 (April 2013).

———. *Mayor Grom.* "Chumnoy Doktor. Chast' 7," vol. 1, no. 8 (May 2013).

———. *Mayor Grom,* vol. 1, no. 9 (June 2013).

Gabrelianov, Artem, Fedotov, Evgeniy, and Vasin, Andrey. "Imia emu Besoboi: chast' 1." *Besoboi,* vol. 1, no. 1 (October 2012): n.p.

Gaddy, Clifford, and Ickes, Barry. *Russia's Addiction: The Political Economy of Resource Dependence.* Washington, DC: Brookings Institution Press, 2008.

Gaidar, Yegor. *Collapse of an Empire: Lessons for a Modern Russia.* Brookings Institution Press, 2007.

———. "Lessons of the Russian Crisis for Transition Economies." *Finance & Development* (June 1999): 6–8.

Gardner, Jared. "Autobiography's Biography: 1972–2007." *Biography,* vol. 31, no. 1 (Winter 2008): 1–26.

Garland-Thomson, Rosemarie. "Disability and Representation." *PMLA,* vol. 1, no. 2 (March 2005): 522–527.

———. "Seeing the Disabled: Visual Rhetorics of Disability in Popular Photography." *The New Disability History: American Perspectives.* Ed. Paul Longmore and Lauri Umansky. New York University Press, 2001: 335–374.

Gastall, Tom. "CCI: Is the Comic Book Doomed?." *ComicBookResources.com* (July 27, 2011). http://www.comicbookresources.com/?page=article&id=33573.

Gerden, Eugene. "Comics and Graphic Novels: Interview with Russia's Dmitry Yakovlev." *Publishing Perspectives* (June 12, 2019). https://publishingperspectives.com/2019/07/graphic-novel-comics-publisher-russia-dmitry-yakovlev-bumknigo/.

———. "Marvel's Spider-Man Widens His Web in Russia: Eksmo-AST Buys into Comics." *Publishing Perspectives* (February 9, 2018). https://publishingperspectives.com/2018/02/russia-eksmo-acquires-kofilmo-marvel-comics-publisher/.

Gessen, Masha. *The Future Is History: How Totalitarianism Reclaimed Russia.* Riverhead Books, 2017.

———. "How Russia's Hilarious, Homoerotic 'Satisfaction' Became a Nationwide Meme of Solidarity." *The New Yorker* (January 22, 2018). https://www.newyorker.com/news/our-columnists/how-russias-hilarious-homoerotic-satisfaction-became-a-nationwide-meme-of-solidarity.

Goldschmidt, Paul. "Legislation on Pornography in Russia." *Europe-Asia Studies,* vol. 47, no. 6 (September 1995): 1–10.

———. "Pornography in Russia." *Consuming Russia: Popular Culture, Sex and Society Since Gorbachev.* Ed. Adele Marie Barker. Duke University Press, 1999: 318–336.

González-Gallego, Rubén. *White on Black.* Trans. Marian Schwartz. Harcourt, 2007.

Goralik, Linor. *Found Life: Poems, Stories, Comics, a Play, and an Interview.* Ed. Ainsley Morse, Maria Vassileva, and Maya Vinokour. Columbia University Press, 2018.

Gorbunov, Andrey. "Pavel Astakhov v Ekaterinburge: 'Izdateli dolzhny sami iz'iat' *Tetradi Smerti* iz prodazhi." *Komsomolskaia Pravda* (April 3, 2013). https://www.crimea.kp.ru/daily/26057.4/2967108/.

Gorlova, Lyudmila. "Komiks kak sistema kodov." *Izotekts: stat'i i komisky.* Ed. Aleksandr Kunin. RGBM, 2010: 63–74.

Goscilo, Helena. "The Body Breached: Post-Soviet Masculinity on Screen." *The Cinematic Bodies of Eastern Europe and Russia: Between Pain and Pleasure.* Ed. Ewa Mazierska et al. Edinburgh University Press, 2016: 89–109.

———. "Perestroika and Post-Soviet Prose: Dazzle to Dispersal." *A History of Women's Writing in Russia.* Ed. Adele Marie Barker and Jehanne M. Gheith. Cambridge University Press, 2002: 297–312.

———. "Putin's Performance of Masculinity." *Putin as Celebrity and Cultural Icon.* Ed. Helena Goscilo. Routledge, 2013: 180–207.

Goscilo, Helena, and Yana Hashamova. "Introduction—Cinepaternity: The Psyche and Its Heritage." *Cinepaternity: Fathers and Sons in Soviet and Post-Soviet Film.* Ed. Helena Gosilo and Yana Hashamova. Indiana University Press, 2010: 2–25.

Graham, Seth. "Chernukha and Russian Film." *Studies in Slavic Cultures,* no. 1 (2000): 9–27.

———. "Two Decades of Post-Soviet Cinema: Taking Stock of Our Stocktaking." *KinoKultura,* no. 21 (July 2008). http://www.kinokultura.com/2008/21-graham.shtml.

———. "The Wages of Syncretism: Folkloric New Russians and Post-Soviet Popular Culture." *The Russian Review,* no. 62 (January 2003): 37–53.

Grayson, Nathan. "Overwatch Comic Not Released in Russia Because of Gay Propaganda Law." *Kotaku* (December 20, 2016). https://kotaku.com/overwatch-comic-banned-in-russia-over-gay-propaganda-la-1790343967.

Griffin, Michael, and Dara Waldron. "Across Time and Space: The Utopian Impulses of Andrei Tarkovsky's *Stalker.*" *Exploring the Utopian Impulse: Essays on Utopian Thought and Practice.* Ed. Griffin. Lang, 2007: 257–272.

Groensteen, Thierry. *The System of Comics.* Trans. Bart Beaty and Nick Nguyen. University Press of Mississippi, 2007.

Gruntovskiy, A. *Russkiy Kulachniy Boi: Istoriia, Etnografiia, Tekhnika.* TOO Tekhnologiia Avtomatizirovannykh System, 1998.

Guillory, Sean. "Dermokratiya, USA." *Jacobin* (March 2017). https://www.jacobinmag.com/2017/03/russia-us-clinton-boris-yeltsin-elections-interference-trump/.

GULAG History Museum. *Vy-zhivshie: Sbornik graficheskikh novell.* Muzey istorii GULAGa, 2019.

Gulin, Igor'. "Grafika izmeneniia." *Kommersant',* no. 6 (June 4, 2012). https://www.kommersant.ru/doc/1944236.

Gustafson, Thane. *Wheel of Fortune: The Battle for Oil and Power in Russia.* Harvard University Press, 2017.

Hacking, Ian. *Rewriting the Soul: Multiple Personality and the Sciences of Memory.* Princeton University Press, 1995.

Handelman, Stephen. *Comrade Criminal: Russia's New Mafiya.* Yale University Press, 1995.

Harding, Luke. "Human Rights Lawyer Murdered in Moscow." *The Guardian* (January 19, 2009). https://www.theguardian.com/world/2009/jan/20/russia-lawyer-murder.

Hartblay, Cassandra. "Good Ramps, Bad Ramps: Centralized Design Standards and Disability Access in Russian Urban Infrastructure." *American Ethnologist,* vol. 1, no. 44 (January 2017): 1–14.

Hatfield, Charles. *Alternative Comics: An Emerging Literature.* University Press of Mississippi, 2005.

———. "Comic Books." *Comics Studies: A Guidebook*. Ed. Charles Hatfield and Bart Beaty. Rutgers, 2020: 25–39.

———. "Fearsome Possibilities: An Afterword." *Uncanny Bodies: Superhero Comics and Disability*. Ed. Scott T. Smith and José Alaniz. Penn State University Press, 2019: 217–224.

Hatty, Susan. *Masculinities, Violence, Culture*. Sage, 2000.

Herman, David. "Storyworld/umwelt: Nonhuman Experiences in Graphic Narratives." *SubStance*, vol. 40, no. 1 (2011): 156–181.

Hibbs, Bryan. "Rewarding Publishers for Their Behavior." *ICV2* (January 6, 2010). http://www.icv2.com/articles/news/16596.html.

Higgins, Andrew. "He Found One of Stalin's Mass Graves. Now He's In Jail." *New York Times* (April 27, 2020). https://www.nytimes.com/2020/04/27/world/europe/russia-historian-stalin-mass-graves.html.

Holmgren, Beth. "Bug Inspectors and Beauty Queens: The Problems of Translating Feminism Into Russian." *Genders 22: Postcommunism and the Body Politic*. Ed. Ellen E. Berry. NYU Press, 1995: 15–31.

Huang, Cheng-Wen, and Arlene Archer. "Fluidity of Modes in the Translation of Manga: The Case of Kishimoto's *Naruto*." *Visual Communication*, vol. 13, no. 4 (2014): 471–486.

Human Rights Watch. *Abandoned by the State: Violence, Neglect and Isolation for Children with Disabilities in Russian Orphanages*. 2014.

———. *Barriers Everywhere: Lack of Accessibility for People with Disabilities in Russia*. 2013.

———. *"I Could Kill You and No One Would Stop Me": Weak State Response to Domestic Violence in Russia*. 2018.

Humphrey, Caroline. *The Unmaking of Soviet Life: Everyday Economies after Socialism*. Cornell University Press, 2002.

Husband, William B. "The New Economic Policy (NEP) and the Revolutionary Experiment: 1921–1929." *Russia: A History*. Ed. Gregory L. Freeze. Oxford University Press, 1997: 263–290.

Hutchinson, Samuel. "Whacked but Not Forgotten." *The New York Times* (April 13, 1997). https://www.nytimes.com/1997/04/13/magazine/whacked-but-not-forgotten.html.

Iamshanov, Boris. "Slukhi idut na popravku." *Rossiyskaia Gazeta*, no. 15 (8069) (January 25, 2020). https://rg.ru/2020/01/25/krasheninnikov-raziasnil-kliuchevye-momenty-predlagaemyh-izmenenij-v-konstituciiu.html.

Iarskaia-Smirnova, Elena. *Odezhda dlia Adamy i Evy: ocherki gendernykh issledovanii*. INION RAN, 2001.

Ignatenko, Mariia. "Khikhus o festivale KomMissiia." *Bolshoi Gorod* (May 7, 2012). http://bg.ru/society/hihus_o_festivale_kommissiya-10870/.

InoTV. "Vladimir Putin stal zvezdoy komiksov." *RT* (June 19, 2011). https://russian.rt.com/inotv/2011-06-19/Vladimir-Putin-stal-zvezdoj-komiksov/.

Iorsh, Aleksei. "Musia Pinkenzon." KomMissia 2010 Festival Catalog. KomMissia, 82–93.

Iossel, Mikhail. "The 1980s American Soap Opera That Explains How Russia Feels about Everything." *Foreign Policy* (July 24, 2017) https://foreignpolicy.com/2017/07/24/american-soap-opera-explains-how-russia-feels-about-everything-santa-barbara-trump-putin/.

Isova, Mariia. "Respekt i uvazhukha na Vinzavode." *Nezavisimaia Gazeta* (May 1, 2012). http://www.ng.ru/culture/2012-05-01/100_vinzavod.html.

Jones, Gerard. *Killing Monsters: Why Children Need Fantasy, Super Heroes, and Make-Believe Violence*. Basic Books, 2002.

Kaganovsky, Lilya. *How the Soviet Man Was Unmade: Cultural Fantasy and Male Subjectivity under Stalin.* University of Pittsburgh Press, 2008.

Kaindl, Klaus. "Comics in Translation." *Handbook of Translation Studies,* vol. 1. Ed. Yves Gambier and Luc van Doorslaer. John Benjamins, 2010: 36–40.

Kalenik, Sergey. "Chelovek kak vse—Epizod 1: Skrytaia ugroza." *Superputin.ru* (2011). http://superputin.win/episode1.html.

Kamyshevskaia, Alena. *Moi seks.* Boomkniga, 2014.

Karpova, Anna. "Sozdatel' 'Vatnika' Anton Chadskiy: Kak ia stal rusofobom." *Snob* (October 14, 2014). https://snob.ru/selected/entry/82278/.

Kenez, Peter. *A History of the Soviet Union from the Beginning to the End.* 2nd ed. Cambridge University Press, 2006.

Khachaturov, Mikhail. "Boomfest. 10 let." *Izotekts: stat'i i komiksy* (2015): 24–28.

Khanukaeva, Raisa. "Elena Avinova: 'Russkii komiks poka podrostok." *Eksmo.ru* (June 22, 2017). https://eksmo.ru/interview/elena-avinova-russkiy-komiks-poka-podrostok-ID7064119/.

Kharms, Daniil. *Today I Wrote Nothing: The Selected Writings of Daniil Kharms.* Trans. and ed. Matvei Yankelevich. Overlook Duckworth, 2007.

Khikhus. "Krasnaia Shapochka: rozhdestvenskaia skazka." *Almanakh: Volshebnie Komiksy.* Kom-Missiia, 2003: 42–43.

Khmelnitskiy, Dmitriy. "Osobo opasnye kartinki." *Terra Incognita,* no. 8/18 (August 2003). http://terraincognita.spb.ru/n18/index2.htm.

King, David. *The Commissar Vanishes: The Falsification of Photographs and Art in Stalin's Russia.* Canongate, 1997.

Klimenko, Ekaterina V. "Building the Nation, Legitimizing the State: Russia—My History and Memory of the Russian Revolutions in Contemporary Russia." *Nationalities Papers* (2020): 1–17.

Klimova, Ksenia. "Steps." *Present Imperfect: Stories by Russian Women.* Ed. Ayesha Kagal and Natasha Perova. Westview Press, 1996: 141–144.

Klyuchareva, Natalya. "One Year in Paradise." Trans. Mariya Gusev. *Rasskazy: New Fiction from a New Russia.* Ed. Mikhail Iossel and Jeff Parker. Tin House, 2009: 343–364.

Køhlert, Frederik Byrn. *Serial Selves: Identity and Representation in Autobiographical Comics.* Rutgers University Press, 2019.

Kolchevska, Natasha. "Circles of Hell, Circles of Life: Two Responses to Violence in Gulag Memoirs." *Times of Trouble: Violence in Russian Literature and Culture.* Ed. Marcus C. Levitt and Tatyana Novikov. University of Wisconsin Press, 2007: 222–235.

Kolgarev, Igor.' "On riadom." Moscow International Festival of Drawn Stories KomMissia 2005 Catalog. KomMissiia, 2005: n.p.

Kolokoltsev, Mikhail. "'Vidish' komiksy? A oni est'!': komiks-industriia v RF sokratilas' na 70% iz-za koronavirusa." *Geek City* (June 5, 2020). https://78.ru/articles/2020-06-05/vidish_komiksi_a_oni_est_komiksindustriya_v_rf_sokratilas_na_70_izza_koronavirusa.

Kolomenskiy, Iuriy. "Obzor: Moy Seks." *Spidermedia* (December 11, 2014). http://spidermedia.ru/blog/transistor/obzor-komiksa-moy-seks.

Komardin, Konstantin. Interview with author. Prague, fall 2011.

Komsomol'skaia Pravda. "Avtor komiksa o tiumenskom supergeroe sobiraet den'gi na izdanie final'noi istorii." *Komsomol'skaia Pravda* (July 17, 2018). https://www.tumen.kp.ru/daily/26855/3897948/.

Kon, Igor.' "Muzhkie Issledovaniia: Meniaiushchiesia muzhchiny v izmeniaiushchemsia mire." *Vvedenie v gendernie issledovaniia, chast' I.* Ed. Irina Zherebkina. Aleteiya, 2001.

———. "Sexuality and Culture." *Sex and Russian Society.* Ed. Igor Kon and James Riordan. Indiana University Press, 1993: 15–44.

Korobkova, Evgeniia. "Perevodchiki komiksov predlagaiut sozdat' slovar' zvukopodrazhanii." *Izvestiia* (August 10, 2015). https://iz.ru/news/589735.

Koroleva, Alena. "V samarskoi oblasti proizoshlo sobytie predskazannoe karikaturistom Elkinom 4 goda nazad . . ." *The Insider* (October 12, 2019). https://theins.ru/news/181223.

Kostenko, Aleksandr. "Interv'iu s Vladimirom Morozovym, rukovoditelem Zangavar." *Comics Boom* (December 11, 2018). https://vk.com/@comicsboom-intervu-s-vladimirom-morozovym-rukovoditelem-zangavar.

Kostin, Semen. "Neizvestnaia industriia: interv'yu s rossiyskimi izdateliami mangi. Kak ustroen rynok mangi v Rossii i kak on poiavilsia." *DTF* (October 9, 2018). https://dtf.ru/anime/27462-neizvestnaya-industriyaintervyu-s-rossiyskimi-izdatelyami-mangi.

Kostina, Anastasiia. "Hunting for Reality: An Interview with Marina Razbezhkina." *Film Quarterly,* vol. 73, no. 3 (Spring 2020): https://filmquarterly.org/2020/02/27/hunting-for-reality-an-interview-with-marina-razbezhkina/.

Kotkin, Stephen. *Magnetic Mountain: Stalinism as a Civilization.* University of California Press, 1995.

Kovalev, Alexei. "Russia's Attempt to Say Nyet to Foreign Words Is Comical." *The Guardian* (June 20, 2014). https://www.theguardian.com/commentisfree/2014/jun/20/russia-nyet-foreign-words-duma.

Kozhevnikov, Igor.' *Betmen v Rossii.* Tien, 2017.

———. *Cherez krov' i stradanie.* Tien, 2017.

———. Interview with author. St. Petersburg, September 2013.

———. "Mishka." *Veles,* no. 7 (1995): 50.

Kravchenko, Alexander, and Svetlana Boiko. "What Is Happening to Russian? Linguistic Change as an Ecological Process." *Russian Journal of Communication,* vol. 6, no. 3 (2014): 1–14.

Kravtsova, Mariia. "Marginal'niy zhanr?" *Artkhronika,* no. 8 (2006): 90–93.

Kresling, Pavel. "On prosto ne umeet risovat': tiumenskoe komiks-podpol'e." *Zapovednik* (November 23, 2017). https://zapovednik.space/material/on_prosto_ne_umeet_risovat.

Kriukov, Denis. "Energiia na styke kadrov." *Kursomaniia* (ca. 2012). [link inaccessible]

Kubeeva, Polina. "Zhelteiushchie mal'chiki v glazakh." *Izvestia* (July 24, 2002). http://main.izvestia.ru/print/?id=21508.

Kuhlman, Martha, and Alaniz, José. "General Introduction: Comics of the 'New' Europe." *Comics of the New Europe: Reflections and Intersections.* Ed. Martha Kuhlman and José Alaniz. Leuven University Press, 2020: 7–24.

Kukulin, Ilya. "Cultural Shifts in Russia since 2010: Messianic Cynicism and Paradigms of Artistic Resistance." *Russian Literature,* no. 96–98 (2018): 221–254.

Kunin, Aleksandr. "13 millionov rublei na komiksy!" *Khroniki Chedrika* (December 19, 2015). [link no longer accessible]

———. "5 let Tsentru komiksov i vizual'noi kul'tury RGBM." *Izotekts: stat'i i komiksy* (2015): 5–10.

———. "Aleksey Iorsh: o zhizni i smerti geroev." *Khroniki Chedrika* (July 19, 2012). http://chedrik.ru/2012/iorsh/.

———. "Dmitriy Iakovlev: Poezdka v Angulem. Do i posle." *Khroniki Chedrika* (2010). http://chedrik.ru/2010/poezdka-v-angulem/.

———. "Ikonicheskiy povorot." *Izotekts: stat'i i komiksy* 2011. RGBM, 2011: 5–10.

———. Interview with author. Moscow, September 2013.

———. Interview with author. Moscow, July 2017.

———. "Istoriia ne dolzhna povtoriatsia!" *Izotekst 2012/2013: stat'i i komiksy.* RGBM, 2013: 5–10.

———. "K chitateliu!" *Izotekts: stat'i i komiksy* (2010): 3–6.

———. "Khoroshikh veshchei bylo mnogo!" *Territoriia L* (July 13, 2018). https://gazetargub.ru/?p=8650.

———. "Komiks industriia: Chernye piatna i belye dyry." *Khroniki Chedrika,* no. 0 (2009): 2–7.

———. "Komiks v Rossii." *Bibliografiia,* no. 4 (2013): 45–55.

———. "KomMissiia. 15 let." *Izotekts: stat'i i komiksy* (2015): 11–23.

———. "Lena Uzhinova: razgovor na slozhnye temy." *Territoriia L* (November 15, 2018). https://gazetargub.ru/?p=9452.

———. "Moskovskiy tsentr komiksov as is." *Izotekts: stat'i i komiksy* 2011. RGBM, 2011: 107–112.

———. "O zhizni i smerti geroev." *Khroniki Chedrika,* no. 0 (2009): 46–49.

———. Personal correspondence. January 20, 2019.

———. Personal correspondence. February 19, 2020.

———. "Pro KomMissiiu i 'ideal'niy' komiks-festival.'" *Khroniki Chedrika,* no. 0 (2009): 8–9.

———. "Sotsial'niy rossiyskiy komiks." *Khroniki Chedrika* (March 18, 2019). http://chedrik.ru/2012/socialnyj-rossijskij-komiks/.

Kurilla, Ivan. *PONARS Eurasia Policy Memo,* no. 331 (August 2014): 1–5.

Kushnir, Daria. "Why Russian Indie Book Publishers Are Fighting the Conservative Mainstream." *The Calvert Journal* (May 29, 2020) https://www.calvertjournal.com/features/show/11839/independent-book-publishers-russia-z.

Kutuzov, Kirill. "Amerikanskie meynstrim-komiksy na russkom." *Izotekst* (2015): 128–134.

Kuznetsova, Elena. "V Peterburge otkroiut pervuiu v Rossii biblioteku mangi." *Fontanka* (February 3, 2020). https://calendar.fontanka.ru/articles/9191/.

Lapina-Kratasiuk, Elena. "Konstruirovanie real'nosti v SMI." *Russian Cyberspace,* vol. 1, no. 1 (2009): 61–69. http://www.russian-cyberspace.com/pdf/issue1/Media-Constructions-of-Reality_E-Lapina-Kratasyuk.pdf.

Larionova, Galina. "Poteriat'sia ili naytis'?" *Megabayt* (August 10, 2019). https://mbradio.ru/publication/3252/.

Lavrent'eva, Ol'ga. *ShUV.* Boomkniga, 2016.

———. *Survilo.* Boomkniga, 2019.

Leblanc, Philippe. "Rounding Up the 2018 Ignatz Award Winners and SPX Controversies." *The Beat* (September 21, 2018). https://www.comicsbeat.com/rounding-up-the-2018-ignatz-award-winners-and-spx-controversies/.

Lefèvre, P. "Some Medium-Specific Qualities of Graphic Sequences." *SubStance,* vol. 40, no. 1 (2011): pp. 14–33.

Legislation Online. "Article 282 Criminal Code [excerpt]." *Legislation Online* (n.d.). https://www.legislationline.org/documents/id/4028.

Leitch, Thomas M. *Film Adaptation and Its Discontents: From Gone with the Wind to the Passion of the Christ.* Johns Hopkins University Press, 2007.

Lent, John. "Cartooning, Public Crises and Conscientization: A Global Perspective." *International Journal of Comic Art,* vol. 10, no. 1 (Spring 2008): 352–384.

Lenta.ru. "Khudozhnik v invalidnom kresle zavis na stene pered pandusom v nikuda." *Lenta.ru* (July 12, 2019). https://lenta.ru/news/2019/07/12/performance/.

Levada Center. "Nostal'giia po SSSR." December 25, 2017. https://www.levada.ru/2017/12/25/nostalgiya-po-sssr/print/.

Levin, Bob. "Something of Value." *The Comics Journal* (February 6, 2017). http://www.tcj.com/something-of-value/.

Levy, Clifford J. "It Isn't Magic: Putin Opponents Vanish from TV." *The New York Times* (June 3, 2008). https://www.nytimes.com/2008/06/03/world/europe/03russia.html.

Liashchenko, Dmitriy. "Kuda dvizhetsia russkiy komiks." *Nishevoe isskustvo: kak komiksy vyzhivaiut i razvivaiutsia v Rossii.* Self-published blog, n.d. [2019]. http://9art.tilda.ws/move.

Lin, E. "Peculiarities of Modern Language Situation: Borrowings in Russian Language." *Tambov University Review,* vol. 10, no. 150 (2015): 200–205.

Linton, Simi. *My Body Politic: A Memoir.* University of Michigan Press, 2006.

Lipatov, Aleksei. "Stalin protiv Gitlera." *Al'manakh risovannykh istorii,* no. 3 (2005): 133–145.

Lipovetskiy, Mark. "Vsekh liubliu na svete ia!" *Iskusstvo Kino,* no. 11 (2000): 55–59.

Lisitsyn, Evgeniy. "IMKhO: Nelitsenzionnaia manga v Rossii." *Spidermedia.ru* (December 12, 2017). http://spidermedia.ru/comics/unlicensed-manga-in-russia.

Litichevskii, Georgii. "Estetika komiksa v sovremenom iskusstve." *Izotekst* (2010): 17–32.

Lomasko, Victoria. "How to Change Your Constitution in a Health Crisis." *The Nib* (August 6, 2020). https://thenib.com/how-to-change-your-constitution-in-a-crisis/.

———. *Other Russias.* Trans. Thomas Campbell et al. N+1, 2017.

Lomasko, Viktoriia. Email interview. November 2012.

———. Interview with author. Moscow, September 2013.

——— (Solglyadatay). "Chast' pervaia. Sotsial'nye komiksy v SMI. Blogery-Komiksisty." *Live Journal* (June 21, 2011). http://soglyadatay.livejournal.com/97196.html.

——— (Solglyadatay). "Chast' vtoraia. Sudebniy komiks/Graficheskiy reportazh s protsessa/Dokumental'niy komiks." *Live Journal* (July 5, 2011). http://soglyadatay.livejournal.com/97577.html#cutid1.

——— (Soglyadatay). "Pro rabotu s migrantami." *Live Journal* (October 20, 2012). https://soglyadatay.livejournal.com/128483.html.

———. "Viktoriia Lomasko o sotsial'noi grafike." *Otkrytaia Rossia* (November 8, 2014). https://openrussia.org/post/view/797/.

Lomasko, Viktoriia, and Nikolaev, Anton. *Zapretnoe iskusstvo.* Boomkniga, 2011.

Longo, Chris. "Bubble Comics, Comic Con Russia, and the Country's Comics Revolution." *Den of Geek* (July 18, 2016). https://www.denofgeek.com/us/books-comics/comics/257096/bubble-comics-comic-con-russia-and-the-countrys-comics-revolution#disqus_thread.

Lovell, Stephen, and Menzel, Birgit, eds. *Reading for Entertainment in Contemporary Russia: Post-Soviet Popular Literature in Historical Perspective.* Sagner, 2005.

Maas, Katerina. "Sozdatel' Tiumena rasskazal v Tomske, kak zhivetsia nezavisimym khudozhnikam-komiksistam v Sibiri." *Tomskiy Obzor* (November 14, 2017). https://obzor.city/article/556630--sozdatel-tjumena-rasskazal-v-tomske-kak-zhivetsja-nezavisimym-hudozhnikam-komiksistam-v-sibiri.

Madden, Matt. "A History of American Comic Books in Six Panels." *Matt Madden's Blog* (2012). http://mattmadden.blogspot.com/2012/08/a-history-of-american-comic-books-in.html.

Maguro, Iuliia. "Istoriia mangi v Rossii (1988–2014)." *Manga v Iaponii i Rossii.* Ed. Iuliia Magera. Comics Factory, 2015: 256–294.

———. "Istoriia poiavleniia pervykh iaponskikh komiksov na russkom iazyke." *Iaponskie issledovaniia,* no. 4 (2018): 6–23.

————. "Russkaia manga v poiskakh sobstvennogo puti." *Manga v Iaponii i Rossii.* Ed. Iuliia Magera. Comics Factory, 2015: 184–224.

Majsova, Natalija. "The Hazy Gaze of the *Bogatyrs* of the Russian *Byliny.*" *Teorija in Praksa,* no. 53 (April 2016): 906–919.

Makarova, Elizaveta. "Chelovek-Pauk perebralsia v Eksmo-AST." *Kommersant',* no. 7 (January 17, 2018). https://www.kommersant.ru/doc/3521778.

Maksimova, Svetlana, ed. "Comics in Education: Are They Useful?" Trans. Seth Graham. *International Journal of Comic Art,* vol. 7, no. 1 (Spring 2005): 75–94.

Mann, Thomas. *The Magic Mountain.* Trans. H. T. Lowe-Porter. Vintage, 1992.

Mansurov, N. S. "Children's Publications in the Soviet Union." *Comics and Visual Culture: Research Studies from Ten Countries.* Ed. Alphons Silbermann. K. G. Saur, 1986: 134–148.

Martem'ianov, Maksim. "Gabrelianovy i rossiyskaia imperiia komiksov." *GQ Russia* (May 6, 2014). https://www.gq.ru/entertainment/gabrelyanovy-i-rossijskaya-imperiya-komiksov.

Martynov, Kirill. "Pomnit' vse. Piat' let nazad ubili Borisa Nemtsova." *Novaia Gazeta* (February 28, 2020). https://novayagazeta.ru/articles/2020/02/27/84089-pomnit-vsyo.

Masing-Delic, Irene. *Abolishing Death: A Salvation Myth of Russian Twentieth-Century Literature.* Stanford University Press, 1992.

Maslov, Nikolai. *Il Était Une Fois La Sibérie. Première Epoque: Le Paradis des Hommes.* Trans. Joëlle Roche-Parfenov. Actes Sud BD, 2010.

————. *Siberia.* Soft Skull Press, 2006.

Matveeva, Anna. "Komiksy: chitat' ili smotret'?" *Artgid* (May 8, 2013). https://artguide.com/posts/353.

Mazanov, Artem. "Magazin komiksov Chuk i Gik zaiavil, chto Bilayn blokiruet SMS o komiksakh iz-za slova 'miks.' Operator otritsaet." *TJ Journal* (April 8, 2019). https://tjournal.ru/tech/92661-magazin-komiksov-chuk-i-gik-zayavil-chto-bilayn-blokiruet-sms-o-komiksah-iz-za-slova-miks-operator-otricaet.

McCauley, Martin. "From Perestroika towards a New Order: 1985–1995." *Russia: A History.* Ed. Gregory L. Freeze. Oxford University Press, 1997: 383–421.

McCloud, Scott. *Understanding Comics.* Kitchen Sink Press, 1993.

McIlvenny, Paul. "The Disabled Male Body Writes/Draws Back: The Graphic Fictions of Masculinity and the Body in the Autobiographical Comic *The Spiral Cage.*" *Revealing Male Bodies.* Ed. Nancy Tuana et al. Indiana University Press, 2002: 100–124.

Menzel, Birgit. "Russian Science Fiction and Fantasy Literature." *Reading for Entertainment in Contemporary Russia: Post-Soviet Popular Literature in Historical Perspective.* Ed. Stephen Lovell and Birgit Menzel. Sagner, 2005: 117–150.

Merino, Ana. *El Cómic Hispánico.* Ediciones Cátedra, 2003.

Messner, Michael. *Politics of Masculinities: Men in Movements.* Sage, 1997.

Metelitsa, Katia, Kachaev, Valeriy, and Sapozhkov, Igor'. *Anna Karenina by Leo Tolstoy.* Mir Novykh Russkikh, 2000.

Mikhailov, Egor. "Ia ne khochu, chtoby komiks byl krasivym: interv'iu s sozdatelem supergeroia Tiumena." *Afisha Daily* (September 5, 2018). https://daily.afisha.ru/brain/9929-ya-ne-hochu-chtoby-komiks-byl-krasivym-intervyu-s-sozdatelem-neftyanogo-supergeroya-tyumena/.

Mikhalkov, Nikita. *Besogon: Rossiia mezhdu proshlym i budushchim.* Izdatel'tsvo E, 2016.

————. "The Function of a National Cinema." *Russia on Reels: The Russian Idea in Post-Soviet Cinema.* Ed. Birgit Beumers. I. B. Tauris: 50–53.

Mikheev, Aleksey. "Onkolog Aleksey Maschan: 'Situatsiia s lekarstvami blizka k katastrofe.'" *Miloserdie.ru* (February 4, 2020). https://www.miloserdie.ru/article/onkolog-aleksej-maschan-situatsiya-s-lekarstvami-blizka-k-katastrofe/.

Mikisha, Viktoriia. "Delo Iuli Tsvetkovoy—politicheskoe." *Novaia Gazeta* (June 28, 2020). https://novayagazeta.ru/articles/2020/06/28/86050-delo-yuli-tsvetkovoy-politicheskoe.

Mikkonen, Kai. "Focalization and Comics: from the Specificities of the Medium to Conceptual Reformulation." *Scandinavian Journal of Comic Art,* vol. 1, no. 1 (Spring 2012): 70–95.

———. "The Implicit Narrator in Comics. Transformations of Free Indirect Discourse in Two Graphic Adaptations of *Madame Bovary*." *International Journal of Comic Art,* vol. 13, no. 2 (Fall 2011): 473–487.

Miktum, Vladislav. "Interv'iu s avtorom i khudozhnikom Georgiem Litichevskim." *Spidermedia* (March 13, 2016). http://spidermedia.ru/comics/intervyu-s-avtorom-i-hudozhnikom-georgiem-litichevskim.

Miller, Christopher. "The Tabloid King Who Shapes How Russians See the World." *Mashable* (June 16, 2015). https://mashable.com/2015/06/16/lifenews-mastermind/.

Miskarian, Kara. "TV—glavniy konkurent komiksov v Rossii." *Artkhronika,* no. 8 (2006): 84–89.

Mitchell, W. J. T. "Beyond Comparison." *A Comics Studies Reader.* Ed. Jeet Heer and Kent Worcester. University Press of Mississippi, 2009: 116–23.

Mochulsky, Fyodor. *Gulag Boss: A Soviet Memoir.* Trans. Deborah Kaple. Oxford University Press, 2011.

Molot. "Importozameshchenie shagaet po strane." *Live Journal* (August 11, 2015). https://van-der-moloth.livejournal.com/143351.html.

Moore, Alan, and Gibbons, Dave. *Watchmen* (New Edition). DC Comics, 2014.

The Moscow Times. "Putin Crowned SuperPutin at New Art Exhibition in Moscow." *The Moscow Times* (December 8, 2017). https://www.themoscowtimes.com/2017/12/08/putin-crowned-superputin-at-new-art-exhibition-in-moscow-a59869.

My—chast' obshchestva. "Chetyre etapa zhizni Iuriia Kuznetsova." *My—chast' obshchestva,* no. 1 (December 2000): 30–33.

Naiman, Eric. *Sex in Public: The Incarnation of Early Soviet Ideology.* Princeton University Press, 1997.

Narozhniy, Dmitriy. *Vitaliy, nemodniy illiustrator.* Komil'fo/Live Bubbles, 2015.

Naylor, Aliide. "St. Petersburg Exhibition Censored and Closed." *The Moscow Times* (October 12, 2015). https://www.themoscowtimes.com/2015/10/12/st-petersburg-exhibition-censored-and-closed-a50223.

Neliubin, Nikolay. "'Vystavki komiksov otkryvaet direktor Ermitazha.' Izdatel' komiksov otvetil Medinskomu na repliku pro 'debilov.'" *Fontanka.ru* (September 4, 2019). https://calendar.fontanka.ru/articles/8628/print.html.

Nenilin, Aleksandr. "Dmitriy Yakovlev." *Petersburg.ru* (2012). https://peterburg.ru/people/dmitriy-yakovlev.

The New Yorker. "Martin Amis in Conversation with Olga Slavnikova." *The New Yorker* blog, (June 13, 2012). https://www.newyorker.com/books/page-turner/martin-amis-in-conversation-with-olga-slavnikova.

Nikanorov, Aleksei. "Inspektor Klash." *Komiksolet* (2001). https://www.comicsnews.org/comics/inspektor-klash/page1.

Nikitina, Iuliia. Email interview. February 2016.

———. *Kniga Tela.* Live Bubbles, 2015.

————. "Razdelenie: komiks o boli i ne tol'ko tela." *Regnum* (June 23, 2017). https://regnum.ru/news/2291345.html.

Nikitinskiy, Leonid. "Chto takoe 'Kafka Kodeks." *Novaia Gazeta* (August 22, 2018). https://novayagazeta.ru/articles/2018/08/13/77482-chto-takoe-kafka-kodeks.

Nikolayenko, Olena. "The Revolt of the Post-Soviet Generation: Youth Movements in Serbia, Georgia and Ukraine." *Comparative Politics*, vol. 39, no. 2 (January 2007): 169–188.

Norris, Stephen M. *Blockbuster History in the New Russia: Movies, Memory, and Patriotism.* Indiana University Press, 2012.

Norton, Paul. "Slow Steps to Mobility." *Moscow Guardian* (September 24, 1993): 8–11.

Novaia Gazeta. "V Nizhegorodskoi oblasti poiavilsia banner s izobrazheniem Stalina i nadpis'iu 'I'll Be Back.'" *Novaia Gazeta* (December 22, 2019). https://novayagazeta.ru/news/2019/12/22/157858-v-nizhegorodskoy-oblasti-povesili-banner-so-stalinym-i-nadpisyu-i-ll-be-back.

Novinite. "Sofia Graffiti Fans Mourn Soviet Memorial's New Look." *Novinite.com* (June 22, 2011). https://balkaninsight.com/2011/06/22/soviet-army-monument-in-sofia-washed-clean-overnight/.

Novye Izvestiia. "'Chernaia kniga' Sobianina: za 7 let v Moskve sneseno 159 pamiatnikov." *Novye Izvestiia* (July 18, 2018). https://newizv.ru/news/city/18-07-2018/chernaya-kniga-sobyanina-za-7-let-v-moskve-sneseno-159-pamyatnikov.

NPR. "Graphic Novel about Holocaust *Maus* Banned in Russia for Its Cover." *All Things Considered* (April 28, 2015). https://www.npr.org/2015/04/28/402856064/graphic-novel-about-holocaust-maus-banned-in-russia-for-its-cover.

Odintsova, Tat'iana. "Lavka komiksov. Skol'ko prinosit torgovlia kartinkami." *RBK Gazeta* (March 23, 2016). https://www.rbc.ru/newspaper/2016/03/24/56f269ec9a7947efd02791d0.

Ostrovsky, Arkady. "Rocking the Kremlin." *The Economist* (August/September 2017). https://www.1843magazine.com/features/rocking-the-kremlin.

Otkrytye Media. "'Ia ni khrena ne kul'turniy chelovek.' Ministr kul'tury Ol'ga Liubomiva—o sebe, Putine i pravoslavii." *Otkrytye Media* (January 22, 2020). https://openmedia.io/infometer/ya-ni-xrena-ne-kulturnyj-chelovek-ministr-kultury-olga-lyubimova-o-sebe-putine-i-pravoslavii/.

Oushakine, Sergei. *The Patriotism of Despair: Nation, War, and Loss in Russia.* Cornell University Press, 2009.

Pal'veleva, Liliia. "Nesmeshnye kartinki. Sbornik komiksov o zhertvakh GULAGa." *Radio Svoboda* (March 31, 2019). https://www.svoboda.org/a/29851508.html.

Panfilov, Fedor. "My dolzhny sozdat' svoy, russkiy komiks." *Colta.ru* (May 8, 2014). https://www.colta.ru/articles/media/3131-my-dolzhny-sozdat-svoy-russkiy-komiks.

Pankin, Aleksei. "A Bad Track Record." *Russia Profile*, vol. 3, no. 4 (May 2006): 43.

Paperno, Irina. "Exhuming the Bodies of Soviet Terror." *Representations*, vol. 75, no. 1 (Summer 2001): 89–118.

Parker, John R. "Censoring America: Comics, Propaganda and the Information War, Part II." *Comics Alliance* (March 21, 2017). https://comicsalliance.com/comics-and-propaganda-part-two/.

————. "The Russia House of Ideas: An Interview with Russian Comics Publisher Bubble." *Comics Alliance* (March 31, 2017). https://comicsalliance.com/bubble-comics-interview/.

Parson, Sean, and Schatz, J. L. "Introduction: The Purpose and Intent of Our Project." *Superheroes and Masculinity: Unmasking the Gender Performance of Heroism.* Ed. Sean Parson and J. L. Schatz. Lexington, 2020: 1–11.

Pavlovskiy, Aleksei. "Komiks kak bukvar.'" *Oktiabr'*, no. 8 (2017). https://magazines.gorky.media/october/2017/8/komiks-kak-bukvar.html.

———. "Proshloe i budushchee Rossii v komiksakh *Veles* (1991–1995)." *Izotekts: Sbornik materialov II Konferentsentsii issledovatelei risovannykh istorii 17–19 maia 2017.* Ed. Aleksandr Kunin and Iuliia Magera. RGBM, 2017: 43–61.

———. "'Russkaia gotika' i simuliatsiia smerti: 'ShUV' Ol'gi Lavrent'evy." *Russkiy komiks bez slov* (September 16, 2016). https://vk.com/rkbzz?w=wall-128635046_6.

———. "Strakh komiksa: komiksofobiia v sovetskom soiuze." *Izotekts: Sbornik materialov Konferentsii issledovatelei komiksov 19–20 maia.* Ed. Aleksandr Kunin and Yulia Magera. RGBM, 2016: 86–96.

Pelevin, Viktor. *Homo Zapiens.* Trans. Andrew Bromfeld. Penguin, 2002.

———. *Omon Ra.* Trans. Andrew Bromfield. New Directions, 1992.

———. *The Sacred Book of the Werewolf.* Trans. Andrew Bromfeld. Viking, 2008.

Phillips, Sarah D. "'There Are No Invalids in the USSR!': A Missing Soviet Chapter in the New Disability History." *Disability Studies Quarterly,* vol. 29, no. 3 (2009). http://dsq-sds.org/article/view/936.

Pinchuk, Alina. "Ni sbezhat,' ni spriatat'sia." *Radio Svoboda* (February 4, 2020). https://www.svoboda.org/a/30413897.html.

Plungian, Nadia. "Immersivnoe iskusstvo freski." *Colta* (September 27, 2018). https://www.colta.ru/articles/art/19257-immersivnoe-iskusstvo-freski.

Po, Alisa. "Festival' 'KomMissiia' tayno pokinul 'Vinzavod.'" *The Village* (May 18, 2012). https://www.the-village.ru/village/city/city/113591-komik.

Polak, Kate. *Ethics in the Gutter: Empathy and Historical Fiction in Comics.* The Ohio State UP, 2017.

Polygaeva, Daria. "Dokopalis' do myshei: Izdatel' i perevodchik—o zaprete komiksa *Maus.*" *The Village* (April 27, 2014). https://www.the-village.ru/village/city/situation/213657-maus.

Pomerantsev, Igor'. "Khudozhnik v zone." *Radio Svoboda* (July 31, 1998). http://www.svoboda.org/programs/OTB/1998/OBP.09.asp.

Pomerantsev, Peter. *Nothing Is True and Everything Is Possible: The Surreal Heart of the New Russia.* PublicAffairs, 2014.

Pomerantsev, Peter, and Weiss, Michael. "The Menace of Unreality: How the Kremlin Weaponizes Culture and Money." *The Interpreter* (2014). https://imrussia.org/media/pdf/Research/Michael_Weiss_and_Peter_Pomerantsev__The_Menace_of_Unreality.pdf.

Ponosov, Il'ia. "V Nizhnem Novgorode zakryli kafe, otkuda vygnali sestru Vodianovoi." *Rossiyskaia Gazeta* (August 13, 2015). https://rg.ru/2015/08/13/reg-pfo/cafe-anons.html.

Postema, Barbara. *Narrative Structure in Comics: Making Sense of Fragments.* RIT Press, 2013.

Powell, Bill, and Matthews, Owen. "Moscow on the Make: Amid Wildness and Decadence, a City That Once Epitomized Drabness Fights to Reinvent Itself." *Newsweek* (September 1, 1997): 36–38.

Project Respect. "Comics as a Social Statement." May 2011. http://www.respect.com.mx/en/news/2-news/10-roundtable.

———. "Manifesto." May 2011. http://www.respect.com.mx/en/manifesto.

Prorokov, Grigoriy. "Komiksy i graficheskie romani: vosem' vazhneishikh izdatel'stv i glavnye proizvedeniia, kotorye vyshli po-russki." *Afisha* (August 3, 2011). https://daily.afisha.ru/archive/vozduh/archive/9841/.

Reed, Ryan. "Watch Pussy Riot's Disturbing Protest Video *Chaika*." *Rolling Stone* (February 3, 2016). https://www.rollingstone.com/politics/politics-news/watch-pussy-riots-disturbing-protest-video-chaika-229985/.

Regnum. "Slon s ogranichennymi vozmozhnostiami: kogda telo otkazyvaetsia rabotat.'" *Regnum* (April 14, 2017). https://regnum.ru/news/2263134.html.

———. "Vladimir Putin: 'Raspad SSSR—krupneyshaia geopoliticheskaia katastrofa veka.'" *Regnum* (April 25, 2005). https://regnum.ru/news/polit/444083.html.

Remnick, David. *Lenin's Tomb: The Last Days of the Soviet Empire*. Vintage, 1994.

———. *Resurrection: The Struggle for a New Russia*. Random House, 1997.

———. "The Tsar's Opponent." *The New Yorker* (September 24, 2007). https://www.newyorker.com/magazine/2007/10/01/the-tsars-opponent.

Revzin, Grigoriy. "Futbol'shisty." *Snob*, no. 2 (29) (February 2011): 15–17.

Reynolds, Richard. *Super Heroes: A Modern Mythology*. University Press of Mississippi, 1992.

Rhoades, Shirrel. *Comic Books: How the Industry Works*. Peter Lang, 2008.

Ria Novosti. "Aktivisty 'Khriushi protiv' rasshiriat geografiiu aktsii 'Esh' rossiyskoe.'" *Ria Novosti* (July 30, 2015). https://ria.ru/20150730/1154382902.html.

———. "V Moskovskoi finansovo-promyshlennoi akademii budut prepodavat' komiksy." *Ria Novosti* (May 30, 2011). https://ria.ru/20110530/381815010.html.

Robinson, Sally. *Marked Men: White Masculinity in Crisis*. Columbia University Press, 2000.

Robski, Oksana. *Casual*. Trans. Antonina W. Bouis. Regan, 2006.

Rogers, Douglas. *The Depths of Russia: Oil, Power, and Culture after Socialism*. Cornell University Press, 2015.

Rokossovskaia, Ariadna. "Respekt v tvoem bagazhe." *Rossiyskaia Gazeta* (December 13, 2011). http://www.rg.ru/2011/12/13/hudozniki.html.

Romanov, Pavel, and Iarskaia-Smirnova, Elena. *Politika invalidnosti: sotsial'noe grazhdanstvo invalidov v sovremmenoi Rossii*. Nauchnaia kniga, 2006.

Roth, Andrew. "Russian Antifascist Group Given 'Monstrous' Jail Terms." *The Guardian* (February 10, 2020). https://www.theguardian.com/world/2020/feb/10/russian-anti-fascist-group-network-jail.

———. "Thousands March in Moscow Demanding Open City Elections." *The Observer* (August 10, 2019). https://www.theguardian.com/world/2019/aug/10/thousands-march-in-moscow-disqualification-city-elections.

Rothrock, Kevin. "Gone Mad with Political Correctness: How Russia's Anti-Fascist Censorship Has Jumped the Shark." *Meduza* (April 27, 2015). https://meduza.io/en/feature/2015/04/27/gone-mad-with-political-correctness.

Rovbut, Dar'ia. "Prikliucheniia Tiumena i ego druzei." *Tiumenskiy kur'er* (April 3, 2018). http://tm-courier.ru/archives/140738.

Rudak, Vladimir. Interview with author. Seattle, October 2017.

Rudak, Vladimir, and Uzhinova, Lena. *Ia—slon!* Boomkniga, 2017.

Rykovtseva, Yelena. "Youth's New Take on Rebellion." *Russia Profile*, vol. 3, no. 3 (March, 2006): 35.

Sacco, Joe. "Chechen War, Chechen Women." *Journalism*. Metropolitan, 2012: 29–69.

Sadekova, Suriia. "Komiksy, eto uzhe seryozno. Sotheby's provodit pervye torgi, posviashchennye etomu zhanru." *The Art Newspaper Russia*, no. 03–04 (July-August, 2012): 49.

Said, Edward. *Orientalism*. Vintage, 1978.

Sakov, Vladimir. Interview with author. Moscow, June 1996.

Samutina, Natal'ia. "Iaponskie komiksy manga v Rossii: vvedenie v problematiku chteniia." *Novoe Literaturnoe Obozrenie*, no. 160 (June 2019). https://www.nlobooks.ru/magazines/novoe_literaturnoe_obozrenie/160_nlo_6_2019/article/21799/.

———. Personal correspondence. February 2020.

Santoro, Frank. "The Bridge Is Over." *Comics Comics* (August 1, 2009). http://comicscomicsmag.com/2009/08/bridge-is-over.html.

Savelyeva, Natalia. "How 'Love What You Do' Went Wrong in an 'Academic Sweatshop' in Siberia." *Open Democracy* (March 13, 2020). https://www.opendemocracy.net/en/odr/how-love-what-you-do-went-wrong-in-an-academic-sweatshop-in-siberia/.

Sbornik Komiksov. "Nemnogo istorii." *Sbornik Komiksov,* no. 1 (1991): n.p.

Scarry, Elaine. *The Body in Pain: The Making and Unmaking of the World.* Oxford University Press, 1985.

Shapiro, Joseph. *No Pity: People with Disabilities Forging a New Civil Rights Movement.* Times Books, 1993.

Shcherbinovskaia, Elena, and Sergey Gavrish. *Tayna beloy volchitsy.* Nitusov Press, 2003.

Schilter, David. Personal correspondence. January 9, 2020.

Schmitz-Emams, Monica. "Graphic Narrative as World Literature." *From Comic Strips to Graphic Novels: Contributions to the Theory and History of Graphic Narrative.* Ed. Daniel Stein and Jan-Noël Thon. De Gruyter, 2013: 385–406.

Schuckman, Emily. "Doubly 'Other': The Prostitute as Lesbian in *Land of the Deaf* and *Inhale-Exhale.*" *Beyond Little Vera: Women's Bodies, Women's Welfare in Russia and Central/Eastern Europe.* Ed. Angela Brintlinger and Natasha Kolchevska. The Ohio State University, Dept. of Slavic and East European Languages and Literatures: The Center for Slavic and East European Studies, 2008: 29–54.

Sekulić, Aleksandra. "Reality Check through the Historical Avant-garde: Danilo Milošev Wostok." *Comics of the New Europe: Reflections and Intersections.* Ed. Martha Kuhlman and José ASaniz. Leuven University Press, 2020: 67–81.

Semenova, Elena. "Doroga iz zheltogo kirpicha." *Novaia Gazeta* (July 7, 2018). http://www.ng.ru/ng_exlibris/2018-07-05/10_7259_road.html.

Semenyuk, Oleg. "Comics Art in the USSR: A Short Overview (1917–1985)." Trans. José Alaniz. *International Journal of Comic Art,* vol. 7, no. 1 (Spring/Summer 2005): 56–63.

Serebrianskiy, Sergey. "Izdateli. Bum komiksov v Rossii. Chto govoriat izdateli." *Mir Fantastiki,* no. 128 (April, 2014). https://www.mirf.ru/comics/bum-komiksov-v-rossii-izdateli.

Sergiev Grad. "Shkol'nitsa iz Sergieva Posada stala pobeditel'nitsey rossiyskogo konkursa komiksov, predstaviv interesnuiu rabotu." *SergievGrad.ru* (August 16, 2019). https://www.sergievgrad.ru/news/2685242/skolnica-iz-sergieva-posada-stala-pobeditelnicej-rossijskogo-konkursa-komiksov-predstaviv-interesnuu-rabotu.

Shagina, Elizabeta. "Posle Komiksa: katalog vystavki." *Posle Komiksa.* Erarta Museum of Modern Art, 2014.

Shamarina, Olesiia. "Realii i fantastika nachala 1990-kh: 'Reanimator,' 'Maksim,' i 'Andrey Brius—agent Kosmoflota.'" *Izotekst: stat'i i komiksy* (2015): 83–89.

Shamil & Co. "Vot shto byvaet s temi, kto p'et moloko vmesto piva!" *Noviy Komiks,* vol. 1, no. 3 (November 20–December, 20, 2001): 22.

Shelin, Sergey. "Ia ne protestuiu, ia pokazyvaiu." *Rosbalt* (February 16, 2014). http://www.rosbalt.ru/main/2014/02/16/1233320.html.

Shenkman, Jan. "Liudi ne prostye. Vremia prostykh zakonchilos." *Novaia Gazeta,* no. 136 (December 4, 2019). https://novayagazeta.ru/articles/2019/12/02/82966-boris-kupriyanov-lyudi-ne-prostye-vremya-prostyh-zakonchilos.

Sheregi, F. E. "Molodezhniy ekstremizm kak kharakternaia cherta neblagopoluchnykh obshchestvennykh sistem." *Rossiyskaia molodezh': problemy i resheniia.* Ed. Russian Federal Agency for Education. Tsentr Sotsial'nogo Prognozirovaniia, 2005: 438–455.

Sherwin, Emily. "Russia: Feminist Activist Could Face Prison for Vagina Drawings." *Deutsche Welle* (July 7, 2020). https://www.dw.com/en/russia-feminist-activist-could-face-prison-for-vagina-drawings/a-54070289.

Shil'kovskaia, Ania. "'As kagakod sernitam komion: rossiyskaia perevodchitsa i finskaia khudozhnitsa ozhivliaiut finno-ugorskie iazyki (komiksami!)." *Meduza* (November 25, 2017). https://meduza.io/shapito/2017/11/26/as-kagakod-syornitam-komion-rossiyskaya-perevodchitsa-i-finskaya-hudozhnitsa-ozhivlyayut-finno-ugorskie-yazyki-komiksami.

Shurmina, Natalia. "Russian Who Played *Pokemon Go* in Church Avoids Jail Term." *Reuters* (May 10, 2017). https://www.reuters.com/article/us-russia-blogger-pokemongo/russian-who-played-pokemon-go-in-church-avoids-jail-term-idUSKBN1870L7.

Sibnovosti. "Perviy magazin komiksov otkrylsia v Novosibirske." *Sibnovost.ru* (June 27, 2013). http://nsk.sibnovosti.ru/culture/240688-pervyy-magazin-komiksov-otkrylsya-v-novosibirske.

———. "V Novosibirske otkryli perviy za Uralom tsentr komiksov." *Sibnovosti.ru* (September 20, 2017). http://nsk.sibnovosti.ru/culture/356228-v-novosibirske-otkryli-pervyy-za-uralom-tsentr-komiksov.

Sidorov, Aleksandr. "Pochemu mne nenavistniy komiksy." *Novaia Gazeta* (September 20, 2019). https://www.nvgazeta.ru/news/12370/566144/.

Sikorskaia, Tat'iana, and Akishin, Askol'd. "Podarok." *Igrushka i podarki dlia vrozlykh i detey,* no. 1 (January 2006): 46–47.

Sikoryak, R. *Masterpiece Comics.* Drawn and Quarterly, 2009.

Silverman, Kaja. "Historical Trauma and Male Subjectivity." *Psychoanalysis & Cinema.* Ed. Ann Kaplan. Routledge, 1990: 110–127.

Sloane, Wendy. "Mafia Thwarts 'Golden Age' of Russian Media." *Christian Science Monitor* (July 20, 1994). https://www.csmonitor.com/1994/0720/20091.html.

Slotkin, Richard. *Gunfighter Nation: The Myth of the Frontier in Twentieth-Century America.* Atheneum, 1992.

Smirnov, Dmitriy. "Pribyl' ne iskliuchaetsia . . ." *Komiksolet* (2000). http://comics.aha.ru/rus/articles/7.html.

Smirnov, Dmitriy, and Ross, Andrey. "Kanikuly Maksa—1." *Velikolepnye Prikliucheniia,* vol. 1, no. 21 (2002): 1–12.

Smith, Hedrick. *The Russians.* Ballantine, 1976.

Smith, Martin Cruz. "Moscow Never Sleeps." *National Geographic* (August 2008): 106–133.

Smith, Sidonie. "Human Rights and Comics: Autobiographical Avatars, Crisis Witnessing and Transnational Rescue Networks." *Graphic Subjects: Critical Essays on Autobiography and Graphic Novels.* Ed. Michael A. Chaney. University of Wisconsin Press, 2011: 61–72.

Sohlman, Eva, and MacFarquhar, Neil. "A Diary from a Gulag Meets Evil with Lightness." *The New York Times* (January 3, 2008). https://www.nytimes.com/2018/01/03/arts/design/gulag-museum-moscow-diary.html.

Sokolov, Boris. "Vladimir Sorokin: Oprichnina—ochen' russkoe iavlenie." *Grani* (August 21, 2006). https://graniru.org/Culture/Literature/m.110108.html.

Solzhenitsyn, Aleksandr I. *The Gulag Archipelago I–II*. Trans. Thomas P. Whitney. Harper & Row, 1973.

Solzhenitsyn, Aleksandr. *We Never Make Mistakes: Two Short Novels*. Trans. Paul W. Blackstock. W. W. Norton, 1963.

Sorokin, Vladimir. *Day of the Oprichnik*. Trans. Jamey Gambrell. Farrar, Straus and Giroux: 2011.

Sorrosa, Raúl. "Anna Politkovskaya: Una Muerte en Una Democracia Fallida." *Chasqui*, no. 96 (December 1, 2014): 24–30.

Sosedov, Filipp, and Onishchenko, Roman. No Title. *Panteon: Kult Dvulichia*, vol. 1, no. 3 (August 2013): n.p.

Spidermedia. "Comic Con Russia 2016: Interv'iu s Annoy Rud.'" *Spidermedia* (October 21, 2016). http://spidermedia.ru/comics/comic-con-russia-2016-intervyu-s-annoj-rud.

Spiridov, V. "Zolotaia lozh.'" *KOM-OK*, 1990: 15.

Stanley, Alessandra. "Sexual Harassment Thrives in the New Russian Climate." *The New York Times* (April 17, 1994). http://query.nytimes.com/gst/fullpage.html?res=9C03EFDF1731F934A 25757C0A962958260.

Stein, Daniel. "Popular Seriality, Authorship, Superhero Comics: On the Evolution of a Transnational Genre Economy." *Media Economies: Perspectives on American Cultural Practices*. Ed. Marcel Hartwig et al. Wissenschaftlicher Verlag Trier, 2014: 133–157.

Stites, Richard. *Revolutionary Dreams: Utopian Vision and Experimental Life in the Russian Revolution*. Oxford University Press, 1989.

Strukov, Vlad. "Possessives and Superlatives: On the Simulation of Democracy in Russia." *Russian Cyberspace*, vol. 1, no. 1 (2009): 31–39.

Styshneva, Evgeniia. "Samye risovannye investitsii." *Kommersant' Den'gi* (July 31, 2006). https://www.kommersant.ru/doc/693844.

Suslova, Ekaterina. "Vam slovo, narisovanniy personazh!" *Komp'iuArt*, no. 6 (June 2008). http://www.compuart.ru/article.aspx?id=19145&iid=888.

Szabłowski, Witold. *Dancing Bears: True Stories of People Nostalgic for Life under Tyranny*. Trans. Antonia Lloyd-Jones. Penguin Books, 2018.

Takie dela. "V Sankt-Peterburge viydet perviy v Rossii graficheskiy roman o zhizni cheloveka s invalidnost'iu." *Takie dela* (March 23, 2017). https://takiedela.ru/news/2017/03/23/invalid_kniga/.

Talashin, Aleksandr. "Komiks *Soiuzniki* (Vypuski 1 i 2)—Povod dlia gordosti." *Kotonavty* (February 7, 2017). https://meownauts.com/soyuzniki-review-2/.

Taussig, Michael. *The Nervous System*. Routledge, 1992.

Taylor, Adam. "Putin Says He Wishes the Soviet Union Had Not Collapsed. Many Russians Agree." *Washington Post* (March 3, 2018). https://www.washingtonpost.com/news/worldviews/wp/2018/03/03/putin-says-he-wishes-he-could-change-the-collapse-of-the-soviet-union-many-russians-agree/.

TBK. "Sati Kazanova: 'Moi fond ne zanimaetsia bol'nymi, kosymi, krivymi, prosti Bozhe, det'mi.'" *TBK* (September 19, 2016). https://www.tvk6.ru/publications/news/21017/.

Terent'ev, Mikhail. Interview with author. Moscow, January 2002.

Tishchenkov, Oleg. *Kot X*. Artemy Lebedev Studio, 2013.

Treisman, Daniel. "Why Vladimir Putin Is Shaking Up Russia." *CNN.com* (January 15, 2020). https://www.cnn.com/2020/01/15/opinions/putin-constitutional-changes-treisman/index.html.

Tropkina, Ol'ga. "Perviy kadr." *Rossiyskaia Gazeta*, no. 0 (3919) (November 9, 2005). https://rg.ru/2005/11/09/putin-bondarchuk.html.

Trudov, Maksim. "Nechestniy obzor: Ia—slon!" *Comicstrade.ru* (April 27, 2017). http://comicstrade.ru/2017/04/trudov-slon/.

Turgenev, Ivan Sergeevich. "The Russian Language." *The Essential Turgenev.* Ed. Elizabeth Cheresh Allen. Northwestern University Press, 1994: 883.

Tvorchestvo. "Iazikom Satiry." *Tvorchestvo,* no. 7 (1987): n.p.

UPI. "Yeltsin's Approval in Single Digits." *UPI* (April 5, 1999). https://www.upi.com/Archives/1999/04/05/Yeltsins-popularity-in-single-digits/8155923284800/.

Ushakin, Sergey. "Vidimost' muzhestvennosti." *O Muzhe(N)stvennosti: sbornik statei.* Ed. Sergey Ushakin. Novoe Literaturnoe Obozrenie, 2002: 479–503.

Ustinova, Irina P. "English in Russia." *World Englishes,* vol. 24, no. 2 (June 2005): 239–252.

Uzhinova, Lena. "Nakhodka v Besovtse." *Novaia Gazeta* (August 5, 2019). https://novayagazeta.ru/articles/2019/08/05/81494-nahodka-v-besovtse.

———. "Pro glaz." *Komikser,* no. 1 (1999): 16–17.

Vagabova, Said. "Not Welcome in Daghestan—Anime, K-pop, and Rap." *OC Media* (February 5, 2018). https://oc-media.org/features/not-welcome-in-daghestan-anime-k-pop-and-rap/.

Vargol'skaia, Virdzhiniia. "Art rezidentsiia za prava cheloveka." *Radio Prague* (December 22, 2016). https://ruski.radio.cz/art-rezidenciya-za-prava-cheloveka-8205312.

Vasilyeva, Maria. "Russian LGBT Activist Fined for 'Gay Propaganda' Family Drawings." *Reuters* (July 10, 2020). https://www.reuters.com/article/us-russia-activist-court/russian-lgbt-activist-fined-for-gay-propaganda-family-drawings-idUSKBN24B2IY.

Veles-VA. "Biografii." Veles website. http://veles-va.ru/comics/content/biogr.html [link no longer accessible].

———. "Katalog komiksov." Veles website. http://veles-va.ru/comics/content/coms.html [link no longer accessible].

———. "Nemnogo istorii." Veles website. http://veles-va.ru/comics/index.html [link no longer accessible].

Velitov, Alim. "Batman." *Almanakh: Volshebnie Komiksy.* KomMissiia, 2003: 10.

———. "Kerdyk" *Almanakh: Volshebnie Komiksy.* KomMissiia, 2003: 11.

———. "Sem' rekomendatsii." *Izotekst: stat'i i komiksy.* RGBM, 2014: 117–120.

Venkatraman, Sakshi. "Russian Voters Back Referendum Banning Same-Sex Marriage." *NBC News* (July 2, 2020). https://www.nbcnews.com/feature/nbc-out/russian-voters-back-referendum-banning-same-sex-marriage-n1232802.

Vergueiro, Waldomiro C. S. "Brazilian Superheroes in Search of Their Own Identities." *International Journal of Comic Art,* vol. 2, no. 2 (Fall 2000): 164–177.

Versaci, Rocco. *This Book Contains Graphic Language: Comics as Literature.* Continuum, 2007.

The Village. "Supermen vmesto Stalina: 10 komiksov o Rossii, kotorye kogo-nibud' oskorbiat.'" *The Village* (January 23, 2018). https://www.the-village.ru/village/weekend/weekend-guide/299046-smert-stalina-komiksy.

Vishnevetskaia, Iuliia, and Yashnov, Misha. "V poiskakh geniia iz sovetskoy psikhushki." *Meduza* (August 4, 2019). https://meduza.io/feature/2019/08/05/v-poiskah-geniya-iz-sovetskoy-psihushki.

Vladimirskiy, Vasiliy. "Nauka o komiksakh: opyt refleksii." *Rara Avis* (June 28, 2016). http://rara-rara.ru/menu-texts/nauka_o_komiksah_opyt_refleksii.

Volegov, Vladimir. "Chernaia Zvezda." *Noviy Komiks,* vol. 1, no. 3 (November 20–December, 20, 2001): 6–10.

———. "Versace." *Noviy Komiks,* vol. 1, no. 1 (2001): 5–9.

Volkova, Natal'ia. "Komiks 'Ia—slon!': uvechnomu cheloveku neobkhodimo imet' tolstuiu kozhu." *Miloserdie.ru* (May 19, 2017). https://www.miloserdie.ru/article/komiks-ya-slon-uvechnomu-cheloveku-neobhodimo-imet-tolstuyu-kozhu2/.

Vol'tskaia, Tat'iana. "Rossiia—ptitsa, a ne medved.'" *Radio Svoboda* (November 21, 2015). https://www.svoboda.org/a/27375443.html.

Vorobeva, Polina. "Aleksei Volkov: 'Ia mnogo chitaiu pro deyateley komiksov proshlogo." (August 31, 2017). https://geekster.ru/novosti/aleksej-volkov-ya-mnogo-chitayu-pro-deyatelej-komiksov-proshlogo/.

Voronkova, Anna. "Komiks zavoevyvaiut MGU." *Izotekst: stat'i i komiksy* (2012–2013): 68–75.

———. "Komu i zachem nuzhny sotsial'nye risovannye istorii?" *Izotekst: stat'i i komiksy* (2014): 61–65.

Walicki, Andrzej. *A History of Russian Thought from the Enlightenment to Marxism.* Trans. Andrews-Ruseicka. Stanford University Press, 1979.

Walker, Shaun. "Putin Approves Legal Challenge That Decriminalizes Some Domestic Violence." *The Guardian* (February 7, 2017). https://www.theguardian.com/world/2017/feb/07/putin-approves-change-to-law-decriminalising-domestic-violence.

Weissman, Benjamin M. *Herbert Hoover and Famine Relief to Soviet Russia, 1921–1923.* Hoover Institution Press, 1974.

Whitlock, Gillian. "Autographics." *Comics Studies: A Guidebook.* Ed. Charles Hatfield and Bart Beaty. Rutgers, 2020: 227–240.

Wicomix. "Retsentsii: Soiuzniki. Vypusk perviy: Pered rassvetom. Chast' pervaia." *Wicomix* (January 27, 2017). https://wicomix.wordpress.com/2017/01/27/ .

Widdicks, Mary. "The Visual Language of Comic Books Can Improve Brain Function." *Quartz* (January 2, 2020). https://qz.com/1777533/reading-comic-books-can-improve-brain-health/.

Williams, Linda. *Hardcore: Power, Pleasure and the Frenzy of the Visible.* 2nd ed. University of California Press, 1999.

Witek, Joseph. *Comic Books as History: The Narrative Art of Jack Jackson, Art Spiegelman, and Harvey Pekar.* University Press of Mississippi, 1989.

Woo, Benjamin. "The Android's Dungeon: Comic-Bookstores, Cultural Spaces, and the Social Practices of Audiences." *Journal of Graphic Novels and Comics,* vol. 2, no. 2 (December 2011): 125–136.

———. "Is There a Comic Book Industry?" *Media Industries,* vol. 5, no. 1 (2018): 27–46.

———. "Reconsidering Comics Journalism: Information and Experience in Joe Sacco's *Palestine.*" *The Rise and Reason of Comics and Graphic Literature.* McFarland, 2010: 166–177.

Worcester, Kent. "Journalistic Comics." *The Routledge Companion to Comics.* Ed. Frank Bramlett, Roy T. Cook, and Aaron Meskin. Routledge, 2017: 137–145.

Yaffa, Joshua. "The Waste and Corruption of Vladimir Putin's 2014 Winter Olympics." *Bloomberg* (February 2, 2014). https://www.bloomberg.com/news/articles/2014-01-02/the-2014-winter-olympics-in-sochi-cost-51-billion.

Yakovlev, Dmitriy. Personal correspondence. December 2019.

———. Personal correspondence. May 2020.

Yandex. "Gibel' istoricheskoi Moskvy—katastrofa dlia goroda." *Yandex.com* (December 4, 2019). https://zen.yandex.ru/media/anashina/gibel-istoricheskoi-moskvy-katastrofa-dlia-goroda-5de7a04c74f1bc00b2a46ff1.

Yermakov, Igor', and Kozhevnikov, Igor'. "Krasnaia krov.'" *Veles.* Vols. 1–4 and 6–7 (1992–1996).

Yermakov, Oleg. *Afghan Tales: Stories from Russia's Vietnam.* Trans. Marc Romano. William Morrow and Co., 1993.

Zagvozdkina, Katia. "Vlasti Moskvy oprovergli informatsiiu o snose kinoteatra 'Khudozhestven niy.'" *Afisha Daily* (December 11, 2019). https://daily.afisha.ru/news/32778-vlasti-moskvy-oprovergli-informaciyu-o-snose-kinoteatra-hudozhestvennyy/.

Zanettin, Federico. *Comics and Translation.* Routledge, 2014.

———. "Translation, Censorship and the Development of European Comics Cultures." *Perspectives,* vol. 26, no. 6 (2018): 868–884.

Zaslavskiy, Mikhail. "Den' rozhdeniia russkogo komiksa." *Izotekts: Sbornik materialov II Konferentsii issledovatelei risovannykh istorii 17–19 maia 2017.* Ed. Aleksandr Kunin and Yuliia Magera. RGBM, 2017: 33–42.

———. Interview with author. Moscow, July 2017.

———. "Ul'ianovskie zhurnaly komiksov *Serezhka* i *Arbuz* (1994–1999): Materiali k publikatsii polnogo elektronnogo arkhiva zhurnalov na 'Komiksolete.' *Izotekts: Sbornik materialov III Konferentsii issledovatelei risovannykh istorii 4 aprelia 2018.* Ed. Aleksandr Kunin and Yuliia Magera. RGBM, 2018: 21–36.

Zaslavsky, Misha, and Akishine, Askold. *Le Maitre & Margueritte.* Trans. Helene Dauniol-Remaud. Actes Sud BD, 2005.

Zdravomyslova, Elena, and Temkina, Anna. "Krisis maskulinosti v pozdnesovetskom diskurse." *O Muzhe(N)stvennosti: sbornik statei.* Ed. Ushakin. NLO, 2002: 432–451.

Zelenova, Mary. "Invisible Children: Russia's Dima Yakovlev Law." NATO Association of Canada (February 1, 2017). http://natoassociation.ca/invisible-children-russias-dima-yakovlev-law/.

Zhulikov, Aleksei. Interview with author. Tbilisi, Georgia, December 2019.

Zolotukhina, Darya. "Young People Find Solidarity in the Act of Being Different." *Russia Beyond the Headlines* (November 25, 2010). http://rbth.com/articles/2010/11/25/young_people_find_solidarity_in_the_act_of_being_different05145.html.

INDEX

STUDIES IN COMICS AND CARTOONS

JARED GARDNER, CHARLES HATFIELD, AND REBECCA WANZO, SERIES EDITORS

LUCY SHELTON CASWELL, FOUNDING EDITOR EMERITA

Books published in Studies in Comics and Cartoons focus exclusively on comics and graphic literature, highlighting their relation to literary studies. The series includes monographs and edited collections that cover the history of comics and cartoons from the editorial cartoon and early sequential comics of the nineteenth century through webcomics of the twenty-first. Studies that focus on international comics are also considered.